The Palgrave Series on Chinese Law

Series Editor
Dayuan Han
Law School
Renmin University of China
Beijing, China

The Chinese legal system is complex, sometimes contradictory, and misunderstood. This series, edited by the dean of one of China's most prominent law schools, will serve as a basic reference point for legal scholars, sinologists, and international relations scholars, explaining and clarifying the realities of China's legal system.

More information about this series at
http://www.palgrave.com/gp/series/15719

Danling Yu

Chinese Business Law

palgrave
macmillan

Danling Yu
China Foreign Affairs University
Beijing, China

The Palgrave Series on Chinese Law
ISBN 978-981-13-0901-4 ISBN 978-981-13-0902-1 (eBook)
https://doi.org/10.1007/978-981-13-0902-1

Library of Congress Control Number: 2018958587

Cover illustration: © Juhani Viitanen / Alamy Stock Photo
Cover Design by Tjaša Krivec

This Palgrave Macmillan imprint is published by the registered company Springer Nature Singapore Pte Ltd.
The registered company address is: 152 Beach Road, #21-01/04 Gateway East, Singapore 189721, Singapore

Acknowledgements

Accomplishing a scholarly work on the core subjects of Chinese business law in the English language has never been an easy task for me. I would like to compare this experience to the life journey of a pioneering legal academic.

First, I would like to thank my dearest father who encouraged me to undertake this strenuous but daunting task. I took up the idea of this project first with Renmin University of China Press that responded with such enthusiasm and vigor that it quite overwhelmed me. I was happy though, among other things, that a major part of legal rules, values, and principles of Chinese corporate law, foreign investment law, and securities law unique to Chinese legal culture have finally been translated and would be made comprehensible upon completion of this book. After Chinese Business Law was published, several important national business laws were revised and regulations enacted. While preparing for an international edition by Palgrave Macmillan, I knew that I would need a major revision. As the subjects changed rapidly, I referred to the fundamentals and focused the revision on the core legal rules and constraints underlying Chinese business legal governance.

During the many years of preparing to write the book, I have been very blessed by the love, inspiration, and courage of my family. I reflect upon these years with a magnificent feeling of happiness and profound gratitude.

The other person I would like to thank is our immortal and eternal Frederick F. Chopin who has forever been inspiring me with his generosity, humanity, and sublime beauty of music in the lonesome and most often desolate hours of composition.

And last but not the least, my heartfelt thanks go to Palgrave Macmillan for its vision, professionalism, and dedication in making this book a reality.

Contents

CHAPTER 1

Corporate Law

1.1 The Evolution of Corporate Law in China

Corporate law in China was developed as part of efforts to reform the overall business law framework beginning in the late 1970s. Legal reforms were initiated at the start of the *gaige kaifang* 'reform and opening up' period by large business entities in both the state and non-state sectors. Consequently, not only did state-owned businesses benefit from the reforms but so did private enterprises. The ensuing economic reform testified to the need for a standardized national legal framework for business that could guide corporate associations and organizations. It took until 1993 however for this standardized framework to be validated by the National People's Congress, the legislature of China, as the Company Law of 1993.

The promulgation of the Company Law of 1993 facilitated a series of economic reforms that transformed China's economy from a planned to a market-oriented system. The law then underwent a series of amendments and revisions by the National People's Congress in 1999 and 2004, again in 2005, effective on January 1, 2006, and again in December 2013, effective from March 1, 2014. Each revision marked a milestone in the development of Chinese corporate law. The first revision, in 1999, resolved, among other things, the issue of supervision and management of state-owned companies and aimed at promoting growth of high technology by condoning a higher level of recognition of technological contributions to corporations' registered capital. The second revision, in 2004,

D. Yu, *Chinese Business Law*, The Palgrave Series on Chinese Law,
https://doi.org/10.1007/978-981-13-0902-1_1

among other things, abolished governmental approvals that had previously been necessary for the issuance of above par value stocks. The revision of 2005 provided a basic legal framework by adopting a more balanced approach to modern corporate governance. Revisions of the Company Law in 2013 abolished the minimum registered capital contribution requirement for corporations. Under the newly-revised corporate law, not only was no minimum registered capital required, but the requirement of an initial contribution of registered capital and the proportion of cash in the registered capital contribution, were also abolished.[1] The revised Company Law of 2013 replaced the paid-in contributions of registered capital requirement with a registered capital by subscription requirement. Under the new subscription system, shareholders had to agree to their subscribed amount, contribution methods, and contribution timing. The revised law no longer required a paid-in minimum registered capital. The timetable for the contribution, the investment certificate, and the registration of paid-in registered capital at the company registration authority will be discussed further later in this chapter.

1.2 Legal Framework

The current corporate law regime consists of Chinese constitutional law, national laws promulgated by the Chinese National People's Congress, regional and local laws enacted by regional and local legislative authorities, administrative rules and regulations enacted by the Chinese State Council and departmental rules issued by cabinet departments under the State Council.

As the fundamental law of the country, the Constitution of the People's Republic of China and its subsequent amendments, provides the overall governance structure for the regulation of all corporations. Lending legitimacy to the existence and establishment of corporations, the Constitution states that economic ownership exists in a tiered ownership system comprising both public and private elements. Private ownership coexists with public ownership, with public ownership at the core.[2] Constitutional law allows for different modes of distribution, giving validity to both publicly

[1] The Company Law of the People's Republic of China, art. 7, art.23, art.26, art.32, art.77, art. 80 and art. 83 (2014) (P.R.C.).

[2] The Constitution of the People's Republic of China, art. 6, (2005) (P.R.C.).

and privately-owned economic entities. Constitutionally, private business has a legitimate place in the economic system, with the government taking on the role of protecting the lawful rights and interests of economic individuals and private businesses via encouragement, support and guidance.[3]

In addition to China's constitutional law, the main body of law that governs corporations in China comprises the Company Law, the Civil Law, the Securities Law, the Bankruptcy Law, and the Commercial Banking Law. If a corporation involves foreign investment interests, it is also subject to laws related to foreign investment (FIE law). These include the Equity Joint Venture Law (EJV Law), the Cooperative Joint Venture Law (CJV Law), and the Wholly Foreign-owned Enterprise Law (WFOE Law).

Administrative rules and regulations are another important part of the governing regime. Administrative rules and regulations are issued by the State Council, with authorized agency departments tasked with exercising regulation and supervising corporations. The departments that issue rules governing corporations are principally the State Administration of Industry and Commerce (SAIC), the State Administration of Foreign Exchange (SAFE), the State Administration of Taxation (SAT), the State Asset Supervision and Administration Commission (SASAC), and the China Securities Regulatory Commission (CSRC).

1.3 Corporations

1.3.1 General Introduction

A corporation is an artificial entity created by law to act within the scope of the law to achieve designated purposes. Being an artificial entity, a corporation can act only through agents. Those agents are officers and managers who are entrusted to act on behalf of the corporation.

A corporation has the capacity to undertake civil actions, and these may include owning property, entering into contracts, and suing or being sued in the name of the corporation. In theory, a corporation may enjoy a perpetual existence. Under the law, a corporation is a legal person with independent business property, and may exercise property rights thereto.

The essence of a corporation is limited liability. As the corporation owns corporate assets, shareholders no longer own those assets or capital

[3] The Constitution of the People's Republic of China, art. 11, (2005) (P.R.C.).

once they have been contributed to the corporation. The corporation is liable for its debts with regard to all its assets. Shareholders are liable for corporate debts regarding the shares they own or contributions they have made to the corporation. Corporation agents, namely officers and managers, are not generally liable for the debts of the corporation. This is the core value of corporate limited liability. Company Law, however, does impose certain personal liabilities on shareholders. They may be, especially controlling shareholders, held personally liable for any abuses of their position within the corporation. To find otherwise would be tantamount to condoning an abuse of the limited liability protection of the corporation by giving wrongdoers an unfair advantage over creditors in terms of rights and interests.

1.3.2 Piercing the Corporate Veil

The revised Company Law of 2005 codified 'corporate veil piercing' as legal doctrine. Intended to impose liability upon shareholders, especially controlling shareholders, who are found to have abused their positions, it describes the process of removing the corporate legal personality identity in order to call shareholders or a shareholder of a corporation to account. The doctrine can be applied in circumstances where a shareholder abuses the independent identity of the juridical person of the corporation or their limited liability to evade their liability with respect to a debt payment or where a shareholder co-mingles their personal funds with the assets of the corporation. An example of this might be when the sole shareholder of a company uses its funds and assets as their own. The legal significance of this doctrine is to minimize the absolute effect of limited liability borne by a corporate entity.

Despite its fairly recent codification, the courts had been applying the principle of corporate veil piercing before 2006. The first instance was a 1994 Supreme Court decision in response to an inquiry made by the Guangdong High Court. Its response was that corporate veil piercing was permissible if the actual capital contribution made to a corporation was less than the sum of registered capital of the company. Undercapitalization was thereafter a consideration in applying the doctrine. Interestingly, later revisions of the corporate law did not include the response of the Supreme People's Court of 1994 in its codification that undercapitalization might be considered a factor in cases of corporate veil piercing.

The Company Law of 2005 offered two more provisions regarding the doctrine of corporate veil piercing. Article 20 of the law states that 'where any shareholders of a corporation evades payment of its debt by abusing the independent identity of juridical person or the shareholder's limited liability, thus seriously damaging the interests of creditors, it shall bear joint liabilities for the debts of the corporation.' Article 20 focuses on two factors that the courts should consider in deciding to pierce the corporate veil, namely (1) whether the abuse resulted in non-payment of debts, and (2) whether this non-payment caused any actual injury to the creditor. Article 64 of the law provides for a commingling of funds in a sole shareholder limited liability corporation, in that 'if the shareholder of a one-person limited liability corporation is not independent from their own property, they shall bear joint liabilities for the debts of the corporation.'

Currently, in deciding whether or not to pierce the corporate veil, the court applies these two factors. The legal focus of concern remains the protection of creditors' rights. The doctrine in effect grants the court more discretion in holding shareholders liable for abusing their position. The law does not suggest the presence of fraud is a factor for judicial consideration. Relevant judicial practice suggests that courts tend to follow a narrow reading of the law and limit the application of the doctrine to circumstances that concern the protection of creditors' interests.

1.4 Types of Corporations

1.4.1 Limited Liability Corporations and Joint Stock Corporations

There are two main types of corporation in China. They are the limited liability company (LLC) and the joint stock limited company (JSC).

A LLC is usually a privately-held, small-scale entity, owned by a limited number of shareholders who enjoy rights in proportion to their capital contributions. They may, however, agree otherwise with respect to their rights regarding management and profit if agreed to by all shareholders and included in the articles of incorporation. They may also make decisions with respect to the structure and management of the company if included in the articles of incorporation. In general, the law lends a greater degree of management and operational freedom to limited liability companies.

A JSC is usually a medium to large scale enterprise. The governance structure is composed of a shareholder meeting, a board of directors, a board of supervisors, and a body of executive management. It has limited liability. It may be established upon the issuance of stocks to incorporators and may issue one part of its stocks to incorporators and the other to investors. In a partial purchase of stocks, incorporators must purchase a required 35 per cent minimum of the total number of the stocks of the corporation. The corporation may decide to issue shares to the public or specified investors for subscription. It may also choose to list shares on the stock exchange to become a public corporation.

In practice, a corporation may change from a LLC to a JSC or *vice versa* upon satisfying statutory requirements.

1.4.2 Special Types of Corporations in China

The Company Law sets out special categories for corporations. These are single member LLCs, wholly state-owned enterprises (SOEs), and listed corporations.

1.4.3 The Single Member Limited Liability Company (LLCs)

Single member LLCs or wholly state-owned corporations are limited liability corporations. Listed corporations must be established and organized as joint stock corporations.

A revision under the Company Law of 2005 allowed a single member to establish a limited liability company. Under the previous version of the law, a LLC was required to have a minimum of two shareholders. In practice, there were already single member companies before the Company Law of 2005 came into being. Such companies operated and maintained business activities by having a shadow shareholder. Recognition of the validity of a single shareholder company under the Company Law of 2005 saw the national legislature provide a legal basis for the practice of wholly state-owned companies (SOEs) or wholly foreign-owned enterprises (WFOEs).

Specifically, single member LLCs are companies with one shareholder, who may be a natural or a legal person. A natural person may establish only one single member LLC. Such a LLC may not invest to establish a single person LLC. The Company Law of 2005 determined that the minimum registered capital for such companies was a lump sum of RMB

100,000. The Company Law of 2014 abolished both requirements for establishing a single member LLC.[4]

Upon filing for company registration, a LLC with a single shareholder is required to state that it is solely funded by one natural or legal person as shown on the company business license. A single member LLC may use a simplified style of management. Any shareholder meeting decision is required by law to be made in writing and kept with the company. An audited financial statement at the end of each fiscal year is also required.

By virtue of the legislative validation of single member LLCs, a foreign individual investor may set up a wholly foreign-owned enterprise (WFOE). They are required, however, to comply with all the relevant provisions of the Company Law and the Wholly Foreign-owned Enterprise Law.

1.4.4 Wholly State-Owned Enterprises (WFOE)

A wholly state-owned enterprise is another type of corporation that is specific to China.

A wholly state-owned enterprise (WFOE) is a LLC established through investment by the state. Here, the state refers to agencies authorized by the State Council or local authorities that manage and supervise state-owned assets by acting as capital contributors or shareholders.

The State-owned Assets Supervision and Administration Commission of the State Council (SASAC) and its local offices may authorize the board of directors of a wholly state-owned enterprise to exercise certain functions of the shareholder meeting and decide with respect to company priorities. Such delegated authority to the board of directors may not, however, include decisions about mergers, divisions, dissolutions, petitions for bankruptcy, or any increase or decrease in a corporation's registered capital or the issuance of corporate bonds. Decision-making power and authority regarding the aforementioned major corporate activities shall be examined by SASAC and reported to the relevant people's government authorities for approval.

The chairperson, vice chairperson, directors, or senior managers of a wholly state-owned corporation may not hold concurrent positions in any other LLC, joint stock corporations (JSC), or any other type of economic entity unless specifically approved and permitted by SASAC.

[4] The Corporate Law of the People's Republic of China, art. 59 (2014) (P.R.C.).

1.4.5 *Public Corporations*

Public corporations are JSCs that may trade shares on the stock exchange. The listing of the shares or stocks of joint stock corporations needs to be approved by the relevant government authority. The China Securities Regulatory Commission (CSRC) is the main authority responsible for this approval. As such, the governance framework for a joint stock corporation is the Company Law and the Securities Law.

1.5 Establishment of a Corporation

1.5.1 *General Guidelines*

This section will introduce ways in which one may establish a corporation.

The corporate law prescribes legal requirements with respect to the establishment of a corporation. The major requirements are as follows:

(i) There must be a sufficient number of incorporators.
(ii) There is no statutory minimum registered capital.
(iii) The incorporator shall prepare the articles of incorporation.
(iv) The corporation shall have a name and domicile.
(v) The issuance of shares of a joint stock corporation shall comply with the law.

1.5.2 *Incorporators*

An incorporator is a person who prepares the filing of necessary documents for registration and takes both internal and external steps to form and establish a corporation. Under the law, incorporators shall proceed in compliance with the provisions set out under the law and satisfy qualification requirements. As incorporators, they are required to exercise their rights and perform their obligations, and they may be subject to legal liabilities if they violate the law.

The statutorily required number of incorporators for a LLC is a minimum of two persons up to a maximum of 50 persons. A JSC may have up to 200 shareholders. At least half of a JSC's incorporators, who may be of any nationality, should reside in China. A natural person, partnership, or corporation that has not been otherwise prohibited from becoming an incorporator may serve as one. A person with limited civil capacity, however, may not.

An incorporator is obligated under the law and articles of incorporation to perform certain obligations. Such obligations include making full capital contribution payments for the limited liability corporation. The Company Law of 2005 requires that the incorporators pay no less than 20 per cent of registered capital prior to the establishment of a limited liability corporation. The remaining portion is required to be paid within two years of the corporation's establishment. The possible exception is the payment of a capital contribution for an investment company. In such a case, the incorporators shall pay the remaining portion within the five years of the initial lump sum having been paid. The Company Law of 2014, however, has done away with the statutory minimum registered capital requirement and the statutory contribution timetable. Incorporators are left to decide for themselves with regard to their contribution of registered capital. They are only required to subscribe to the registered capital in writing at the time of the corporation's establishment and registration.

The incorporators of a JSC may agree with respect to their rights and obligations and provide for their agreements in the articles of incorporation. A JSC may be established by either issuing all stocks to the incorporators or issuing part of the stocks to the public. If it is established by issuing all of the stocks to the incorporators, they must subscribe to the full amount of shares prescribed in the articles of incorporation. If it is established by issuing part of the stocks to the public, they are required to subscribe to no less than 35 per cent of total shares. Subscribers shall then pay their subscription or face penalties.

An incorporator in breach of subscription obligations shall pay compensation to nonbreaching subscribers. An incorporator or a shareholder who fails to make a payment under the subscription agreement or fails to make a payment according to the timetable is required to make up the defaulted amount owed to the corporation. The other defaulting and non-defaulting shareholders shall bear joint and several liability for the debts owed to the corporation.

The Company Law prescribes the liabilities that an incorporator of a JSC should shoulder. Under the law, an incorporator shall assume the following liabilities:

(i) If the incorporation fails, the incorporators shall bear joint and several liability for the debts and expenses resulting from any pre-establishment activities. The incorporators shall also be liable for refunding the paid-in capital plus any interest.
(ii) If an incorporator negligently infringes the interest of the corporation during its establishment, it shall be held liable for any damages.
(iii) A person who fraudulently registers a corporation shall rectify the situation and pay a fine issued by the registration authority. If the circumstances are serious, the corporation's registration will be cancelled or its business license revoked.

1.5.3 Capital

The concept of registered capital has been awarded much importance under the law. The Company Law of 2014 abolished the minimum registered capital requirement and the statutory timetable for making registered capital contributions.

In general, the concept of registered capital is equivalent to that of equity. In a limited liability corporation, registered capital amounts to a capital contribution by shareholders. In a joint stock corporation, registered capital is the total amount of equity subscribed to by incorporators or the total amount of equity paid by incorporators and public investors.

Under the Company Law of 2005, the minimum capital required for a limited liability corporation was set at RMB 30,000 and the minimum for a single member limited liability corporation was set at RMB 100,000. The requirement for a joint stock corporation was set at RMB 5 million. The revised Company Law of 2014 abolished the relevant requirement regarding registered capital by no longer requiring a minimum capital contribution, a paid-in capital contribution, or required an initial installment payment. By this means, the law has turned a system of paid-in capital registration into one of registered capital subscription. The corporation is responsible for the veracity underlying its subscription capital on its own terms. The threshold setting up a corporation has been considerably reduced, and paid-in capital is no longer required at the time of registration.

The capital contribution to a corporation may be made in cash or in lawfully transferable noncurrency property. The latter is regarded as a noncash form of contribution. This may include intellectual property rights and land use rights. However, labor services, credit, the name of a natural person, business reputation, a franchising right, or a property with secured interest are unacceptable registered capital contributions.[5]

The requirement laid out in the Company Law of 2005 regarding the minimum cash capital contribution for a limited liability corporation was abolished under the Company Law of 2014. It should be noted that the use of noncash property as a capital contribution must be evaluated and verified by the relevant authorities. Legal requirements have been imposed on the evaluation of any noncash contribution to disallow for any over- or under-valuation.

With regard to investment in any corporation other than an investment corporation, the law has removed a number of restrictions on corporations. Currently, a corporation may effectively invest in enterprises that are limited liability corporations or joint stock corporation. But it is prohibited from investing in a general partnership as a general partner. As such, the law has left the issue of investment up to the corporation itself.

1.5.4 Articles of Incorporation

The articles of incorporation of a corporation establish the constitution of a corporation. They exert a binding power on shareholders, directors, supervisors, and senior management officers. The law defines senior management officers as the manager, deputy manager, person in charge of financial affairs, and secretary of the board of directors of a public corporation. A corporation's articles of incorporation may stipulate any other person as a senior management officer as well. The articles of incorporation are agreed to and written by the incorporators. They need to be adopted at the inaugural assembly of the corporation if it is to be established by the issuance of shares. The articles of incorporation may be amended but any amendments must be filed for registration. Generally, the articles of incorporation address the following important information:

(i) Details of the corporation, its name, domicile, business scope, and subscription of its registered capital;

[5] The Regulations on the Administration of the Registration of the Registered Capital of Corporations, SAIC, art. 8 (2007).

(ii) Information about shareholders and their rights;
(iii) Information regarding corporate structure and shareholder meetings as well as the board of directors; and
(iv) Circumstances under which the corporation may be dissolved and procedures regarding liquidation.

1.5.5 Name and Domicile

A corporation must have a name and place of residence. The place of residence is what it is referred to as the domicile. The name and domicile of a corporation need to be set out in the first clause of the articles of incorporation. The name of the corporation, once approved and registered with the corporation registration authority, enjoys legal protection.[6] The naming of the corporation must comply with the relevant provisions of the Company Law and administrative regulations such as the Regulations on the Administration of the Registration of Corporations of 2005.

A corporation should seek approval for its chosen name prior to establishment. Having been approved, the name will be reserved for six months during which time it may not be used for other business activities or transferred.[7]

A corporation must have domicile, a legal address that serves as its main office. A corporation may only have one domicile authorized with the registration authority, according to the jurisdiction of the registration authority.[8]

A corporation established as a LLC will indicate that it is a limited liability corporation by incorporating 'limited liability corporation' or 'limited corporation' in its name. Likewise, a JSC will indicate that it is a joint stock corporation by incorporating 'joint stock limited corporation' or 'joint stock corporation' in its name. The Administrative Rules on the Registration of the Names of Enterprises[9] and the Implementing Measures

[6]The Regulations on the Administration of the Registration of Corporations, State Council, art. 11 (P.R.C.).

[7]Regulations on Administration of Corporation Registration, State Council, art. 17 to 19 (P.R.C.).

[8]The Regulations on the Administration of the Registration of Corporations, State Council, Art. 12 (P.R.C.).

[9]The Administrative Rules on the Registration of the Names of Enterprises, SAIC (1991).

of the Regulations concerned[10] provide details instructions on the naming of corporations.

1.5.6 Establishment Procedures

With respect to the establishment of a corporation, incorporators will first formulate articles of incorporation. The articles of incorporation are largely a product wherein shareholders or incorporators record their agreements with respect to their rights and obligations. This is not subject to any governmental approval. The next step for incorporators and investors is completion of capital contributions in accordance with their ratio of subscription agreed in the articles of incorporation. Finally, incorporators will carry out the registration procedure at the corporation registration authority. Registrants may complete the application via facsimile, electronic mail, or other electronic means. The registration authorities will request, among other things, the name and domicile of the corporation, the name of the legal representative, the type of enterprise, the business scope, the term of business operation, and the names of shareholders or incorporators.

The State Administration of Industry and Commerce (SAIC) acts as the registration authority along with its regional and local offices. SAIC refers to the national office in Beijing while regional and local offices exist throughout the country.

The national office of SAIC regularly handles the registration of foreign invested enterprises, the registration of state-owned corporations with capital contributions represented by the State Administration of State-owned Asset Commission (SASAC) and other corporations having SASAC as an investor and holding more than 50 per cent of the shares, and the registration of other corporations required by law or administrative regulations to be registered with the national office of SAIC.

SAIC may delegate some of its registration duties to local offices. Foreign investors are advised to check with SAIC to gain information regarding local or regionally authorized registration options.

Usually, local or regional SAIC offices handle the registration of state-owned corporations and corporations in which SASAC is an investor with

[10] The Measures Implementing the Administrative Rules on the Registration of the Names of Enterprises, SAIC (2004).

50 per cent or less of shares.[11] A corporation invested in by individuals will register with the local or regional SAIC office. Joint stock corporations may register with the city level SAIC office.[12]

If a corporation is established by public stock issuance, the law requires incorporators to publish a prospectus and prepare the necessary stock subscription forms. The forms usually include the number of stocks subscribed to by each of the incorporators, the value and the issuing price of the stock, the purpose of financing, the rights and obligations of the subscribers, and the representation that the subscribers will revoke the subscriptions if the offering is undersubscribed on the closing date. Otherwise subscribers will pay according to the number of stocks to which they have subscribed.

1.5.7 Inaugural Assembly

An inaugural assembly is a meeting of incorporators or subscribers in which decisions are made regarding the establishment of the corporation prior to the implementation of registration procedures.

When the incorporators hold their inaugural assembly, they must inform subscribers of the date upon which the inaugural assembly is to take place or publicly announce the date of the assembly 15 days in advance. At the inaugural assembly, incorporators will adopt the articles of incorporation, elect members of the board of directors and the board of supervisors, and examine the value of noncash contributions by incorporators. A resolution adopted at the inaugural assembly requires an affirmative vote by the incorporators or subscribers representing more than 50 per cent of the voting shares of those present at the meeting. Within a period of 30 days after an inaugural assembly, the board of directors will file a registration application with the local, regional, or national SAIC office. If satisfied that the necessary documents have been submitted, the SAIC office will proceed to register the corporation. SAIC will issue a business license to the corporation with the name, domicile, scope of business, and name of the corporation's legal representative. The date of

[11] The Regulations on the Administration of the Registration of Corporations, State Council, art. 7 (2005).

[12] The Regulations on Administration of the Registration of Corporations, State Council, art. 8 (2005).

issuance of the business license is the date on which the corporation is established.

1.6 Corporate Capital and Corporate Finance

1.6.1 Corporate Capital

In general, the capital of a corporation includes equity capital, debt, and capital generated by the corporation during its conduct of business and operations. The narrow position on corporate capital holds that it includes only the equity of a corporation. Under the law, equity is total contributions from shareholders at the time of the corporation's establishment, as stated in the articles of incorporation. Debts, short term or long term, may be raised from financial institutions, shareholders, or public investors. Capital generated by the corporation is its internally generated funds. These internally generated funds are retained earnings, distributions to any wealth accumulation fund, and funds from corporate asset transfers.

A corporation's legal person has independent property and proprietary rights. A corporation owns corporate property in the name of the legal person and is liable to debts to the extent of corporate property.

1.6.2 Equity Capital

Equity appears in many forms. In China, most often, one form of equity is registered capital. Under the law, registered capital is the total amount of the property subscribed to by shareholders at the time of the establishment of a corporation. The law provides that registered capital is the amount of capital contribution subscribed to by shareholders for a limited liability corporation. Insofar as a joint stock limited liability corporation is concerned, registered capital is the total amount of equity subscribed to by promoters.

The practice of requiring minimum registered capital has undergone certain changes. Firstly, there was the minimum registered capital requirement under the Company Law of 2005. The minimum registered capital requirement for a joint stock limited liability corporation was RMB five million or more and RMB 30,000 for a limited liability corporation. The minimum registered capital should be written into the corporate articles of incorporation and registered with the registration authority to be examined and confirmed by the registration authority. Moreover, registered capital should have been either paid up at the time the corporation was founded or paid in installments. The Company Law of 2014 abolished the minimum registered capital requirement and the statutory scheduled payment.

1.6.3 Forms of Contribution

Shareholders of a limited liability corporation or promoters of a joint stock limited liability corporation may contribute either with tangible property or intangible property, such as IP rights and land use rights. Intangible property for the purpose of contribution must be evaluated, appraised, and confirmed so as to discourage over- or under-valuation. When making contributions, if in the form of cash, the shareholder shall deposit cash into the corporation's bank account. If property, usage rights shall be transferred from the shareholder to the corporation. Once the contribution is complete, the law requires shareholders to produce a report and asset examination authorization certificate.

For a joint stock limited liability corporation established by way of promotion, the registered capital is the total amount of equity subscribed to by promoters at the corporation registration authority. The Company Law of 2014 no longer requires an initial contribution of 20 per cent of the registered capital or more.

For an investment corporation, the requirement is that the contribution needs to be made and completed within five years of a corporation's establishment, under the Company Law of 2005. This requirement has been removed from the Company Law of 2014. For a limited liability corporation, the requirement for a noncash contribution is the same as required of a joint stock limited liability corporation by way of promotion. After the contribution or subscription is made, the promoters or subscribers are required to approach the asset evaluation agency for the issuance of an asset evaluation report and certificate of asset evaluation.

1.7 Rights of Shareholders

Shareholders' main rights are to profit and participate in the management of the corporation. The right to profit includes the right to share in the profit distribution of the corporation, the right to the residual asset distribution of the corporation, and the right to subscribe to new shares. The right to participate in the management of the corporation includes the right to vote, the right to call a shareholder meeting, and the right to inspect the corporation's books and records. The right to share in profit distribution may only be realized if only operational conditions permit. Profit distribution can only be made when the corporation has a net profit after any losses has been made up and the withdrawal of lawfully established funds has been completed. The right to residual asset distribution may be exercised under the condition that all debt obligations have been met. The shareholders may have the right to subscribe to the newly issued shares of the corporation on a pro rata basis. The right to vote is the major manifestation of a shareholder's right to participate in the management of the corporation. The shareholder meeting operates under the condition of one-share-one-vote. The resolution of a shareholder meeting must be approved by the majority of shareholders present. A shareholder's right to know refers to the right to know the operational conditions and financial conditions of the corporation and the right to propose and make enquiries regarding the situation of the corporation. Recently, the Supreme People's Court issued Judicial Interpretation IV, giving a narrow reading of the exercise of this right. This will be discussed further later in this chapter.

The shareholders of a LLC may inspect the corporation's articles of incorporation, resolutions of shareholder meetings, resolutions of meetings of the board of directors, resolutions of the board of supervisors, financial and accounting reports as well as accounting records, and make copies thereof. Nonetheless, the right to know is not totally unrestricted. A corporation to be inspected may decline a request from a shareholder if it finds any impropriety in such request that may harm the corporation.

Another manifestation of a shareholder's right to participate in the management in the corporation is the right to sue. The law provides for this if any shareholder has inflicted harm upon the interests of other shareholders or the conduct of the senior management or the directors of the board has encroached upon the interests of the shareholders. Under such circumstances, the shareholder may exercise the right to sue.

1.8 Corporate Finance

1.8.1 General Concept

The capital of a JSC may be divided into shares, with each share being of equal value. The smallest unit of capital of a corporation is one share. Shares come in the form of corporation stock, and can be either common or preferential. Shareholders vote according to the principle of one-share-one-vote and enjoy rights in proportion to the extent of their shareholding. Rights include the right to profit and the right to vote. The right to profit is the right to receive dividends and the right to receive a proportion of the residual property of the corporation upon liquidation. Normally, the rights associated with each type of share are more or less similar, but common shareholders, however, may enjoy a wider range of rights. They have voting and decision-making rights with regard to major corporate affairs. Meanwhile, the right to profit held by common shareholders may be exercised only after that of preferred shareholders.

The Company Law of 2014 does not, however, specifically provide for any preferred shares issued by a corporation. Article 132 empowers the State Council to stipulate other kind of shares other than common stocks in its rules and regulations. Preferred shares are, in fact, adopted in practice by Chinese corporations. The practice with regard to preferred shares is rather similar to that in the civil law countries and common law countries. Preferred shareholders are given preference over common shareholders in profit distribution and receipt of residual assets in terms of sequence. However, preferred shareholders have no right to vote and participate in the management of the corporation.

1.8.2 Types of Stocks

Stocks are categorized as either registered stocks or bearer stocks. Registered stocks are normally issued by a corporation to its promoters and legal person shareholders. Such stocks require a registry of the names of the promoters and the names of the legal persons. Upon transfer, the name of the transferee shareholder is required to be registered with the corporation to validate the transfer. Bearer stocks, as the term suggests, do not need to be registered with the corporation and can be transferred upon endorsement.

1.9 Corporate Governance

Corporate governance institutions consist of a shareholder meeting, a board of directors, and a board of supervisors. The shareholder meeting is a major part of a corporation's governance system. The shareholder meeting acts by way of resolutions which should be executed by the board of directors. Excepting a wholly state-owned enterprise or a single shareholder limited liability corporation, a limited liability corporation or a joint stock limited liability corporation is required under the law to have shareholder meetings.

The board of directors is the institution responsible for the execution of the business affairs of a corporation. The directors on the board will be elected at the shareholder meeting. In a limited liability corporation established without a board of directors, the executive director is responsible for corporate business affairs. The establishment of the board of directors is mandatory under the law.

The board of directors may hire managers. Managers are agents who are responsible for executing the decisions and resolutions of the board. The power of decisions rests with the board of directors, not with the managers.

The Company Law requires the establishment of the board of supervisors to supervise the execution of business affairs by directors and managers and the financial and operational conditions of the corporation. The board of supervisors reports to the shareholder meeting. The shareholder meeting elects supervisors. The employee representatives on the board of supervisors are elected by the employee representative assembly.

A limited liability corporation without a board of supervisors may have one to two supervisors. A board of supervisors is likewise mandatory.

1.9.1 The Shareholder Meeting

The Company Law gives broad powers to the shareholder meeting including decision-making powers regarding the operational and investment plans of the corporation, electing or changing directors or supervisors who are non-employee representatives, making decisions regarding compensation matters involving directors and supervisors, approving the report of the board of directors and the report of the board of supervisors, approving financial and fiscal plans and any profit distribution plan, making decisions with respect to any increase or decrease of registered capital, resolving with respect to bond issuance, mergers, divestitures, change of corporate form, dissolution, or liquidation, and amending the articles of incorporation.

There are regular shareholder meetings and special shareholder meetings. In a LLC, regular shareholder meetings are often scheduled meetings, and special shareholder meetings can be called by proposal made by shareholders with one-tenth of the votes or with one-third of the votes by the board of supervisors.

In a JSC, regular shareholder meetings tend to be held annually. The law provides that a JSC may call for a special shareholder meeting if there is no quorum present at a board of directors meeting, if requested by shareholders holding 10 per cent or more of the shares of the corporation singularly or jointly, if the board of directors deems it necessary, or if proposed by the board of supervisors.

The shareholder meeting of a LLC will be called for or presided over by a majority of shareholders. The shareholder meeting of a JSC will be called for by the board of directors and presided over by the chair of the board of directors.

A shareholder meeting resolution may either be a regular or a special resolution. Article 104 of the Company Law of 2014 provides that a shareholder resolution shall be approved by one half of voting shareholders present at the meeting. This is what it is referred to as a regular resolution of a shareholder meeting. However, a resolution to amend the articles of incorporation, an increase or decrease of registered capital, mergers, divestitures, dissolution, or change in corporate form will require a special resolution of the shareholder meeting, approved with two-thirds or more by those shareholders present at the meeting.

The approval of the shareholder meeting is required for the transfer of major corporate assets or the provision of an external guarantee. A public corporation will need the approval of the shareholder meeting with two-thirds vote of the shareholders present at the meeting if within one year it will have transferred its major assets or provided a guarantee exceeding 30 per cent of the capital of the corporation. Shareholders in a limited liability corporation will vote in proportion to their equity contribution whereas shareholders in a joint stock limited liability corporation will enjoy one-share-one-vote.

Voting to elect the directors of the board of directors may adopt either straight or cumulative voting. The law provides that the shareholder meeting to elect directors or supervisors may adopt cumulative voting in accordance with the articles of incorporation or resolutions of the shareholder meeting. Cumulative voting is a voting method that improves minority shareholders' chances of naming representatives on the board of directors. In regular or statutory voting, shareholders must apportion their votes equally among candidates for directors.

Cumulative voting allows a shareholder to cast all of its votes for one candidate. Let us assume one vote per share, a shareholder owns 100 shares, and there are six directors to be elected. The regular method will allow the shareholder to cast 100 votes for each of the six candidates for a director, to the total of 600 votes. The cumulative voting method will allow the same 600 votes to be cast for one candidate or split as the shareholder wishes.

Proxy voting is provided for under the law; a shareholder may attend a shareholder meeting by way of a proxy. Proxy voting is only applicable to a joint stock limited liability corporation in China.

1.9.2 The Board of Directors

The law provides for the constituent number of a board of directors for both a LLC and a JSC. A LLC must have a board of directors comprising of between three and thirteen persons. A JSC must have one with between five to nineteen persons. A LLC that is small in scale or with a limited number of shareholders, and has not established a board of directors, may have one executive director.

The members of the board of directors are elected by the shareholders. One thing to note is that the board of directors of a limited liability corporation must include employee representatives who have been elected at an employee representative assembly if such corporations are invested in by more than two state-owned enterprises or more than two state-owned investment entities. The functions and powers of the board of directors are provided for under the law. The board of directors is accountable to shareholders by calling and reporting to the shareholder meeting, executing the resolutions of the shareholder meeting, making decisions regarding operational and investment plans, producing an annual fiscal budgetary plan and profit distribution plan, as well as plans regarding an increase or decrease in registered capital and bond issuance, formulating plans regarding mergers, divestitures, changes of corporate form or dissolutions, making decisions regarding management structure, appointing or removing managers, making decisions regarding their compensation matters and appointing or removing deputy managers or financial officers, making decisions regarding their compensation, and formulating the basic management system of the corporation. The board of directors may have other functions and powers as provided for in the articles of incorporation.

A corporation will have one chairperson and deputy chairpersons. The election of a chairperson or deputy chairperson requires a simple majority vote by the board directors. The law provides that the chairperson calls for and presides over board of director meetings and examines the execution of any resolutions made by the board of directors.

The meeting of the board of directors may either be a regular scheduled meeting or a special meeting. The law allows the articles of incorporation to provide for the meeting of the board of directors except that a meeting of the board of directors of a joint stock limited liability corporation may only be provided for under the law. A board of directors meeting should take place at least twice annually. It should represent more than one-tenth of votes and represent more than two-thirds of directors, or supervisors may propose a special meeting of the board of directors.

Each director has a single vote. The law gives a relatively freer rein to limited liability corporation regarding procedures and voting methods by the board of directors. A quorum of more than one half of the directors needs to be present at a board of directors meeting. A resolution of the board of directors needs the approval of more than half of all directors.

The term of directors may be decided under the articles of incorporation but may not exceed three years per term. A director may be reelected. Staggered terms are not an option.

A director of a corporation's board may be removed at a shareholder meeting without cause or in a court of law with cause.

The salary, bonuses and stock options paid to a director of a corporation's board will be determined by shareholders at a shareholder meeting.

Board directors may incur liabilities for resolutions of the board of directors. A director who disagrees in writing, however, may be exonerated from their liabilities.

1.9.3 Managers

Managers may make corporation business decisions on their own. The institution of management is not a mandatory establishment under the law that provides that limited liability corporation or joint stock limited liability corporation are permitted to have managers. The articles of incorporation will generally provide for the appointment and removal of managers by the board of directors. In general, the law does not restrict the qualifications of managers nor the number of positions a manager may hold within the corporation. A manager may be a shareholder and a director.

Managers are appointed by the board of directors to be accountable to the board of directors for the operation and management of the corporation, the execution of the resolutions of the board of directors, the formulation of annual operation plans and investment plans, the establishment of management and regulation of the corporation, and making proposals regarding the appointment or removal of deputy managers, financial managers, or any other person in the corporation. Managers may be present during meetings of the board of directors.

The board of directors will decide the remuneration of managers. In a joint stock limited liability corporation, the decision by the board of directors regarding the remuneration of managers will need to be disclosed to the shareholders.

1.9.4 The Board of Supervisors

A board of supervisors will have one chairperson and one deputy chairperson elected by more than half of the supervisors. This may not be fewer than three persons in a limited liability corporation, but if the corporation has only a few shareholders or is otherwise small in scale, the corporation may have just one to two supervisors.

The board of supervisors will include shareholder representatives and employee representatives. The board of supervisors of a joint stock limited liability corporation may not consist of fewer than three persons with appropriate representation from shareholders and employee representatives. Employee representatives will be elected at employee representative assembly or through any other democratic elections for either a limited liability corporation or a joint stock limited liability corporation. Employee representatives are selected in proportion to the number of employees of the corporation. Normally the employee representation shall amount to no fewer than one-third of supervisors on the board of supervisors. The board of supervisors will have a chairperson, elected by more than half of supervisors. Directors or senior managers may not be supervisors.

As in the case of a LLC, directors or senior managers of a JSC may not be supervisors.

A supervisor serves a term of three years and may be reelected. The board of supervisors, or supervisors if there is no board of supervisors, may examine the financial affairs of the corporation, supervise the performance of the directors or supervisors, propose to remove directors or senior managers who are in violation of laws, rules, articles of incorporation, or the resolution of the shareholder meeting, request that directors or senior managers rectify acts contravening the interests of the corporation, propose a preliminary shareholder meeting, submit proposals to the shareholder meeting, and litigate against directors or senior managers in accordance with the law. Supervisors may be present at the meetings of the board of directors and inquire into or propose resolutions to the board of directors. Supervisors may propose a preliminary meeting of the board of supervisors. The board of supervisors may initiate investigations into the business affairs of the corporation and hire accounting firms when needed upon discovery of any irregularities in business operations. The corporation should pay the necessary expenses.

The board of supervisors of a LLC should hold annual meetings while the board of supervisors of a JSC should hold biannual meetings.

1.10 Public Corporations

The regulatory scheme relating to public corporations requires them to comply with not only general laws, rules and regulations governing JSCs but also Securities Law, special trading regulations, administrative rules and stock exchange regulations. The law mainly provides for the organizational structure of a public corporation including procedures for share transfers, the transfer of major assets, the provision of guarantees that exceed the statutory limit, the establishment of an independent directorship, the provision of a secretary to the board of directors, and related transactions of public corporations.

Article 122 of the Company Law of 2014 provides that a transfer of major assets or the provision of a guarantee exceeding 30 per cent of corporation assets within one year requires a shareholder meeting resolution and a vote in favor by more than two-thirds of the shareholders present at the meeting. A transfer of major assets generally means one that exceeds 50 per cent of total assets in the audited consolidated balance sheet of the last fiscal year of the corporation and the transfer of net assets that exceed 50 per cent of net assets in the audited consolidated balance sheet of the last fiscal year of the corporation. The transfer of major assets also includes the transfer of the assets that exceeds the proportion of 50 per cent of the main business volume in the audited consolidated balance sheet of the fiscal accounting year.

1.10.1 Special Provisions for Public Corporations

1.10.1.1 Independent Directors

The Company Law of 2014 obliges public corporations to establish independent directorships. In practice, these have operated several years before being passed into law. An independent director in a public corporation is a director who holds no other posts within the corporation and without any relationships with the corporation or the major shareholders that may hamper the status of independence. An independent director owns the duty of loyalty and duty of care to the public corporation and its shareholders. A public corporation is required to select professionals including at least one accounting professional to serve as an independent director. A public corporation is required to have at least one-third of the board of directors as independent directors. In principle, one may only hold independent directorships at a maximum of five public corporations.

To ensure their independence, the law prohibits certain persons from occupying the post, including staff members of the public corporation, the direct relatives and those with major social relations with the staff, the top ten natural person shareholders and their direct relatives who directly or indirectly hold more than 1 per cent of issued shares of the public corporation, a shareholder unit that directly or indirectly holds more than 5 per cent of the issued shares of the public corporation, the staff members and their direct relatives who hold posts within the top five shareholder units of the public corporation, or persons who provide financial, legal, and consulting services to the public corporation or its affiliates.

The board of directors, the board of supervisors, or shareholders singularly or jointly holding more than 1 per cent of issued shares of the public corporation may propose candidates for the independent directorship subject to the election outcome at the shareholder meeting. The securities supervisory and regulatory agency has the right to conduct an examination of the qualification and independence of an independent director. An independent director may be reelected but for no more than six years in total.

Approval from independent directors regarding major related transactions of the corporation is required before a report regarding the transaction can be submitted to the board of directors. Independent directors may hire independent financial consulting services to make evaluations of such transaction. They may independently hire external audit and consulting agency. An independent director may convey their opinion regarding any damage to the interest and rights of minority shareholders. The powers of independent directors include the right to make proposals regarding the hiring of an accounting firm to the board of directors, a preliminary shareholder meeting to the board of directors, and a meeting of the board of directors. The exercise of the above mentioned powers will require the approval of more than half the independent directors. In addition, an independent director will provide independent opinions regarding the nomination and removal of directors, the appointment or removal of senior managers, and the remuneration of directors and senior managers. The articles of incorporation may provide for any other powers of an independent director.

To help to ensure independence in the performance of their duties, an independent director enjoys equal rights to those of any other director including the right to know about corporate affairs. To achieve this end, an independent director may seek assistance from the public corporation which may not interfere in the work of independent directors. The public corporation will also need to provide necessary working conditions and cooperation to facilitate the performance of the duties of independent directors.

Under the law, a public corporation shall have a secretary to the board of directors be responsible for the organization of shareholder meetings and meetings of the board of directors. A secretary to the board of directors will prepare document depositories, maintain, and manage information and material related to shareholders and be responsible for disclosure of information by the public corporation. Under the law, a secretary to the board of directors is a member of the senior management whose major obligations are to assist in the handling the daily activities of the board of directors. This secretary is subject to appointment or removal by the board of directors.

1.10.1.2 Corporate Representatives

Someone who has taken the role of corporate representative enjoys the right to externally represent the corporation in activities ranging from business operations to negotiation. Under the law, the corporate representative is referred to as a legal representative. The chairperson, executive director, or any manager may act as legal representative of the corporation in accordance with the articles of incorporation.

1.10.1.3 Restrictions and Duties

The law imposes restrictions on the qualifications, duties, and activities of those involved in corporation operations. A person may not serve as a director, supervisor, or senior management officer of a corporation if they (i) lack civil capacity or has only limited civil capacity; (ii) have been sentenced to pay a criminal penalty for corruption, bribery, encroachment of property, misappropriation of property, or disrupting the economic order of the socialist market economy (iii) are a former director, factory director, or manager of a corporation that went bankrupt and was liquidated, were personally liable for such bankruptcy or liquidation, and three years have not passed since the date of completion of the bankruptcy or liquidation proceedings; (iv) have served as the legal representative of a corporation whose business license has been revoked and for which they were personally liable because of a violation of law in the last three years; or (v) have significant overdue personal debts.

The election or appointment of a director, supervisor, or officer who fits the description of any of the above conditions would be invalid. Such director, supervisor, or senior management officer has to be dismissed from the position in question.

Directors, supervisors, and senior managers owe a duty of care as well as a duty of loyalty to the corporation. They must act in ways pursuant to the relevant laws, regulations, and articles of incorporation. No director, supervisor, or senior management officer may take any bribe or other illegal gains by taking advantage of the position nor encroach upon corporation property. Article 149 of the Company Law of 2014 provides a list of acts that violate the duty of loyalty. Any gains thus obtained will be considered illegal and confiscated by the corporation. Individuals involved will be liable for any losses to the corporation. Prohibited acts include (i) misappropriating corporation funds; (ii) depositing corporate funds into an individual bank account; (iii) using corporate funds for loans or guaranties without the approval of the shareholder meeting or board meeting, in violation of the articles of incorporation; (iv) signing a contract or trading with the corporation in violation of the articles of incorporation or without approval by the shareholder meeting; (v) appropriating corporate business opportunities for personal benefit or operating for oneself or another person in competition with the corporation without the approval of the shareholder meeting; (vi) obtaining commission from a corporate transaction; (vii) disclosing corporate secrets without permission; and (viii) performing any other acts inconsistent with the duty of loyalty.

In the event that a director, supervisor, or senior manager breaches their duties, shareholders may pursue legal action against them. Upon the request of shareholders who individually or collectively hold more than 1 per cent of corporate shares, the corporation may, via its board of directors, file a lawsuit against those who allegedly breached their duties. The corporation also may file a lawsuit via its board of supervisors. To be qualified, shareholders must have held more than 1 per cent of corporate shares continuously for more than 180 day. Shareholders may file the suit on their own if they find that the corporation has refused to file such a suit, if there is an emergency such that any delay will cause irreparable harm to the corporation, or if the interests of shareholders are directly jeopardized. If a manager infringes the interests of shareholders in violation of laws, administrative rules and regulations, or the articles of incorporation, the aggrieved shareholders may sue for compensation.

1.10.2 Invalid Corporate Resolutions and Relief

An invalid resolution of the board of directors and a resolution of the shareholder meeting may be cancelled or made void. A resolution is deemed defective if in violation of laws, rules or internal corporate regulations such as the articles of incorporation. The law specifically provides for defective corporate resolutions by means of voidance or cancellation. Article 22 of the Company Law of 2014 provides that resolutions of the shareholder meeting or board of directors are void in contravention of laws, rules, or the articles of incorporation. Shareholders have the right to request the court to cancel any such resolution within 60 days of the date on which the resolution was agreed. The people's court may at the request of the corporation ask the shareholders to provide the corresponding guarantee. Normally, a resolution in contravention of laws or rules is void or is subject to cancellation with regard to the substance of the matter. Procedural matters or voting methods that violate rules, laws, or the articles of incorporation are subject to cancellation, but can only be resolved through the courts.

1.10.3 Fiduciary Duties

The concept of fiduciary duties under the law refers to the duties of care and loyalty. Article 148 of the Company Law of 2014 provides for the fiduciary duties of directors, supervisors, and senior managers. The law requires them observe laws, rules and the articles of incorporation and pay the duties of care and loyalty to their corporation.

Duty of care is the standard a fiduciary must observe to avoid damaging the interests of the corporation. Duty of loyalty refers to the standard of behavior by which fiduciaries place the interest of the corporation above their own. A fiduciary may not accept bribes or illegal income by virtue of their position within the corporation. In addition, they may not usurp corporate property. The law sets forth specific provisions for the duty of loyalty with regard to directors or senior managers. Directors or senior managers may not usurp corporate funds or open personal bank accounts with corporate funds, without approval of a shareholder meeting or board of directors meeting, make a loan to another person with corporate funds, provide a guarantee to another person with corporate fund, enter into a contract with the corporation, transact with the corporation, procure corporate opportunities for itself or the other persons, or accept commission for any transaction between the corporation and any other person. Fiduciaries may not disclose corporate secrets. The law has a catch-all clause to proscribe any act that is in violation of the duty of loyalty.

1.10.4 The Rights and Responsibilities of Fiduciary Duties

Directors, supervisors, senior managers, controlling shareholders, or controlling person owe fiduciary duties to the corporation and shareholders and bear liabilities for breach of fiduciary duties to the corporation and shareholders. Directors, supervisors or senior managers who violate laws, rules or the articles of incorporation and have caused damages will be liable when breaching fiduciary duties. The law also provides for the liability of directors, supervisors, or senior managers that act against the interests of the corporation in conducting related transactions.

Shareholders owe fiduciary duties to each other, especially in cases in which the interests of majority shareholders or controlling shareholders run counter to the interests of minority shareholders. Shareholders are required to observe laws, rules and the articles of incorporation not to abuse shareholder rights and damage the interests of the corporation or the interests of other shareholders. A controlling shareholder is a shareholder with more than 50 per cent of shares of a limited liability corporation or a joint stock limited liability corporation. A shareholder may still be a controlling shareholder with less than 50 per cent of corporate shares if they exercise major influence over the resolutions made at a shareholder meeting. A controlling person may indeed not be a shareholder, but be able to exercise control over the corporation through investment, agreements or other arrangements.

1.11 Duty of Care

Duty of care refers to the performance of obligations by directors or senior managers in compliance with a reasonable degree of care. Duty of care is the basis for judging whether a particular behavior by a director or senior manager is negligent or not. Directors or senior managers may be deemed negligent if duty of care is breached and found liable for damages. In discussions on duty of care, the important component is the business judgment rule. Designed to shield directors or senior managers from harassment lawsuits following business failures, it is, in fact, a safe harbor rule. In principle and practice, the standard for failure to satisfy the business judgment rule is gross negligence. As a rule that enjoys general practice in countries like the United States, it has not been tested much in Chinese courts. It is not clear that the law provides shelter by way of the business judgment rule even though courts tend to defer to corporate management's business judgment.

1.11.1 Duty of Loyalty

Duty of loyalty refers to a standard of behavior by which a fiduciary shall place the interests of the corporation above their own. A fiduciary may not accept bribes or illegal income by virtue of their position within the corporation. In addition, they may not usurp corporate property.

Duty of loyalty has two components: first, directors or senior managers may not place their own interests above the corporation's and shareholders; and second, they may not exploit their position in the corporation for their own benefit.

The law sets forth specific provisions relating to the duty of loyalty. Directors or senior managers may not enter into self-dealing transactions or transactions in which there is a conflict of interest. Self-dealing may occur when directors or senior managers represent both sides in a transaction and achieve an optimal outcome for both sides. Duty of loyalty may be an issue when directors or senior managers transfer their own property to the corporation. The law provides that directors or senior managers may not enter into contracts or transact with the corporation in contravention of the articles of incorporation or without the approval of the shareholder meeting. The law does not prohibit self-dealing but subjects such transactions to the approval of the shareholder meeting or the provisions of the articles of incorporation.

The law requires that controlling shareholders, controlling persons, directors, supervisors, or senior managers, shall not damage the interests of the corporation by exploiting their relationship with the corporation, in case liabilities and damages ensue. These relationships are defined as those between a majority shareholder, controlling person, director, supervisor or senior manager, and the enterprises directly or indirectly controlled by such persons. Related transactions may be regarded as a special type of self-dealing. The law is more interested in requiring the related persons not to exploit the related relationships to damage the interests of the corporation than aiming to prohibit self-dealing acts altogether.

Usurpation of corporate opportunities may be considered a major breach of duty of loyalty. The duty of loyalty prohibits directors or senior managers from usurping corporate opportunities to benefit themselves. Under the law, the directors or senior managers may procure corporate opportunities to benefit themselves or the others only with the consent of the shareholder meeting.

Duty of loyalty includes the duty not to compete with the corporation. The law provides that neither directors nor senior managers may engage in similar business to that of the corporation for their own or for the others without the prior consent of the shareholder meeting. The shareholder meeting must consent to business conducted in competition with the corporation for such conduct to be permissible. The law condones such transactions if the competitive action is conducted upon receiving the consent of the shareholder meeting.

1.11.2 Derivative Litigation

A derivative lawsuit may be initiated by a shareholder who, on behalf of the corporation, brings a lawsuit against a wrongdoer for acts committed in the instance that the corporation fails to remedy the wrong. A derivative lawsuit may deter wrongdoings against the corporation to protect the interests of the corporation and minority shareholders in the event that there is a breach of fiduciary duty. It is a substitute relief mechanism that ultimately helps to enforce fiduciary duties on the part of directors, supervisors, and senior management. The derivative lawsuit doctrine was established in common law countries and soon met with widespread acceptance in civil law countries. China is one of the countries to have adopted a derivative lawsuit doctrine.

A derivative lawsuit is different from a shareholder lawsuit or direct shareholder lawsuit. The latter addresses a wrong directly inflicted upon the shareholder. The legal authority for a derivative lawsuit is based on the Company Law of 2014. The law endorses a shareholder's right to bring a lawsuit against any act in contravention of the interests of the corporation and the shareholders, in violation of the laws, rules, regulations, and the articles of incorporation, by directors, senior managers, supervisors or any other third persons. This particular article serves as an important legal basis upon which the mechanism of derivative lawsuit is founded. The law also prohibits the abuse of shareholders' rights and provides for liability on the part of wrongdoers if the abuse causes damages to other shareholders' interests.

In a derivative lawsuit, the original litigation right rests with the corporation. The shareholder derives the derivative litigation right from the original right. The plaintiff shareholder may pursue a derivative lawsuit in the interests of the corporation. The corporation as beneficiary reaps any ultimate reward of the litigation. A derivative lawsuit should proceed in accordance with a set of special procedures under the law which may be terminated or dismissed upon noncompliance of these special procedures.

Shareholders of a limited liability corporation may act as plaintiff in a derivative lawsuit without restrictions. Shareholders of a joint stock limited liability corporation however, need to maintain their shareholder status for at least 180 days or singularly or jointly hold more than 1 per cent of the shares of the corporation to be able to sue in a derivative lawsuit. The defendant in a derivative lawsuit may be any person to have violated the interests of the corporation. In practice, the defendants may be directors, supervisors or senior managers. Derivative lawsuit could be directed against a controlling shareholder or a person in actual control of the corporation. The law provides that a shareholder has the duty to observe laws, rules, regulations and the articles of incorporation in exercising shareholder rights and that they may not damage other shareholders' interests.

A shareholder who is to initiate a derivative lawsuit must first make a pre-lawsuit demand on the corporation to take any necessary action to litigate the wrong in the first place. Only after the corporation fails to take any such action may the shareholder bring a derivative lawsuit. The pre-lawsuit demand is meant to exhaust internal remedy options in the corporation before shareholders resort to the extraordinary relief of a derivative lawsuit. To satisfy the pre-lawsuit demand requirement, the shareholder is required to file a written request to the board of supervisors or the board of directors to ask to litigate the wrongdoing in court. It is also acceptable for the shareholder to go directly to court in the name of the corporation in the case of a hard to remedy emergency that would inflict harm on the interests of the corporation. In such an instance, the requirement to make a pre-lawsuit demand is excused. Otherwise, upon receipt of a written demand from the shareholder, the corporation has a statutory period of 30 days to respond. If the corporation fails to respond within 30 days, the shareholder may bring the case to court. Under either circumstances, the burden of proof is on the litigating shareholder.

1.12 Corporate Changes

1.12.1 Mergers and Divestitures

1.12.2 Corporate Mergers

A merger refers to the combining of two corporate entities in accordance with legal procedures by way of a merger agreement. Under the law, a corporate merger may either take the form of a merger or a consolidation. In a merger, one corporation is merged into another, with the former being dissolved. Under this type of merger, the corporation that is still in existence after the merger will retain its original name before the merger and will inherit the proprietary rights and the rights of the creditors of the corporation that has been merged. In the meantime, the merging corporation will be continuing to undertake the debt obligations of the corporation that has been merged. Under a consolidation, two or more separate corporate entities will become a new corporate entity with the former two or more entities being dissolved.

Chinese Company Law provides procedural requirements for a merger. A merger requires the resolution of the meeting of shareholders. For a limited liability corporation and joint stock limited liability corporation, a two-thirds vote of shareholders at the shareholder meeting is required. The law requires the corporation to produce an asset and liability statement and balance sheet. The balance sheet needs to include all tangible and intangible properties of the corporation, real properties, cash, and any other form of properties of the corporation. The corporation is required to notify its debtors within 10 days of the date of the resolution approving the merger and publicize the merger within 30 days in newspapers. This notification requirement gives creditors the time to exercise their rights to raise any discrepancies regarding the payment of debts. Within this prescribed period of time, normally within 30 days upon the receipt of notification by the creditor, they are deemed to have agreed to the merger if no discrepancies have been raised.

A corporate merger brings with it certain legal consequences, such as the dissolution of a corporation, corporate changes, the transfer of corporate rights and obligations, and fulfillment of the requirement to register the merger.

A corporation going through a merger is not required to go through dissolution procedures under the law. The corporation that remains after the merger will need to amend its articles of incorporation. Such amendment will be accomplished at a shareholder meeting after the merger. Under a consolidation merger, the new corporation may call for an establishment meeting to formulate new articles of incorporation. The principle for a merger or consolidation is that the rights and obligations of the corporation will be inherited by the existing corporation, and all proprietary rights will be inherited without condition. Any property that has been transferred after the merger will need to be registered with the authorities by the new corporation in accordance with required procedures. Any debts that have been inherited by the corporation are required to be registered with the corporation registry. A post-merger corporation shall be registered with the corporation registry authority or relevant governmental department. A corporation that is dissolved should proceed with the required cancellation procedures at the corporation registry authority. A newly established corporation shall proceed with establishment registration with the corporation registry authority.

1.12.3 Divestitures

A divestiture refers to when a corporation divests its properties to become two or more corporate entities. It may take place in one of two forms. The first is a corporation that has divested a portion of its properties or business to form a new corporate entity or several new corporate entities. With such a divestiture, the corporation may still remain in existence. The second form of divestiture, also referred to as a dissolution divestiture, is a corporate act by which the original corporation, with all its properties, becomes two or more new corporations after divestiture and the original corporation is dissolved.

A divestiture must be approved by resolution at a shareholder meeting. A two-thirds vote in favor is required for either a limited liability corporation or a joint stock limited liability corporation. The law requires that the corporation under a divestiture should produce its balance sheet and asset liability statement for review at a shareholder meeting. The corporation shall notify its creditors within 10 days of the date of resolution and publicize the divestiture in the newspaper for 30 days. The parties involving in a corporate divestiture may agree in writing as to the division and payment of debt obligations of the corporation. The law requires that the debt obligations of the corporation before the divestiture shall be inherited by the corporation surviving the divestiture with the latter bearing joint and several liabilities in default of the parties' agreement to the contrary. A divestiture may also result in a merger, consolidation, dissolution, corporate changes or the establishment of a new corporation. A corporation after divestiture will be required to go through proper cancellation procedures or establishment registration formalities with the corporation registry. The law provides that following divestiture, a corporation shall register for changes with the corporation registry. A corporation that has been dissolved after divestiture is required under the law to register its cancellation. If a new corporation is established as a result of a divestiture, the law requires a newly established corporation to proceed with establishment registration with the corporation registry.

1.12.4 Changes in Capitalization

Changes in capitalization generally refer to either an increase or decrease in the capitalization of a corporation. An increase of capitalization either refers to an increase in total registered capital, an increase of the face value of shares, or an increase in the capital contribution. A new share issuance or debt to equity swap will affect an increase in the capitalization of the corporation. An increase in the face value of the shares is to increase the value per share without increasing the total amount of shares in the corporation. If a limited liability corporation requires an increase in contribution, the corporation may increase shareholders' capital contributions on a pro rata basis or it may invite external investors into the corporation. A joint stock limited liability corporation may issue new shares to increase its capitalization. Such new issuance may be a public subscription or a subscription by the original shareholders. Under normal circumstances, the corporation's original shareholders will enjoy preemptive rights to purchase new shares. A debt to equity swap by a joint stock limited liability corporation is an alternative way to effect change in corporate capitalization.

The statutory procedures for an increase in corporate capitalization should be approved by a super majority vote of shareholders. The law requires a two-thirds vote in favor for either a limited liability corporation or a joint stock limited liability corporation. Any corporation that has increased its registered capital must register the increase with the corporate registry. A corporation may also decrease its capitalization, including the face value of shares, the capital contribution or the total quantity of shares. A decrease in the face value of shares refers to a decrease of the value per share without changing the total quantity of shares of the corporation. A reduction in capital contribution or a reduction of the total quantity of shares means a reduction of the contribution to the corporation or a reduction of the total quantity of shares of the corporation. A corporation will normally buy back its shares for capitalization reduction. One thing to note is that in the event that a corporation chooses to buy back its shares, within 10 days of the buyback, it must proceed to cancel the shares that have been bought back. The statutory requirement for the procedure of reduction of capitalization is rather similar to that required by an increase in capitalization. Normally, a reduction of capitalization needs a two-thirds vote by shareholders. Likewise, the corporation is also required to produce a review of assets and liabilities and a balance sheet for the reduction of registered capital for shareholders. The corporation shall notify its creditors within 10 days of the date of the resolution approving the reduction and put up a public notice in the newspaper within 30 days. Upon receipt of the notification, debtors may, within 30 days, approach the corporation for debt payment or request the provision of a guarantee of debt obligations. Similarly, the corporation after the reduction of the registered capital shall register the changes with the corporation registry.

1.12.5 Termination of a Corporation

1.12.6 Dissolution

The dissolution of a corporation refers to the termination of the legal person identity of a corporation upon the occurrence of a certain event. The legal person identity of the corporation remains until the corporation is wound-up which may happen after dissolution. A corporation may become dissolved in the cases of a merger or divestiture. A dissolved corporation must go through the statutory process of dissolution.

A dissolution may be either a voluntary dissolution or an involuntary dissolution. A voluntary dissolution occurs when the corporation dissolves itself upon the occurrence of a certain event on its own volition. Such an event may be prescribed under the articles of incorporation of the corporation or by a shareholder meeting resolution. A corporation may prescribe under the articles of incorporation such instances as may trigger a dissolution. For example, the articles of incorporation may provide for specific terms of the corporation. Upon the occurrence of the expiry of the term, the corporation will become dissolved pursuant to the articles of incorporation. Modern corporate law is generally of the opinion that a corporation may exist in perpetual terms. The articles of incorporation may provide, however, a specific term for the corporation. Otherwise, the corporation may exist perpetually in theory.

An involuntary dissolution is the dissolution of a corporation pursuant to an act under the law or an administrative order.

Statutory dissolution is a type of involuntary dissolution. Statutory dissolution prescribes a set of circumstances upon the occurrence of which a dissolution under the law or rules and regulations is caused. For instance, a merger or divestiture may be a cause for dissolution. A dissolution may be pursuant to an administrative order which is an order issued by the department in charge of the dissolution. An administrative order for dissolution includes circumstances of the revocation of the business license or the closure of the business. The law regards the revocation of the business license or closure of the business as a valid cause for dissolution.

The judgment from a court may also constitute an order to dissolve a corporation. A court is authorized within its judicial power to dissolve a corporation. Such order of the court for dissolution may be requested by shareholders by petitioning the court. Under the law, shareholders with

10 per cent voting rights of the corporation may petition the court to dissolve the corporation, in the absence of alternatives, upon the occurrence of the prescribed conditions. Such conditions may include poor management by the corporation that causes material loss to shareholder interests. Another situation for involuntary dissolution is what it is described in the law pursuant to which the shareholders may petition the court for dissolution when the corporation faces a deadlock. In the event of a deadlock, shareholders may exercise the right to petition the court for dissolution. The court is at its discretion to make a decision as to whether to issue an order to dissolve the corporation.

When a corporation is in bankruptcy proceeding, the corporation will become dissolved and terminated upon completion of the bankruptcy procedures.

1.12.7 Liquidation

Liquidation refers to a series of acts and procedures that bring about a division of the corporate property and a closure to the legal relationships of the corporation. After a corporation is dissolved and wound up, the legal person identity of the corporation is then terminated. The legal person status of a corporation retains legal validity after the dissolution but before the liquidation process. Before a corporation can be completely wound-up, the legal capacity to exercise its relevant rights is limited to the execution of liquidation duties. The corporation is forbidden from engaging in any other business activities for profit. As soon as a dissolved corporation enters into the liquidation process, the corporate institution endowed with the powers of the corporation will cease to be effective. The persons in charge of the liquidation process will represent the corporation in execution of the necessary corporate functions including, but not limited to, notifying creditors, winding up any unfinished business activities, paying any taxes that are due, distributing residual property, and participating in any litigation.

Under the law, liquidation is categorized as voluntary liquidation, prescribed liquidation, or bankruptcy liquidation.

Voluntary liquidation refers to a liquidation that is initiated and organized by the corporation. A corporation may engage in voluntary liquidation upon the occurrence of certain events that are provided for under the articles of incorporation or pursuant to a dissolution resolution of the shareholder meeting. The occurrence of dissolution triggering events may include the revocation of a corporation's business license, the closure of corporate business, or a petition filed by shareholders with the court to terminate the corporation.

A corporation that has been dissolved must establish a liquidation committee within 15 days of the occurrence of an event that has triggered dissolution. The liquidation committee shall consist of shareholders for a limited liability corporation and directors or persons designated by the shareholder meeting for a joint stock limited liability corporation. The controlling shareholders, directors, and managers will bear civil liabilities for any damages to the property of the corporation or the rights of the shareholders in the event that the corporation fails to pass the voluntary liquidation process.

The prescribed liquidation process refers to a process by persons designated by the court to conduct liquidation by a petition of the interested parties concerned.

Bankruptcy liquidation is a corporate liquidation process under the bankruptcy law. In theory, a corporation that has declared bankruptcy will go through bankruptcy procedures to liquidate and wind up business. If the liquidation committee finds corporate assets to be insufficient to pay its debts, the corporation will file for bankruptcy with the court. The liquidation committee shall transfer the relevant liquidation matter to the court after it issues a declaration of bankruptcy. The chief responsibilities of the liquidation committee are to perform its functions under the law. The committee will produce an asset and liability statement and balance sheet, notify the debtors of the corporation within 10 days of the establishment of the liquidation committee, handle any unfinished corporate matters, pay taxes that are due, pay the debts of the corporation, formulate a liquidation plan that should be submitted for confirmation at the shareholder meeting or the court, distribute any residual property after payment of the corporation's debts, and represent the corporation in civil litigation matters. The sequence for payments should be liquidation expenses, salaries, social security expenses, taxes, and corporation's debts. For any residual property, the corporation will distribute its residual property to the shareholders pro rata. The committee members may be liable for any damages to the interests of the corporation and creditors due to intentional or material negligence.

The liquidation process will be terminated upon submission of the application for cancellation of the business registration with the corporation registration agency on production of a report by the liquidation committee that has been confirmed at the shareholder meeting or in court.

1.13 The Transformation

1.13.1 Registered Capital

Over the course of a decade, corporate law in China has undergone many changes. The recent changes that have come into being with the revised Company Law of 2014 are the result of fruitful experiments arising from years of implementation of the paid-in registered capital system. A payment of 100 per cent of the registered capital at the time of establishment used to be required. This means that if a corporation had registered capital of RMB one million, before 2005 it would have been obliged to pay it all before operations began. Under the Company Law of 2005, this was reduced to a 20 per cent downpayment at the time of registration, with the remaining amount to be paid up within the first two years for an LLC and within the first five years for an investment corporation. The Company Law of 2014 eliminated these restrictions, which means that a single member LLC is no longer required to pay all its registered capital at once.

Clearly, the objective for this reform was to broaden access to the establishment of corporations. The reform was initially implemented in the Shanghai Free Trade Zone, the Shenzhen Free Trade Zone, and in other key cities. Setting up a corporation has become more user-friendly and the threshold has been considerably lowered. Literally speaking, one may set up a corporation for RMB 1 under the latest Company Law. Article 7 of the Company Law of 2014 abolished the 'paid-in capital' requirement for establishing a corporation. Article 23 revised the Company Law of 2005 regarding minimum registered capital by providing for subscribed capital by shareholders. Article 26 stated that the registered capital of a LLC is the contribution subscribed to by shareholders registered on the corporation registry unless otherwise provided by law. The requirement under the Company Law of 2005 regarding the minimum registered capital of a single member LLC and the one-time contribution has been abolished. The requirement for one-time or installment contributions for corporations in general has been abolished under the Company Law of 2014. Articles 76 and 80 in conjunction with Article 83 of the Company Law of 2014 provide that the articles of incorporation designate share contributions for establishing a JSC and shareholders are required to subscribe in writing and pay as agreed.

Nevertheless, inconsistencies under the Securities Law, Criminal Law, Foreign Investment Law, and numerous administrative rules have inevitably arisen. For example, the Supreme Court issued a Judicial Interpretation dealing with failed paid-in capital situations. Criminal law has made provisions against the crime of defrauding the system of registered capital with sentences of up to three years' imprisonment and penalties. Such inconsistencies undoubtedly need to be reconciled with and addressed in future rounds of legislation. The relevant administrative rules regarding the registration of corporations will be subject to major changes or may even be repealed.

1.13.2 Shareholder Rights and Corporate Governance

Post-2014, China has witnessed a surge in lawsuits and disputes about corporate governance and shareholder rights, accounting for more than 60 per cent of the total number of lawsuits and disputes involving corporate issues during this period. In August 2017, the Supreme People's Court issued Provisions on Some Issues Concerning the Application of Corporate Law of the People's Republic of China (IV) (Judicial Interpretation IV). This was in response to a rapid increase in corporate lawsuits and the practice of divergence of opinions in court and legal practice. It purported to strengthen shareholders' rights protection and enhance the level of corporate governance by providing uniform answers to many of the problems that have surfaced in law and practice.

Judicial Interpretation IV provided an interpretation of the law covering such issues as the legal effect of shareholder resolutions, the right to profit distribution, preemptive rights, and shareholder representative litigation. It has, among other things, clarified the relationship between the effect of resolutions and litigation to establish the validity of resolutions. As shareholders may have access to their corporation's files and records, Judicial Interpretation IV specified that shareholders may check corporate accounting books and that the shareholders may use hired services to assist in their investigations. Regarding profit distribution, the Supreme Court generally stands by the principle of business judgment and corporate autonomy. The Court made it clear in the Judicial Interpretation that a shareholder requesting a corporation to distribute profits should submit a resolution of the shareholders' meeting or a general meeting of shareholders specifying the distribution plan. Judicial Interpretation IV also provided remedies for damages unto the distribution rights of shareholders by stipulating that the judiciary may intervene properly to correct wrongs on the part of the corporation when shareholders abuse their rights and damage the interest of the corporation and other shareholders by failing to make profit distribution. Judicial Interpretation IV also went to great lengths to delineating a boundary of preemptive shareholder rights in equity transfers. It clearly rejected the argument that a transfer in violation of preemptive rights would automatically be invalidated. Rather, Judicial Interpretation IV states that the non-shareholder transferee may request the transferring shareholder to assume relevant contractual liabilities to protect the interests and rights of the bona fide purchaser.

In general and specific terms, Judicial Interpretation IV is a much welcomed move toward granting judicial relief in the case of injury to shareholders' rights by conferring protection upon minority shareholders, restraining conflicts of interest among shareholders, and between shareholders and the corporation, and attempting to avoid corporate deadlock, all with the aim of helping create a sounder business environment.

CHAPTER 2

Foreign Investment Law

During the 1970s, the government began working towards the liberalization of foreign direct investment in China. This led to major policy changes with respect to laws governing foreign investment and foreign invested enterprises. The government issued policies to stimulate creativity and productivity in the general population in order to promote economic growth. It was during this period and the subsequent three decades of reform that China witnessed the gradual formulation of a governance framework for foreign investment and foreign invested enterprises.

China's entry into the World Trade Organization (WTO) between 2001 and 2005 spearheaded a new stage of growth and development. With entry into the WTO, China enhanced its level of undertakings and commitments to international economic development. The speed at which China started attracting foreign investment also accelerated after WTO entry. During the Tenth Five-Year Plan period, approximately USD 383 billion in foreign capital was invested, of which USD 286 billion was in the form of foreign direct investment.

In general, foreign businesses in China include those invested in by corporations or individuals from Hong Kong, Macau, and Taiwan. These investment businesses are referred to as foreign invested enterprises (FIEs). An FIE may take the form of a Sino-Foreign Equity Joint Venture (EJV), a Sino-Foreign Contractual Joint Venture (CJV), a Wholly Foreign Owned Enterprise (WFOE), a Foreign Invested Joint Stock Limited Corporation (foreign JSC), or another form of investment permitted by law. A foreign

D. Yu, *Chinese Business Law*, The Palgrave Series on Chinese Law,
https://doi.org/10.1007/978-981-13-0902-1_2

investor may be either a natural person with foreign citizenship or a legal person with foreign domicile who engages in direct investment in China. A foreign investor may be a foreign corporation, an enterprise, an economic organization, or a foreign individual and may be from Hong Kong, Macau, or Taiwan. A foreign investor is subject to foreign investment law, as well as the governing rules and regulations. *Sanzi qiye fa*, otherwise known as 'The Three Foreign Investment Laws' were formulated to govern the sphere of foreign investment and FIEs. These three laws provide a legal foundation for the establishment of foreign invested enterprises. They are the Sino-foreign Equity Joint Ventures Law (EJV Law), the Sino-foreign Contractual Joint Ventures Law (CJV Law), and the Wholly Foreign-Owned Enterprises Law (WFOE Law). The EJV Law was promulgated by the National People's Congress on July 1, 1979 and revised on April 4, 1990. Implementing Rules were enacted by the State Council on September 20, 1983 and amended on December 21, 1987. The CJV Law was promulgated by the National People's Congress on April 13, 1988. The National People's Congress promulgated the WFOE Law on April 12, 1986. In 1990, the Implementing Rules were enacted by the State Council. On January 10, 1995, the former MOFTEC issued Provisional Regulations on Certain Issues Concerning the Establishment of Foreign Invested Joint Stock Limited Corporations. These regulations provide the standard for establishing JSCs and serve as a supplement to the three forms of foreign investment.

FIE laws governing foreign investment and the subsequent relevant rules and regulations provide specifically for the establishment, operation, management, termination, and liquidation of FIEs. They protect the rights and interests of domestic and foreign investors equally. Upon entry into the WTO and in order to comply with WTO commitments, the Chinese government updated many of its laws and regulations governing foreign investment. The establishment and growth of the Shanghai Free Trade Zone, other free trade zones and the future establishment of free ports have demonstrated the beginnings of comprehensive legal reform and change in relation to foreign investment. Recently, the central government has made yet more effort to modernize foreign investment regulations with the installation of the special entry control system. Under this system, foreign investment projects are no longer required to gain prior administrative approval on an individual case basis unless they fall within a specified industry or industries on the special entry control list, or are listed on a negative list. This marks a change in the foreign investment regulatory environment from one of administrative approval to one of negative list management. This will be discussed further later in this chapter.

2.1 The Evolution of Chinese Foreign Investment Law

FIE law on foreign investment enterprises is modeled on international business practices but tailored to suit the needs and demands of a country like China, a country which has experienced fundamental economic, political and social change in recent decades. FIE law has proved instrumental in serving the state's more open policy towards attracting foreign investment, economic cooperation and technology exchange. After entering WTO, China's National People's Congress revised the WFOE and CJV Laws of October 2000 as well as the EJV Law of March 2001. This enabled China to conform with new WTO commitments. Consequently, the Implementation Rules for the WFOE Law and EJV Law were amended in April and July 2001, respectively. These amendments and changes demonstrated efforts to evolve legislation in order to cope with an altered environment. Major changes to FIE law included a requirement to balance foreign exchanges accounts, develop raw material supply localization, and report enterprise production plans and export achievement requirements. Although they were an important component of earlier FIE law, the above requirements were not included in the revised laws. For example, Article 20 of former CJV Law required CJVs to maintain a balance between foreign exchange income and expenses. Section 3, Article 18 of the former WFOE Law required WFOEs to maintain a balance of foreign-exchange receipts and disbursements. The CJV and WFOE Laws removed these requirements. A WFOE was previously required to purchase and source its supplies, raw material and fuel on the Chinese domestic market. Article 15 of the revised WFOE Law allowed WFOEs to purchase supplies on either domestic or international markets. Likewise, the former EJV Law required EJVs to prioritize products of local origin on the Chinese domestic market when purchasing raw or semiprocessed materials, fuel and auxiliary equipment. This was despite the provision for EJV acquisition of materials directly from the international market using its own foreign exchange funds. The revised EJV Law allowed EJVs to purchase materials on domestic or international markets. In addition, the requirement for WFOEs to apply advanced technology and equipment and export all or most of their products, was removed. The relevant provision of the revised WFOE law only stated that the establishment of WFOEs must benefit the development of the Chinese national economy and that China encourages the establishment of export-oriented and technologically advanced WFOSs. China's FIE law has never stopped evolving to keep up with the country's constantly changing economic environment. Later FIE legal changes suggest a newly established system of special entry control in foreign investment regulation. This will be discussed more later in this chapter.

2.2 The Governance Regime for Foreign Investment

Since 'Reform and Opening Up' began in China, the Ministry of Commerce, (MOFCOM, formerly MOFTEC), has been the main government department responsible for regulating foreign investment in China. MOFCOM governs the sphere of foreign investment by issuing departmental rules and regulations. During the past three decades of reform it has been de facto legislator of foreign investments. MOFCOM has created a vast number of departmental policies and rules concerning foreign investment and trade, and has also provided general guidance on foreign investment projects. MOFCOM usually takes the lead even when it issues rules in collaboration with other departments.

The National Development and Reform Commission (NDRC) is another important governmental department with responsibility for the macroeconomic management of China. NDRC is considered a major cabinet level ministry under the State Council. It formulates policies for economic and social development, maintains a balance of economic growth, and issues policies to guide reconstruction efforts that shape the future economic system. NDRC is given a broad mandate in relation to the regulation of overall economic activities. It is vested with ultimate authority in deciding how commodities are to be priced. In relation to foreign investment, NDRC is another major department which drafts and updates the Foreign Investment Catalogue and evaluates and approves major foreign investment projects.

The China Securities Regulatory Commission (CSRC) is the agency authorized by the central government to supervise and administrate the securities market. It aims to ensure the orderly and legitimate operation of the securities market in China. CSRC issues rules and regulations on foreign investment in relation to securities.

All foreign investment concerns will inevitably come into contact with the State Administration of Foreign Exchange (SAFE) in relation to foreign exchange matters. SAFE is part of the People's Bank of China (PBOC). As well as other tasks, it is entrusted with the authority to oversee and supervise foreign exchange matters. SAFE carrys out its work by issuing departmental rules on foreign investment in conjunction with other government departments. SAFE is relevant to foreign investment matters when applications are made for registration of foreign exchange matters or in relation to opening a foreign exchange account with it or with its local offices.

The State Administration for Industry and Commerce (SAIC) is an authority directly under the State Council. It is charged with market supervision and regulation and specifically oversees the registration of enterprises and businesses, organizations, and individuals which engage in business activities. SAIC manages the registration of foreign investment matters. SAIC registration gives business licenses to enterprises so that they can operate in China on a legal basis.

The State-owned Asset Supervision and Administration Commission (SASAC) is the major administrative regulator for mergers and acquisitions when state-owned enterprises or state-owned concerns are involved. SASAC was established in recent years in order to try to separate government administration from enterprise management, and business ownership from management power. SASAC performs its investor duties on behalf of the state in relation to all state-owned entities. It has authority to supervise and manage state-owned assets. At national level, SASAC directs and supervises local state-owned asset supervision and administration agencies. As a *de jure* investor, SASAC is a state-owned entity entrusted by the central authorities to undertake experimental reforms and restructure state-owned enterprises.

If a foreign investment concern is engaged in an acquisition involving a state-owned asset or if a state-owned enterprise becomes party to an EJV or CJV, administration by and approval of SASAC is relevant. In such circumstances, the inevitable issues of state-owned asset evaluation and property rights will arise. Concerned parties should seek SASAC approval for such a transaction.

2.2.1 *The Governance Framework for Foreign Investment*

The framework governing foreign investment in China comprises an intricate set of laws, rules, and regulations. Within this domestic governance framework, the Constitution is the paramount law that governs the foreign investment environment. The principal laws that regulate foreign investment are national laws promulgated by the National People's Congress. The main working rules for the direction and regulation of foreign investment are the rules and regulations issued by the State Council or the delegated departments under the State Council.

2.2.2 *The Chinese Constitution*

The Constitution provides the fundamental laws that govern, among other things, foreign investment in China, by permitting and mandating foreign investment. Article 18 of the Constitution is regarded as the constitutional protection clause in relation to foreign investment. It states that China permits foreign enterprises, foreign economic organizations, and foreign individuals to invest in China by establishing various forms of economic relationships with Chinese enterprises and economic organizations in accordance with Chinese law.

2.2.3 *The Laws*

The National People's Congress is responsible for promulgating national laws regarding the establishment, operation, and termination of foreign investment enterprises. FIE law which regulate foreign investment enterprises comprise the EJV Law, the CJV Law, and the WFOE Law. As most foreign investment enterprises choose to establish themselves as corporations, Company Law may be applicable to foreign investment enterprises established as corporations working with default rules for foreign invested LLCs or JSCs on issues not yet provided for under FIE law. If inconsistencies and contradictions occur, the provisions of the EJV Law, the CJV Law, and the WFOE Law will prevail over those of the Company Law.

In addition to the EJV Law, the CJV Law, the WFOE Law, and the Company Law, certain other national laws may also apply to foreign investment enterprises and foreign related merger and acquisition transactions. The civil law, the contract law, the securities law, the law on enterprise income taxation, the law against unfair competition, the property law, and the antitrust law are also relevant to foreign investment concerns. The Civil Law of 1986 is the law that governs property rights and ownership transfers. The Contract Law of 1999 administers foreign economic contracts by Chinese and foreign investors who are parties to foreign investment enterprises. The recently revised Securities Law regulates the issuing and exchange of securities. The Law on Enterprise Income Taxation of 2007 provides a uniform income tax system not specifically related to domestic and foreign investment enterprises. The Law Against Unfair Competitions of 1993, the Property Law of 2007, and the Antitrust Law of 2007 are also applicable to transactions carried out by foreign investment enterprises.

2.2.4 *The Administrative Rules and Regulations*

The organization authorized to issue administrative rules and regulations in accordance with the national legal framework promulgated by the National Peoples' Congress is the State Council. The State Council and its authorized government departments enact rules and regulations in order to manage foreign investment enterprises. Subsequent to the promulgation of national laws, Implementation Rules for the EJV Law, the Implementation Rules for the CJV Law, the Implementation Rules for the WFOE Law, and the Catalogue for the Guidance of Foreign Investment Industries were issued. The rules and regulations issued by the State Council and related departmental authorities constitute the major part of the framework governing foreign investment. Examples of important rules and regulations in relation to foreign investment are the Implementing Opinion on Certain Issues Concerning the Application of the Law on the Administration of Examination, Approval, and Registration of Foreign Invested Corporations issued by SAIC, MOFCOM, China Customs, and SAFE in 2006. As the rules and regulations emanated from specific circumstances, they may be subject to future change in order to reflect the needs of regulators and the demands of foreign investment.

2.3 Foreign Invested Enterprises

In order to qualify as foreign invested enterprises, Chinese law requires no less than 25 per cent of registered capital to be provided by foreign investor(s) in Sino-foreign investment enterprises organized either as an EJV or a CJV. A foreign investor may choose the form of a WFOE if they decide to invest and operate in China without a Chinese partner. Alternative foreign investment vehicles are the JSC, foreign invested investment corporations, or branches of foreign corporations.

2.3.1 *Sino-Foreign Equity Joint Ventures (EJVs)*

Sino-Foreign Equity Joint Ventures (EJVs) are established as LLCs run by Chinese and foreign investors. The EJV Law and its governing rules provide the governing conditions for EJVs to operate. As LLCs, EJVs operate as legal entities that possess an independent capacity for civil liabilities. While the liability of shareholders is limited to their capital contribution, an EJV is liable for its debts to the extent of its assets. For EJVs, a foreign shareholder must hold at least 25 per cent of registered joint venture capital. The Chinese and foreign parties jointly invest, own, and manage the venture. They accept its risks and share its profits and losses in accordance with the proportions of their contribution to the venture. Each party's contribution can be made in cash or in-kind. Such non-cash contributions may include equipment, land-use rights, and office or factory premises.

An EJV is managed by a board of directors and a team of management personnel. If an EJV decides that a shareholder meeting will not act as the highest decision-making authority in the venture, it must establish a board of directors that will do so.

The articles of association of an EJV will determine the size and composition of its board of directors. Parties may appoint and replace directors in accordance with procedures set out in the articles of association. A party will appoint its directors in proportion to its capital contribution and select the chairman and vice chairman from the board of directors. If the chairman is appointed by the Chinese party, the vice chairman will be appointed by the foreign party and vice versa. One director has one vote. The chairman is the legal individual who represents the EJV.

The board of directors will determine business expansion plans, proposals for production and operation, budget, profit distribution plans, remuneration plans, and the appointment of the chairperson, vice chairperson, senior managers, chief engineer, treasurer, and auditors.

The board of directors will exercise its personnel authority to appoint management members for the routine operation of the venture. Management members will include one general manager and one or more deputy managers for the purpose of carrying out the resolutions of the board of directors as well as daily operations and managerial procedures.

2.3.2 *Sino-Foreign Contractual Joint Ventures (CJVs)*

Sino-Foreign Contractual Joint Ventures are also referred to as Sino-Foreign Cooperative Enterprises (CJVs). These kind of ventures are jointly established by Chinese and foreign investment partners in accordance with the CJV Law and its implementing rules. A CJV may be established as a legal person entity or non-legal person entity. If it is established as a legal person entity, it will be organized and managed in much the same way as an EJV. Partners are allowed to invest and contractually delegate management by forming a limited liability corporation.[1] Parties are liable for the debts of the corporation to the extent of their investments unless otherwise stated in the contract. The CJV is liable for the debts of the venture, to the extent of its total assets.

If it is established as a non-legal person entity, the venture is mainly governed by contractual arrangements. This kind of CJV may be set up with each partner retaining a separate legal entity in accordance with Chinese law.[2] If a CJV without legal person status is to operate as a contractual arrangement under a CJV contract, parties will set out their respective rights and obligations in relation to their capital contributions, management, profit, liabilities and investment recoupment arrangements. The law allows for early investment recoupment for the foreign investment partner in advance of the term of the CJV.

The advantage of a CJV is the degree of flexibility with which the parties may operate in relation to profit and loss sharing. Under a CJV, partner profit and loss may be disproportionate to their respective capital contributions to the venture. Investment parties may decide their own rate at which their investment is to be recouped. Such contractual arrangements are subject to the approval of the governing authorities and compliance with the relevant requirements.

A CJV as a legal person entity will establish a board of directors as its highest level of authority. This is similar to the governance structure of an EJV. A CJV as a non-legal person entity may establish a joint managerial committee which is composed of party representatives. This committee will act as the venture's decision-making body. If the chairman is appointed

[1] The Rules Implementing the Sino-foreign Contractual Joint Ventures Law, MOFTEC art. 14 (1995) (P.R.C.).

[2] The Rules Implementing the Sino-Foreign Contractual Joint Ventures Law, MOFTEC art. 50 (1995) (P.R.C.).

by the Chinese side, the vice chairman shall be appointed by the foreign side, and vice versa.

The board of directors or the joint managerial committee can appoint a general manager to take responsibility for the day-to-day operations and management of the CJV. The general manager is held accountable to the board of directors or to the joint managerial committee.

2.3.3 Wholly Foreign Owned Enterprises (WFOEs)

A Wholly Foreign Owned Enterprise (WFOE) is an enterprise owned solely by one or more foreign investors. It is established in accordance with the WFOE Law and its implementing rules. A WFOE is established as a LLC with legal person status. The establishment of a WFOE has many advantages over an EJV or CJV for a foreign investor. In a WFOE, a foreign investor may direct, manage, and operate the enterprise as its sole legal owner. One downside to the WFOE as a form of investment is that it may not engage in business which falls within a "restricted" category on the Foreign Investment Catalogue. Such restriction is not applicable to an EJV or CJV.

2.3.4 Foreign Invested Joint Stock Corporations (Foreign JSCs)

Foreign Invested Joint Stock Corporations (foreign JSCs) are foreign investment enterprises that issue shares for the purpose of establishment. A foreign invested JSC is the same as a regular JSC with regard to share issue requirements. A foreign invested JSC can issue all or a part of its shares to its incorporators. If a part of its shares are issued to the incorporators, a foreign JSC needs to issue a set stock portion to the public as required. The capital of a foreign invested JSC consists of shares owned by Chinese and foreign shareholders. If a foreign invested JSC issues all of its shares to incorporators, at least one of the incorporators needs to be a foreign investor. If a foreign invested JSC issues a part of its shares to the incorporators and the rest to the public, at least one of the incorporators must have been in a continuously profitable state for the three years prior to the establishment of the foreign invested JSC.[3] If such an incorporator

[3]The Regulations on Foreign Invested Joint Stock Limited Corporations, Ministry of Commerce, art. 6 (1995) (P.R.C.).

is a foreign investor, an audited financial report by a foreign CPA registered and residing in the foreign country where the foreign investor is located is required. Shareholding by foreign shareholders shall amount to no less than 25 per cent of the total registered capital, with a minimum set at RMB 30 million.[4]

If approved, a foreign investment enterprise is able to convert to become a foreign investment JSC. A foreign JSC must have a shareholder meeting, a board of directors, and a board of supervisors as parts of its corporate entity.

Foreign invested JSC are governed under a special set of rules and regulations. These rules include the Provisional Regulations on Certain Issues Concerning the Establishment of Foreign Invested Joint Stock Limited Corporations issued by MOFTEC (former MOFCOM) on January 10, 1995. The Company Law provides default rules for matters not covered otherwise by such regulations. If a foreign invested JSC goes public, the Company Law, the Securities Law, and certain other administrative regulations that apply to public corporations become relevant.

2.3.5 Foreign Invested Investment Enterprises

At a certain stage of investment activity and in order to consolidate their investment entities in the country, foreign investment concerns in China can consider establishing foreign invested investment enterprises as corporate vehicles. Foreign invested investment enterprises may enable corporations with multiple investment enterprises already established and invested in China to position themselves in the market in a more advantageous way and to organize operations under one corporate umbrella. These corporations are also referred to as foreign invested holding corporations. Corporations are established as LLCs.[5]

A foreign invested investment enterprises (foreign investment enterprises) may be established in order to engage in venture capital investment in high-tech enterprises yet to be listed on the stock exchange. A foreign invested venture capital enterprise can be established as a legal person.

[4] The Regulations on Foreign Invested Joint Stock Limited Corporations, Ministry of Commerce, art. 2.7 (1995) (P.R.C.).

[5] The Regulations on the Establishment of Foreign Invested Investment Corporations, Ministry of Commerce, art. 2 (2004) (P.R.C.).

Shareholders in foreign invested venture capital enterprises established as legal persons will assume limited liability in proportion to the sum of their capital contributions.

Foreign invested investment enterprises are investment corporations which have been established by foreign investors in the form of a WFOE or a Chinese-foreign JV engaging in direct investment. All foreign investment corporations need approval from MOFCOM. The foreign investment may not be under 10 per cent of capital registered for the Sino-Foreign Joint Venture Investment Corporation. Even though this kind of foreign invested investment corporation may not engage in production activities, these corporations may invest by establishing more FIEs or by taking equity shares in certain other FIEs. Once the foreign investment ratio reaches 25 per cent or more of the registered capital, investment enterprises established or invested in by foreign invested investment corporations are regarded as FIEs. When established, such entities can provide services to their invested enterprises. These services include assisting or representing the invested enterprises in order to purchase machinery, equipment including office equipment, raw materials, components and parts needed in production, selling products manufactured by the entities and providing after sales service. They may further balance foreign exchanges between the entities, provide services for technical support, sales and marketing development, employee training, intra-enterprise personnel management and assisting in the seeking of loans and the provision of security or guarantees. Through scientific research and development centres or offices that might be established in China, high-tech research may be carried out and corresponding products or services may be provided. Consulting services in respect of investment and investment policies may also be provided. If approved by the CBRC, enterprises invested in may be provided with finance.

2.3.6 Branches of Foreign Corporations

Subject to the jurisdiction of Chinese law and while not administered as a legal person, a foreign corporation can establish a branch which may engage in business activities. Under Chinese law, a branch such as this has no civil capacity to independently undertake legal liability. Business activities conducted in China by a foreign branch are for profit. A foreign corporation which is outside the territory of China is liable for how its branch operates its business. When the foreign corporation relinquishes any one of its branches, it must liquidate the branch and pay off the debts according to corporation law. The foreign corporation may only transfer branch assets outside China when the liquidation procedure is completed. Even though it has been established under Chinese law, a foreign branch retains the same corporate citizenship as the foreign corporation.

Foreign corporations that want to establish branches in China need apply for approval to the appropriate authority, and this authority varies depending on the company's main product. For example, MOFCOM is the appropriate authority for a trading concern or manufacturing facility, while the China Banking Regulatory Commission (CBRC) is for a commercial bank. The China Insurance Regulatory Commission (CIRC) is the appropriate authority for an insurance corporation and the General Administration of Civil Aviation of China Corporations is for an air-transportation agent.

2.4 Establishment Procedures and Requirements of Foreign Investment Enterprises

2.4.1 Background and Policy Statements

The fundamental motive for opening up decision-making policy is to promote the development of the Chinese economy with regard to foreign investment opportunities. The establishment of FIEs aims to improve the advancement of science and technology and bring the development of the country into the modern era. The law often explains these purposes in legal statements. For example, the WFOE Law states that the planning of the establishment of WFOEs should favor the development of the national economy, encourage exports and promote the adoption of advanced technology and devices. Still, although regarded as an important element of national modernization, the attraction of foreign direct investment is executed within the confines of fundamental principles in relation to the protection of national security, equality and mutual benefit, and compliance in relation to international practices and customs.

EJV Law expounds that the establishment of EJVs in China by foreign businesses and Chinese corporations must adhere to the "principle of equality and mutual benefit". If a possible foreign direct investment concern is thought to pose harm to sovereignty, social and public interest, national security and laws and regulations, does not conform to the requirements of national economy development, environmental pollution, impairment of a party's rights and interests, or demonstrate obvious inequity in relation to agreements, contracts, or articles of incorporation, it may be refused.

2.4.1.1 Foreign Investment Guidelines and the Catalogue for the Guidance of Foreign Investment Industries

In recent decades, the government issued Foreign Investment Guidelines and the Catalogue for the Guidance of Foreign Investment Industries (Foreign Investment Catalogue). Until systems relating to special entry controls were established in more recent times, these were the main policy guidelines for foreign investment.

The Foreign Investment Catalogue categorized foreign investment businesses and industries into three groups. It set out the criteria for encouragement, prohibition and restriction of foreign investment in various sectors. Foreign investment concerns were required to check the investment catalogue to learn about restrictions and considerations in their sector. The catalogue was updated every few years in order to underscore a policy shift towards restructuring and redirecting growth towards exports. The triple directive on encouragement, prohibition and restriction set out matters related to foreign participation, investment location and foreign ownership percentages. Projects which were not otherwise provided for under those categories were regarded as 'permitted', offering foreign investors the opportunity to invest 'freely.' Foreign investment in 'encouraged' and 'approved' sectors were meet with limited or no restrictions, and examination and approval procedures were quite lenient. All that was required was local level examination and approval. Foreign investment within 'restricted' sectors might be subject to greater scrutiny by the examination and approval authorities and would be managed by a higher level of administration. In some instances, foreign investors in joint ventures were not permitted to assume more than 50 per cent of equity. Unless specifically approved by the authorities, foreign investment projects within 'prohibited' sectors would not be accepted by examination and approval authorities.

In the last few years, policies have changed regarding recycling, clean production, renewable energy utilization, and environmental protection. Since the beginning of the reform period, most foreign direct investment activities were established in southern and eastern coastal regions: the Pearl River Delta area and the Yangtze River Delta area. Historically, these areas have enjoyed preferential policies. The majority of FIEs therefore decided to establish themselves there. In order to encourage more rapid economic growth in the central and western regions, the government formulated policies to shift economic development inland. In 2004, the Catalogue of Priority Industries for Foreign Investment in the Midwest Region (Foreign Investment Catalogue or Midwest Investment Catalogue) was updated and came into effect. This catalogue aimed to boost economic development in the west, encourage foreign investments in central and western regions, attract more advanced technologies, develop competitive industries and enterprises with advanced technologies, and promote the optimization of industrial structures. The establishment of the Shanghai Free Trade Zone and free trade zones in other cities heralded a series of change to foreign direct investment regulations. This has led to government roles and activities in respect of foreign investment being reduced and phased out. The ultimate goal is to offer foreign investors a set of national conditions, thereby removing certain administrative requirements and restrictions. These changes could have a significant direct impact on foreign direct investment regulations. By substituting case by case administrative approval for foreign investment projects, the new governance scheme involved the implementation of a negative list system. This is discussed more in the latter part of this chapter.

2.4.1.2 Foreign Investment Entry Control Measures

The NDRC and MOFCOM recently released a Guidance Catalogue of Foreign Investment Industries (Catalogue). This was revised in 2017. It proposed the development of a negative list of entry for foreign investment which was to be implemented nationwide. Industries that are not on the negative list could, in principle, be permitted without being subjected to restrictive measures. In line with the implementation of special entry control measures, or a negative list regulation, FIE law has been revised in order to set out the legal basis for such a change. The specific revisions are that foreign investment projects that are not within the special entry regulation regime are only required to satisfy recording requirements. In other words, recording is only required for foreign investment projects involving industries that are not on the negative lists under the relevant special entry control measures. The major instrument for foreign investment regulation in the foreseeable future will be negative list management. Apart from restricted foreign investment projects that need approval, all other projects are required to submit to local governmental agency procedures. This negative list practice represents /contributes towards the development of greater transparency, predictability and openness in foreign investment regulation.

The revised catalogue has contributed to the greater opening up of service industries, manufacturing industries and mining industries for foreign investment. It has eliminated restrictions on access to and entry of foreign passenger vehicles in relation to road passenger transport, external cargo handling, credit investigation and rating services, accounting, auditing, large-scale agricultural products, wholesale markets, and integrated water control hubs. Greater access for foreign investment is also provided in relation to the manufacturing of rail transit equipment, automotive electronics and new energy vehicles, motorcycles, edible oils and fats, corn deep processing, fuel ethanol, and the mining industry. The negative list of restricted foreign investment industries includes 35 new varieties of crops and seed production, 28 air traffic control industries and compulsory education establishments.

2.4.2 Capital Issues

2.4.2.1 Total Amount of Investment

FIE law specifically provides for several important principals in relation to foreign investment enterprise capitalization. These are the total amount of investment, registered capital and the ratio requirement between the total amount of investment and registered capital.

The total amount of investment refers to the total of registered capital plus any loans. Registered capital is the paid-in capital of an FIE paid to the investment enterprise when the enterprise is registered with the governmental authorities. When applications to establish enterprises are filed, EJVs, CJVs and WFOEs are required to specify their registered capital and total investment. The stipulated ratio between the two may vary depending on the type of investment project. It is of note that foreign JSCs are not subject to any ratio requirements because the capital of such entities will be divided into shares.

2.4.2.2 Registered Capital

Registered capital of an FIE is the total capital paid to a foreign investment entity. It is the capital subscribed to by all the parties in the venture. Registered capital may be paid in either RMB or a foreign currency as agreed by the parties to the venture. One significant point is that in general, the parties will be liable to debt obligations of the venture to the extent of their registered capital contributions. Another significant point is that the parties will share profit, risks, and losses in proportion to their respective capital contributions. A transfer of registered capital by one party needs to be agreed to by all other parties to the venture. Generally, the non-transferring parties will have a preemptive right to purchase equity offered by the transferring party on the same terms and conditions.

2.4.2.3 Early Recoupment of Investment

There are many factors that foreign investors may wish to consider when choosing a proper corporate form for a foreign JV investment. One important distinction between choosing a CJV over an EJV is that a foreign investor in the CJV may recoup their investment early while a foreign investor in the EJV may not. If a business entity is dissolved, investing parties are generally not entitled to get their investment back. Under the law, investors in a CJV are allowed to receive early recoupment of their investment during the operational period. One popular way of doing this is by means of a distribution of funds to the foreign investor through depreciation of fixed assets. This kind of arrangement has demonstrated how a CJV can be a useful investment vehicle for financing infrastructure projects. According to the administrative rule of the Measures for Examination and Approval of Early Recoupment of Investment from CJVs by their Foreign Investors, the arrangement for early recoupment must be approved by local financial authorities at the provincial level. There are several conditions, however, for early distribution to the foreign investor[6]:

(i) The CJV contract prescribes that all the fixed assets of the CJV will be transferred to the Chinese party at no cost, upon the expiry of the term of the CJV.
(ii) The foreign party will issue a letter of undertaking in order to assume joint and several liability for the debts of the CJV to the extent of the investment and to be recouped in advance.

[6] The Rules Implementing the Chinese Foreign Contractual Joint Ventures Law, Ministry of Commerce, art. 44 (1995) (P.R.C.).

If early recoupment of a foreign party investment is to be made before income tax payment, the CJV needs to apply for examination and approval to the relevant financial and tax authorities.

2.4.3 Contributions

Cash is the common form in which a capital contribution is made. Labour services, credit, the names of natural persons, goodwill, franchise license, and mortgaged assets are excluded from the list of possible types of capital contribution.[7] Investors may use convertible foreign currencies, investment machinery and equipment, industrial property rights and proprietary technology in order to contribute to an investment venture. Contributions which do not take the form of cash must be scrutinized and verified by means of asset evaluation.[8]

Prior to 2014, initial capital contributions by shareholders of foreign invested enterprises were regulated as follows:

(i) If the registered capital payment was to be made in the form of a full lump sum, the enterprise was required to make the capital contribution payment within six months after the date when the corporation was established.

(ii) If payment was to be made by installments, the enterprise was required to make an initial capital contribution of no less than 15 per cent of the total capital contributions.

In either of the above situations, the initial contribution had to be made within three months of the corporation being established. Delay in full or partial payment would be subject to an interest penalty payment in relation to the defaulted amount or loss compensation under the JV contract. After the required registered capital payment was made, registration application for a business license could be made with SAIC or its local office. If a shareholder postponed a capital contribution, that shareholder was

[7] The Regulations on the Corporation Registration and the Regulations on the Administration of the Corporation Registered Capital, art. 8, 28 (P.R.C.).

[8] The Implementing Opinion on Certain Issues Concerning the Application of Law on the Administration of Examination, Approval, and Registration of Foreign Invested Enterprises, art. 10 (P.R.C.).

required to file a registration for modification with SAIC or its local office.[9] The capital contribution could be in the form of properties or property rights free from mortgage or any other types of encumbrances owned by shareholders. If the capital contribution by a Chinese shareholder party involved state-owned assets, it would be necessary to carry out an asset appraisal according to the relevant laws and regulations. In the past, a joint venture contract would usually set a time limit for the making of contributions. If, in the first instance, a shareholder party failed to do this, SAIC would set a time limit for that party to meet contribution obligations. If, in the second instance, the party failed to do this within the time limit set by the authority, the examination and approval authority would intervene in order to cancel and nullify the approval certificate issued to the venture. The SAIC could, eventually, revoke the business license.

The Company Law of 2014 included some important changes that are equally applicable to FIEs as follows:

(i) The abolishing of restrictions on the initial investment ratio, the proportion of the money invested and the time limit for capital contribution to foreign investment companies including contributions from Taiwan, Hong Kong, and Macao investors. Investors are able to decide the size, mode and terms of their investment. The latter was to be clearly shown in the joint venture contract and in the articles of association of the company.

(ii) The restriction on the minimum registered capital of the company is abolished unless otherwise stipulated by laws, administrative regulations and the State Council's decision regarding the minimum registered capital for particular sectors.

These measures were not applied to foreign investment projects approved prior to March 1, 2014.

2.4.3.1 Contributions to an EJV

The law requires shareholders to stipulate the forms of capital contributions in the equity joint venture contract and in the articles of incorpora-

[9] The Implementing Opinion on Certain Issues Concerning the Application of Law on the Administration of Examination, Approval, and Registration of Foreign Invested Enterprises, art. 9.

tion. Shareholders are to jointly assess / evaluate non-cash contributions other than real property. The foreign exchange of capital contribution by the foreign shareholder has to be converted into the RMB or converted into a predetermined foreign currency in accordance with the standard exchange rate announced by the People's Bank of China on the day of submission.[10] The law requires that machinery, equipment, and other materials considered necessary for the production of the joint venture and provided by foreign shareholders should be provided at a price no higher than the current international market rate for similar equipment or materials.[11] The technology and equipment should be of an advanced quality that caters to the needs of the venture. Machinery, equipment, materials, industrial property, or proprietary technologies given by foreign shareholders must be examined and approved by the appropriate authority.[12] The law states that industrial property or proprietary technologies provided by foreign shareholders must 'markedly' improve the performance and quality of existing products, increase productivity and 'notably' conserve raw material, fuel, energy, and power.[13] If the equity joint venture suffers losses emanating from technology and equipment provided by foreign shareholders and known to be outdated, fraud litigation could follow. Non-cash forms of industrial property or proprietary technologies given to the joint venture must be presented in relevant documentation which certifies the validity of patents or trademarks, the basis for determining the price and the agreement about price signed with the Chinese shareholder.[14]

2.4.3.2 Contributions to a CJV

A CJV offers the most flexible form of investment vehicle for foreign and Chinese shareholders. It may be established as a legal person or adminis-

[10] The Rules Implementing the Chinese Foreign Equity Joint Ventures Law, State Council, art. 23 (2001) (P.R.C.).

[11] The Rules Implementing the Chinese Foreign Equity Joint Ventures Law, State Council, art. 24 (2001) (P.R.C.).

[12] The Rules Implementing the Chinese Foreign Equity Joint Ventures Law, State Council, art. 27 (2001) (P.R.C.).

[13] The Rules Implementing the Chinese Foreign Equity Joint Ventures Law, State Council, art. 25 (2001) (P.R.C.).

[14] The Rules Implementing the Chinese Foreign Equity Joint Ventures Law, State Council, art. 26 (2001) (P.R.C.).

tered as a non-legal person.[15] If a CJV is established as a Chinese legal person, the contribution by the foreign shareholder in the CJV may not be less than 25 per cent of the registered capital of the joint venture.[16] If it is not a legal person, the CJV has to satisfy the requirements for capital contribution under the relevant MOFCOM rules.

2.4.3.3 Contributions to a WFOE

The regulatory requirement for non-cash forms of contribution by a WFOE foreign investor is quite similar to the provisions governing the EJV or CJV. Machinery and equipment that is needed for the production and operation of the venture and the purchasing price for the machinery and equipment must not be higher than the fair market price for similar machinery and equipment on the international market.[17] If proprietary technology is to be provided as an investment for a fixed price, the foreign investor will be the owner of the industrial property rights and proprietary technology. Costs for the industrial property rights and proprietary technology must be provided in order to conform to international market general pricing principles.

2.5 Special Considerations for Mergers and Acquisitions

2.5.1 Overview

During the last decade, foreign invested enterprises that have had initial investment success in China, have been venturing into the merger and acquisition market. Foreign investors can consider investing in existing and accomplished domestic enterprises in order to benefit directly from the existing supply chains and distribution networks of established domestic enterprises. Target corporations are usually Chinese domestic corporations with established names and businesses in domestic markets.

[15] The Rules Implementing the Chinese Foreign Contractual Joint Ventures Law, Ministry of Commerce, art. 4 (1995) (P.R.C.).

[16] The Rules Implementing the Chinese Foreign Contractual Joint Ventures Law, Ministry of Commerce, art. 18 (1995) (P.R.C.).

[17] The Rules Implementing the Law on Wholly Foreign-Owned Enterprises, Ministry of Commerce, art. 26 (2001) (P.R.C.).

The move toward conducting mergers and acquisitions by foreign invested enterprises over the past decade marks a change in the direction of foreign investment. While the initial decade of reform can be characterized by an encouragement of foreign investment for an export-driven economy, the second decade was a period in which the momentum for economic growth driven by an inflow of foreign investment continued to develop. The third decade witnessed a marked change in the direction for foreign investment, with it increasingly entering the country in search of domestic market opportunities. The rate of foreign investment inflow has been on the rise, seeking to satisfy growing consumption demand among middle class Chinese. Domestic markets have witnessed record sales volumes for multinational corporation products in and around the period of the 2008 financial crisis.

In 2003, MOFCOM issued Provisional Regulations on Mergers and Acquisitions of Domestic Enterprises by Foreign Investors, aimed at regulating such takeover activities. In 2006, MOFCOM, SASAC, SAT, SAIC, CSRC, and SAFE jointly issued Regulations on Mergers and Acquisitions of Domestic Enterprises by Foreign Investors based on the initial three year trial. On August 30, 2007, China promulgated the Antitrust Law.[18] This law is applicable to domestic and foreign enterprises in respect of mergers and acquisition activities, providing a broad legal framework. Following the promulgation of the Antitrust Law, the regulations for mergers and acquisitions were revised and amended in 2009. The latest amendments provided guidelines on how foreign corporations may apply to merge with or acquire domestic enterprises. Specific guidance is needed for the enactment of the relevant rules of implementation.

Merger and acquisition transactions between domestic enterprises and foreign investors can take the form of share purchases or asset purchases. In share purchases, the foreign investor purchases the shares in a domestic corporation or subscribes to the increased registered capital of the domestic corporation. If more than 25 per cent of shares are purchased, the domestic corporation may become a FIE. Foreign investors in asset purchases will purchase the assets of a domestic enterprise and apply the assets as an investment in order to establish an FIE. Foreign investors may

[18] The Antitrust Law was promulgated by the NPC on Aug. 30, 2007 and became effective on Aug. 1, 2008.

alternatively establish an FIE in order to purchase the assets of a domestic enterprise.

Foreign invested mergers and acquisitions must still be carried out in compliance with the negative list requirement. If the target corporation belongs to a category marked 'restricted' or 'prohibited' for foreign investment, approval would be difficult to secure. If the target corporation is in the industry in which the domestic entity in the corporation is required to have the controlling interest, any foreign investor would need to give up control after the merger and acquisition. Foreign investors will need to seek approval from MOFCOM if the transaction led to foreign control over an enterprise in a critical industry or if the transaction resulted in foreign control of a domestic enterprise with a renowned trademark or a time-honored brand name. If a merger or acquisition transaction involved state-owned assets, the transaction would be governed, among other things, by relevant SASAC rules.

Enterprises with more than 25 per cent of registered capital provided by foreign investors, and established after the mergers and acquisitions will be regarded as FIEs.[19] A domestic investor may establish an FIE by forming an overseas corporation in order to merge with its affiliated domestic corporation. This can be done if the overseas corporation subscribes to more than 25 per cent of any increased registered capital in the domestic corporation or if, after the merger, the enterprise increases the capital to be subscribed to and provided by the overseas corporation to 25 per cent of the registered capital of the corporation.[20] The relevant approval authority of mergers and acquisitions is MOFCOM or at a provincial level, its local offices. The registration authority is SAIC or its authorized local offices. The foreign exchange administrative authority is SAFE or its local offices. The regulations provide detailed information as to the ratio of registered capital and the total amount of investment in a foreign invested enterprise established after an equity merger.

An investor is required to submit the relevant documents in an application to the examination and approval authorities. Document requirements

[19] The Regulations on Mergers and Acquisitions of Domestic Enterprises by Foreign Investors (Mergers and Acquisitions Regulations), MOFCOM, SASAC, SAT, SAIC, CSRC, and SAFE, art. 9(2006) (P.R.C.)

[20] The Regulations on Mergers and Acquisition of Domestic Enterprises by Foreign Investors (Mergers and acquisitions Regulations), MOFCOM, SASAC, SAT, CSRC, and SAFE, art. 9 (2006) (P.R.C.).

vary and depend on the total investment of the proposed foreign invested enterprise, the type of the enterprise and the industry it is engages in. For an equity acquisition, required documents will include a unanimous resolution of the shareholder meeting about the target domestic LLC in respect of the equity purchase or the special resolution of the shareholder meeting of the target domestic JSC in respect of the equity purchase; an application for converting the target domestic corporation into a foreign invested enterprise; the joint venture contract, the articles of incorporation and the purchase agreement; the incorporation certificate, the investor credit certificate which is notarized and attested to according to law and the resettlement plan for the employees of the target domestic corporation.[21]

For an asset purchase, documents required include the resolution of the property holders or the authority of the domestic enterprise in approving the asset sale; the application for the establishment of the foreign invested enterprise; the joint venture contract and the articles of incorporation; the asset purchase agreement between the proposed enterprise and the domestic enterprise or the asset purchase agreement between the foreign investor and the domestic enterprise; the articles of incorporation and the business license of the target domestic enterprise; the notice and public announcement made to the creditors by the target domestic enterprise and the resettlement plan for the employees of the target domestic enterprise together with any relevant approval documents.[22]

The timescale for approval of such a project is 30 days after the authority's receipt of all documents.[23] When approved, the office of SAIC in the locality of the target corporation will issue a registration certificate for the share transfer and the foreign exchange income statement. This certificate provides official proof that the foreign investor has made the equity subscription payment.

[21] The Regulations on Mergers and Acquisitions of Domestic Enterprises by Foreign Investors (Mergers and Acquisitions Regulations), MOFCOM, SASAC, SAT, CSRC, and SAFE, art. 21 (2006) (P.R.C.).

[22] The Regulations on Mergers and Acquisitions of Domestic Enterprises by Foreign Investors (Mergers and Acquisitions Regulations), MOFCOM, SASAC, SAT, CSRC, and SAFE, art. 22 (2006) (P.R.C.).

[23] The Regulations on Mergers and Acquisitions of Domestic Enterprises by Foreign Investors (Mergers and Acquisitions Regulations), MOFCOM, SASAC, SAT, CSRC, and SAFE, art. 25 (2006) (P.R.C.).

When a foreign investor merges, through an asset purchase, with a domestic enterprise, the foreign investor shall file for SAIC registration in order to obtain a business license within 30 days of receipt of the approval certificate.[24] Similar registration procedures need to be completed in respect of mergers of foreign investors with domestic enterprises through equity acquisition. The target domestic corporation needs to complete the registration procedure. Similarly, as in the case of a newly established FIE, the foreign investor concerned is required to file for registration with the relevant departments of taxation, customs, land administration, and foreign exchange control within 30 days of receiving the business license.

2.5.2 *Special Provisions for Mergers and Acquisitions by Foreign Equity*

In merger and acquisition transaction arrangements where an overseas equity provides an inflow of finance, the shareholder of the overseas corporation can purchase the equity interests of a domestic corporation or more shares of the domestic corporation concerned. The general requirements for such overseas corporations are that the jurisdiction where the corporation is registered has a sound legal system, the corporation has a good management record and the corporation has not received any penalties in the preceding three years. The corporation should also be a publicly traded corporation.

The requirements for the equity of the overseas corporation which finances the transaction are that the corporation is lawfully owned by the shareholders, transferable according to the law, free of any ownership disputes, security interests or any other encumbrances, and is listed on an open and lawful overseas securities exchange excluding an over-the-counter exchange. In addition, the transaction price of such equity should have been stable in the preceding year.

Chinese domestic corporations need MOFCOM approval for the transaction to proceed. The corporation will submit the following documents to MOFCOM for the purpose of the approval[25]:

[24] The Regulations on Mergers and Acquisitions of Domestic Enterprises by Foreign Investors (Mergers and Acquisitions Regulations), MOFCOM, SASAC, SAT, CSRC, and SAFE, art. 26 (2006) (P.R.C.).

[25] The Regulations on Mergers and Acquisitions of Domestic Enterprises by Foreign Investors (Mergers and Acquisitions Regulations), MOFCOM, SASAC, SAT, CSRC, and SAFE, art. 32 (2006) (P.R.C.).

(i) A statement regarding changes in equity and the material assets of the corporation in the preceding years.
(ii) A report from a consultant regarding the merger.
(iii) A certificate of incorporation or an identification certificate of the domestic corporation, a certificate of incorporation of the overseas corporation in the proposed merger and the names of the shareholders of the corporations concerned. A statement about the shareholding positions of the shareholders in the overseas corporation with a list of shareholders who hold more than 5 per cent of the overseas corporation.
(iv) The articles of incorporation of the overseas corporation and the guarantee statement by the overseas corporation.
(v) Recent audited financial statements of the overseas corporation and a statement of stock transactions in the preceding six months.

Examination of the application materials and approval process usually takes 30 days. A certificate will be issued indicating 'the merger by foreign investors financed by equity and valid within six months after the certificate issuance' to the investors concerned. When the certificate has been issued, the domestic corporation will file for the registration for conversion into an FIE, for the business license and for a foreign exchange registration certificate.[26]

Within six months of the issuing of the business license, the domestic corporation will apply to MOFCOM and SAFE for approval and for the foreign exchange registration of the overseas investment.[27] The domestic corporation is not allowed to distribute profits, provide a guarantee to any affiliated corporation, transfer equity, reduce the registered capital, liquidate, or dispose of assets until the certificate of approval and the foreign exchange certificate has been issued.

[26] The Regulations on Mergers and Acquisitions of Domestic Enterprises by Foreign Investors (Mergers and Acquisitions Regulations), MOFCOM, SASAC, SAT, CSRC, and SAFE, art. 33 (2006) (P.R.C.).

[27] The Regulations on Mergers and Acquisitions of Domestic Enterprises by Foreign Investors (Mergers and Acquisitions Regulations), MOFCOM, SASAC, SAT, CSRC, and SAFE, art. 35 (2006) (P.R.C.).

Finally, the domestic corporation and the shareholders must file for the registration with the appropriate taxation authority on matters relating to taxation.[28]

2.5.3 Special Provisions for Mergers and Acquisitions by Foreign Equity: Special Purpose Corporations (SPCs)

The Regulations largely address the practice of adopting a special purpose corporation (SPC) which is registered overseas in order to achieve the listing of a domestic corporation on an overseas stock exchange.

A SPC is usually an overseas corporation which is controlled by Chinese investors and is listed on an overseas stock exchange used for realizing shareholder interests in a domestic Chinese corporation. The shareholders of the SPC may use the equity of the SPC in order to finance the purchase of the equity of a domestic corporation and so eventually benefit from a public offering of the latter on the stock exchange. The financial requirement is that the total value of SPC equity shares must not be less than the total value of the equity interest of the target domestic corporation. This kind of evaluation must be done by an asset appraisal firm in China.

It is normally a domestic corporation that initiates the establishment of an overseas SPC. Despite that fact that a SPC is an overseas establishment, it is the domestic corporation that must apply to MOFCOM for approval. The acquisition is regarded as an investment into the overseas enterprise. The domestic corporation applicant will submit the identity certificate of the controlling shareholder of the SPC, the business proposal for an overseas listing of the SPC and the evaluation report by the merger consultant about the potential issuing share price.[29] When MOFCOM's certificate of approval for the overseas investment has been obtained, the incorporator or the controlling shareholder should file for the registration with the local SAIC authority.

After a preliminary examination, MOFCOM is the approval authority for the project application. CSRC is the authority for public listing

[28] The Regulations on Mergers and Acquisitions of Domestic Enterprises by Foreign Investors (Mergers and Acquisitions Regulations), MOFCOM, SASAC, SAT, CSRC, and SAFE, art. 38 (2006) (P.R.C.).

[29] The Regulations on Mergers and Acquisitions of Domestic Enterprises by Foreign Investors (Mergers and Acquisitions Regulations), MOFCOM, SASAC, SAT, CSRC, and SAFE, art. 42 (2006) (P.R.C.).

approval. With CSRC listing approval, the domestic corporation can apply to MOFCOM for the approval certificate. The domestic corporation must apply to MOFCOM for an approval certificate for the FIE and submit the 'proposal for financing proceeds remittance' to MOFCOM, CSRC, and SAIC within 30 days of the completion of the overseas listing of the SPC or the overseas corporation. Within one month of receipt of the FIE approval certificate, the domestic corporation must apply to SAIC and SAFE for a reissue of the FIE business license and foreign exchange registration certificate.[30]

The financing proceeds of SPC overseas offering and trading must be remitted back to China and may be returned to the country through commercial loans to the domestic corporation, by establishing a new FIE, or by merging with a domestic enterprise. One thing to note is that the remittance of the SPC overseas listing proceeds is subject to the relevant laws and administrative regulations on foreign investment and overseas debt. The relevant regulations require that if the SPC distributes profit or dividends to the domestic corporation, or if the domestic corporation receives foreign exchange income from the changes in capital, such profit, dividends, or income must be repatriated into the territory of China within six months of receipt. Profit or dividends can be accrued to the foreign exchange under the current account or settled as foreign exchange. Foreign exchange income that emanates from changes in capital may, after appropriate approval, be deposited in a special account for capital items or settled as foreign exchange.[31]

2.5.4 *Antitrust Examinations*

The regulations relating to the Antitrust Law provide antitrust oversight for cross border mergers and acquisitions. Foreign investors in proposed mergers with a domestic enterprise are required to submit to MOFCOM and SAIC for an antitrust review if any of the following occurs[32]:

[30] The Regulations on Mergers and Acquisitions of Domestic Enterprises by Foreign Investors (Mergers and Acquisitions Regulations), MOFCOM, SASAC, SAT, CSRC, and SAFE, art. 47 (2006) (P.R.C.).

[31] The Regulations on Mergers and Acquisitions of Domestic Enterprises by Foreign Investors (Mergers and Acquisitions Regulations), MOFCOM, SASAC, SAT, CSRC, and SAFE, art. 48 (2006) (P.R.C.).

[32] The Regulations on Mergers and Acquisitions of Domestic Enterprises by Foreign Investors (Mergers and Acquisitions Regulations), MOFCOM, SASAC, SAT, CSRC, and SAFE, art. 51 (2006) (P.R.C.).

(i) The sales turnover of the investor that is to merge with a domestic enterprise in the Chinese market exceeds RMB 1.5 billion in the same year.
(ii) The foreign investor that is to merge with a domestic enterprise has already merged with more than ten domestic enterprises in the associated industries within one year.
(iii) The market occupancy ratio of the investor that is to merge with a domestic enterprise has reached 20 per cent in China.
(iv) The merger will cause the market occupancy ratio of the investor that is to merge with a domestic enterprise in China to reach 25 per cent.

In respect of mergers, a domestic competitor, an appropriate government department or an industrial association may issue a demand to MOFCOM or SAIC to conduct an investigation if a merger will result in a disproportionately large market share and if there is a presence of any other major factor that may materially affect market competition. If MOFCOM and SAIC decide that the proposed merger could cause excessive market centralization, hinder fair competition or damage consumer interest, the administration may convene a hearing and make a decision as to whether to grant approval to the merger within 90 days of the receipt of the complaint.[33]

If the merger may cause excessive centralization in the domestic market, hinder fair competition or damage consumer interests, and if any one of the following is present, the merging party is required to submit the merger proposal in order to seek approval from MOFCOM and SAIC. (i) the overseas investor in a merger with a domestic enterprise owns more than RMB 3 billion of assets within the territory of China; (ii) the sales turnover of the overseas investor in the Chinese market is more than RMB 1.5 billion in the same year; (iii) the market occupancy ratio of the overseas investor and its affiliated enterprises in China has reached 20 per cent (iv) the market occupancy ratio of the overseas investor and its affiliated enterprises in China will reach 25 per cent as a result of the merger, or (v) the merger would result in more than 15

[33] The Regulations on Mergers and Acquisitions of Domestic Enterprises by Foreign Investors (Mergers and Acquisitions Regulations), MOFCOM, SASAC, SAT, CSRC, and SAFE, art. 52 (2006) (P.R.C.).

FIEs in the relevant domestic industries with shares directly or indirectly controlled by the overseas investor. A merger that will improve market condition, ensure the employment of a distressed enterprise, enhance the international competitiveness, or improve the environment may, however, be exempted from MOFCOM and SAIC antitrust examination and review procedures.[34]

With the installation of the negative listing regulation scheme on foreign investment, foreign investors who engage in mergers and acquisitions of domestic enterprises are also required to be compliant with the regulations. Investors who are not subject to the special entry control regulation should provide honest, accurate and full information when filing. Negative listing regulations apply to any foreign investment, expansion of foreign investment and mergers and acquisitions. Record filing is also required of any foreign shareholding exceeding 5 per cent or if there is a change to the comparative control position for foreign invested public corporations and listed companies in the national small to mid-sized company stock transfer system.

2.6 Termination and Liquidation

2.6.1 Introduction

A FIE will terminate when the term designated in the articles of incorporation expires. If shareholders wish for an extension, they can apply 180 days before the term expires. The appropriate authority will make a decision within one month of the granting of an extension.

When a term expires, the FIE is required to establish a liquidation committee in order to conduct an ordinary liquidation under FIE Liquidation Measures. The liquidation proceeding for a bankrupt enterprise will be managed in accordance with the Bankruptcy Law. If an enterprise does not form a liquidation committee, an application for the special liquidation procedure can be made by the board of directors, the joint managerial institution, the shareholders or the creditors.

[34] The Regulations on Mergers and Acquisitions of Domestic Enterprises by Foreign Investors (Mergers and Acquisitions Regulations), MOFCOM, SASAC, SAT, CSRC, and SAFE, art. 54 (2006) (P.R.C.).

2.6.2 Ordinary Liquidation Procedures

A corporation will become involved in liquidation procedures upon the expiry of the term or when the dissolution is approved. The prescribed timescale for liquidation is 180 days from the date of the initiation of the procedures to the date on which the report is due for submission to the examination and approval authority. Within 15 days before the expiration of the term of liquidation, the committee may, however, submit an application to the examination and approval authority for a 90 day extension of the liquidation term.[35]

Those inauthority of the enterprise must establish a liquidation committee within 15 days from the starting of liquidation procedures.[36] When the liquidation committee is established, the enterprise must transfer any liquidation concerned information regarding the accounting statements, the property list, and the list of creditors and debtors to the liquidation committee. The liquidation committee is empowered to liquidate the assets, create a balance sheet and a detailed inventory list of assets and create a liquidation plan. The committee must try to inform unknown creditors and notify known creditors in writing in order to dispose of and liquidate any unfinished business of the corporation, to provide a basis for evaluating and calculating the assets, to pay taxes and fees, to clear claims and debts, and to dispose of any of the remaining assets of the corporation. The liquidation committee will participate in civil lawsuits on behalf of the corporation.[37]

The liquidation committee will submit the balance sheet, the detailed inventory list of assets and the basis for evaluating and calculating the asset and the liquidation plan to the examination and approval authority.

The required schedule for the working of the liquidation committee is set out under the relevant law and rules. Within seven days of the start of the liquidation procedure, the corporation should provide information relating to the name and address of the corporation, the reason for the liquidation and the starting date of the liquidation to the examination approval authorities, the department in charge, the customs authority, the

[35] The Measures on the Liquidation Procedures for Foreign Investment Enterprises, art. 6 (1996) (P.R.C.).

[36] The Measures on the Liquidation Procedures for Foreign Investment Enterprises, art. 8 (1996) (P.R.C.).

[37] The Measures on the Liquidation Procedures for Foreign Investment Enterprises, art. 11 (1996) (P.R.C.).

authority for foreign exchange control, the corporate registration authority, the tax authority and the bank where the corporation has opened its account. If the corporation holds state-owned assets, relevant information will need to be provided to the SASAC.[38]

Within 10 days of its formation, the liquidation committee will notify the creditors and, within 60 days, make a public announcement in a newspaper on at least two occasions.[39] The public announcement should include the name and address of the corporation, the reason for the liquidation, the starting date of the liquidation, the address of the liquidation committee, and a member list of the liquidation committee.

The creditors are generally given 30 days to make claims to the liquidation committee.[40] The claims of known creditors to the corporation may become a part of liquidation claims. The claims of unknown creditors, however, can be made at any time before the final distribution of the remaining assets.

The liquidation committee will register and verify the creditor claims and notify the creditors in writing about the verification result. Creditors who are displeased with the verification result can apply for a re-verification within 15 days of receiving written notice. Creditors who would like to dispute the results of such re-verification may, within 15 days of receiving written notice, litigate in the people's court for a final determination.[41] The liquidation committee may not distribute any assets that are in dispute within the interim proceedings.

Secured creditors will be given priority for payment from the proceeds of the collateral up to the amount of secured claims. The remainder of the assets will be sued to pay off liquidation expenses, wages, labor insurance costs, taxes and debts to shareholders. If the assets do not provide sufficient to pay off the debts, the liquidation committee will apply to the people's court for bankruptcy.

[38] The Measures on the Liquidation Procedures for Foreign Investment Enterprises, art. 16 (1996) (P.R.C.).

[39] The Measures on the Liquidation Procedures for Foreign Investment Enterprises, art. 17 (1996) (P.R.C.).

[40] The Measures on the Liquidation Procedures for Foreign Investment Enterprises, art. 18 (1996) (P.R.C.).

[41] The Measures on the Liquidation Procedures for Foreign Investment Enterprises, art. 21 (1996) (P.R.C.).

The liquidation committee will then deliver a report to the examination and approval authorities in order to secure approval.[42] When approval has been received, the liquidation committee will file for deregistration with the tax and customs authorities and make a newspaper announcement about the termination of the business of the corporation.

When liquidation has been completed, the venture will hand over the corporation documents including accounting vouchers, accounting books, and accounting statements.

2.6.3 *Special Liquidation Procedures*

The original examination and approval authorities of corporations will play a major role in special liquidation proceedings. The authorities will be responsible for setting up a liquidation committee of Chinese and foreign shareholders.[43] The examination and approval authorities will nominate a chairman who will act as the legal person representative. As the highest level of the corporation's authority, the liquidation committee will convene the creditor conference. The chairman of the conference is nominated by the examination and approval authorities. Notice of the conference will be given in writing, 15 days in advance of the conference. A creditor may send an agent to attend the conference.[44] The creditor conference can examine any supporting materials for creditor claims, investigate the circumstances and status of debts, and convey the opinions of creditors about the liquidation plan to the liquidation committee.[45] The liquidation plan and the report of the liquidation committee must be confirmed by the examination and approval authority.

2.6.4 *Changes and Revisions*

During recent years, major changes have taken place in respect of foreign investment regulation schemes by means of the establishment of foreign

[42] The Measures on the Liquidation Procedures for Foreign Investment Enterprises, art. 32 (1996) (P.R.C.).

[43] The Measures on the Liquidation Procedures for Foreign Investment Enterprises, art. 35 (1996) (P.R.C.).

[44] The Measures on the Liquidation Procedures for Foreign Investment Enterprises, art. 40 (1996) (P.R.C.).

[45] The Measures on the Liquidation Procedures for Foreign Investment Enterprises, art. 41 (1996) (P.R.C.).

investment national security review systems, negative list control measures and the adoption of measures to enable more access to the financial services sector by foreign investment in the near future.

2.6.4.1 *Foreign Investment National Security Review*

Since 2011, foreign investment-acquiring Chinese domestic companies have been required to submit applications for foreign investment national security review. The national security review refers to issues concerning national security. It also includes assessing to what extent a proposed acquisition would have an impact on the stability of economic and social life and assessing the research capability of key technology related to national security. Foreign investors who engage in domestic acquisition are requested to file applications to MOFCOM. A joint committee will be established which will comprise the target company, concerned departments from the State Council, industry associations and companies in the same industry. If the joint committee deems it necessary, a decision will be made as to whether or not a national security review should be initiated.

2.6.4.2 *Winds of Change*

The government has established several new actions in relation to foreign investment regulation. The latest further reduces restrictions regarding foreign investment interest shareholding in securities firms and asset management services firms. In the near future, the equity position of foreign investment interest may rise to 51 per cent of shareholding interest. Furthermore, during the next three years, shareholding restrictions are expected to be entirely removed. At present, foreign investment shareholding in foreign invested banks is restricted to 20 per cent whereas foreign investment shareholding in foreign invested securities firms is 49 per cent. Foreign investment securities firms and insurance companies cannot be established as WFOEs. Foreign investment in Chinese banks or financial asset management firms cannot be more than 20 per cent owned by a single investor or 25 per cent owned by multiple investors. It is expected that these restrictions will be abolished and substituted by uniform foreign investment shareholding in banks. In about three years, single or multiple foreign investors should be able to establish life insurance companies in China. The introduction of new rules about foreign investment in new energy cars is expected in 2018 for free trade zone cities and for experimental purposes.

CHAPTER 3

Securities Law

3.1 The Evolution of Securities Law in China

Set up in 1990 and 1991 respectively, the establishment of the Shanghai and Shenzhen Stock Exchanges marked important milestones in the development of China's securities industry. The first securities firm to deal in stock services was established in Shenzhen in 1987, and the first Securities Law was promulgated in 1998. In the interim, a body of administrative rules and regulations were issued to regulate the stock exchanges, supervise securities issuance and exchange, and safeguard justice and fairness in the securities market. The China Securities Regulatory Commission (CSRC) was established by the State Council with delegated powers to regulate and supervise the securities market.

The development of China's securities market emerged out of a period of turbulence and rapidly changing circumstances. The first Securities Law was a welcome act, formulated against a backdrop of inadequate public corporation governance. The interests and rights of investors had hardly been protected at all until then. A securities law was posited as a solution that might offer effective investor protection and endorse standard practice across the country. The Securities Law of 1998 was the first comprehensive law to regulate the securities market in China. Drawing upon past experiences of regulation and supervision, the Securities Law of 1998 brought together administrative rules and regulations into a unified legal framework. It provided legal protection to investors and parties to securities issuance and exchange transactions by forbidding insider trading,

D. Yu, *Chinese Business Law*, The Palgrave Series on Chinese Law,
https://doi.org/10.1007/978-981-13-0902-1_3

market manipulation, and fraud, thus helping to avert financial risk. It also aimed at preventing securities fraud by enhancing standards for public securities issuance, thereby improving the quality of public corporations. Several years into implementation, the national legislature began considering a revision of the law. In 2004 and 2005, the Securities Law was revised twice, enhancing the role of state agency intervention in the securities market. An information disclosure system was introduced, empowering the securities regulatory body, enhancing violation penalties, and strengthening public interest protection. The newly revised law required public corporations to have independent directors and a secretary to the board of directors, and established a accumulative voting and the referral system in securities issuance and transactions. In 2014, the law was revised for the third time. This time, major amendments included, among other things, a requirement to have legal approval for public securities issuance and a requirement regarding the establishment of a syndicate for any securities issuance of over RMB 50 million.

Since 2015, revising the Securities Law has returned to the legislative agenda. One of the most prominent proposals has been a systemic change from a doctrine of approval to one of due care registration insofar as securities issuance is concerned. However, this change is apparently on hold while the securities market goes through many other changes. The legislature has been rethinking the merits of a due care registration system in the wake of unregular market volatility. If the system were to be changed to a registration system, it would probably be a slimmed down version, with emphasis given to the CSRC's supervisory and regulatory role. This will be discussed more later in this chapter.

3.2 Securities

Securities are generally defined as written negotiable instruments with right holders enjoying the rights thereto. Securities are investment rights certificates with designated investor rights including the right to dividends. They are transferrable rights certificates held at the volition of holders, with or without consideration. The essence of securities lies mainly in their transferability. Moreover, securities are of equal face value which enables securities holders to enforce rights and calculate interest upon distribution. As investment certificates, securities investments are naturally subject to a number of market and business risks.

Securities are categorized according to the nature of the rights inherent in the securities or the economic function of the securities. Under Chinese law, if a distinction is made based upon the nature of the rights inherent in the negotiable instruments, securities may be divided into those of property rights, debts, and community member rights. Securities of property rights may take the form of inventory lists or bills of lading. Securities of debts include bills, commercial papers, and debt instruments. Community member securities, with stocks as an example, are securities that bear member rights by individuals or groups of individuals. Categorized by economic function, securities can be divided into proprietary, currency, and capital securities. Proprietary securities are the equivalent of securities of property rights. Currency securities include various types of commercial paper to be exchanged or paid in monetary terms. Capital securities refer to stocks or corporate bonds with investment rights. Civil law regulates proprietary securities, commercial law regulates currency securities, and securities law regulates capital securities. The securities law provides for three main forms of securities, namely stocks, bonds and investment fund shares. Rights instruments and certificates are gaining recognition to also be treated as securities. Financial derivatives, for example, are gaining momentum in this regard.

3.2.1 *Types of Securities*

Before the recent stock market reforms, stocks were categorized based upon the identity of their owner. There were stocks owned by the state, stocks owned by legal persons, and stocks owned by the public. With completion of stock market reforms in 2005, this categorization was retired to the history books and all stocks became A shares on the securities exchanges.

3.2.1.1 Stocks Owned by the State

Stocks owned by the state were stocks in a joint stock limited liability corporation invested by departments or institutions empowered by the state to make investments using state-owned assets.

3.2.1.2 Stocks Owned by Legal Persons

Stocks owned by legal persons referred to stocks owned by legal persons that invested in shares that remained off limits for public circulation in legal person enterprises. Such investments came from legal persons that were either entities with legal person status or social organizations.

Since the founding of the People's Republic of China, most enterprises been been owned by the state. Before 2006, up to 60 per cent of shareholdings of such enterprises could be owned by the state or the legal person of an enterprise. These shares were not for public circulation, meaning they could not be transferred on a stock exchange. The shareholding structure of a public corporation was comprised of stocks owned by the public, the state and the legal person entity. Non-circulation stocks were known as *fei liutong gu* (非流通股), and circulation stocks or *liutong gu* (流通股), were public stocks. The value of these three types of stock was calculated differently. State-owned stocks and stocks owned by legal persons were mostly acquired by negotiation. Public stocks were acquired by bidding on the stock exchange. In other words, these stocks were subject to different modes of acquisition. The process of reform took about seven or eight years to complete and in 2006 nearly all public corporations with these three types of stocks saw their stocks turned into A shares, ending the divided equity shareholding structure. The main method used for stock convergence was payment of a consideration by holders of non-circulation stocks to holders of circulation stocks in exchange for the right to float on the stock exchange. The convergence reform underwent three rounds between 1998 and 2006.

3.2.1.3 Stocks Owned by Public Investors

Stocks owned by public investors were stocks that were tradable and transferrable over the stock exchanges. After the 2006 convergence reform, stocks in China were referred to by categories based on their placement and location. Two main types were established: domestic A and B shares, and overseas H, N and S shares.

3.2.2 Domestic Stocks

3.2.2.1 A Shares

A shares are issued by domestic Chinese issuers, typically a joint stock limited liability corporation, to domestic investors, qualified foreign institutional investors (QFII), and foreign strategic investors upon representation. They are denominated and traded in *renminbi* (RMB) on the Shanghai or the Shenzhen Stock Exchange.

3.2.2.2 *B Shares*

B shares are denominated in RMB but subscribed to and traded in a foreign currency. They are issued and underwritten within China and traded on the Shanghai or the Shenzhen Stock Exchange.

The history of investment in B shares by domestic investors has been interesting. Before February 21, 2001, B shares could not be issued to Chinese citizens living in China. Only foreign individual investors, corporations and entities from foreign countries or those from Hong Kong, Macau, and Taiwan were entitled to become investors. Chinese citizens residing in foreign countries could, however, invest in B shares. After February 21, 2001, local Chinese investors were also permitted to invest in B shares using foreign currency deposited in domestic commercial banks. As of 2001, domestic Chinese issuers could officially issue B shares to both foreign and Chinese investors.

3.2.2.3 *H Shares*

Article 238 of the Securities Law defines H shares as "foreign capital stocks issued by domestic issuers and traded in the foreign market." They are stocks issued by corporations in China whose value is represented in RMB but traded over foreign stock exchanges in foreign currency. Investors once designated these types of securities as H, N, L or S shares. H shares are listed on the Hong Kong Stock Exchange, N shares on the New York Stock Exchange, L shares on the London Stock Exchange and S shares on the Singapore Stock Exchange. Eventually, all these have come to known collectively as H shares.

3.2.2.4 *Red Chip Stocks*

The term 'red chip stocks' has been humorously applied by investors in reference to 'blue chip stocks' on the New York Stock Exchange. Red chip stocks are issued by corporations with a controlling interest from mainland Chinese capital that have been incorporated overseas, usually in offshore tax havens such as British Virgin Islands or Bermuda, but listed on the Hong Kong Stock Exchange. For stocks to be called 'red chip', the controlling mainland Chinese interest is usually no less than 35 per cent of equity in the corporation.

3.2.2.5 *Bonds*

Bonds are certificates held by creditors or debtors. Bonds are issued to investors by governmental agencies, financial institutions, and industrial and commercial enterprises with the payment of interest in accordance with a predetermined rate and repayment of the principal following agreed upon terms. Under the Securities Law, bonds are enforceable debts. In bond-related relationships, investors are creditors and issuers are debtors.

Corporate Bonds

Corporate bonds are certificates of debts issued by corporations that promise to pay interest at an agreed-upon rate and repay the principal to bondholders at the end of an agreed-upon term. Insofar as the corporation is concerned, corporate bonds are debts. In China, only joint stock limited liability corporations may issue stocks but all corporations including limited liability corporations may issue bonds.

The approval authority for corporate bond issuance is the State Council. Qualifications for issuance vary dependent upon the issuer's situation. Corporate bonds may be long, medium, or short term. A long term bond may run for over five years, a medium term bond for up to five years, and a short term bond for just one year. Most corporate bonds are long term while most convertible bonds are medium term or less. An issuer usually provides security for the bond. The current rules and regulations provide that securities may be in the form of a mortgage, guarantee, pledge, or any other bonds, equity or stocks that the issuing corporation owns. An issuing corporation needs to provide full security for convertible corporate bonds. Such security may cover the principal, interest, default penalty, damages and expenses for the exercise of the rights of the bondholders. Conversely, an unsecured bond is a bond unsecured by the issuer.

Government Bonds

Government bonds are public bonds, issued as debt instruments by government authorities at central or provincial level to raise financing or for other designated purposes with a promise to repay the principal and interest at an agreed rate and at a designated time.

Government bonds are either state or local, with the former being debts issued by the central government for a major purpose such as reducing the financial deficit or funding infrastructural projects. This is major form of state credit that is guaranteed by the collection of tax revenue by the central government. With tax incentives for investors, state bonds are subject to less risk and better liquidity, although they do offer lower payment yields. Local bonds are issued by revenue collecting local governments or public institutions for the purpose of local transportation, communications, housing, education, hospital construction, or environmental protection projects. Their repayment is backed by local government tax revenue. Like state bonds, they also provide tax incentives for investors.

Financial Bonds

Financial bonds are issued by banks and non-bank financial institutions for the purpose of acquiring steady financing with a flexible repayment timetable. The interest rate on financial bonds is generally lower than for corporate bonds but higher than for government bonds and fixed term bank deposits. From 1993, financial bonds have not been issued to individual investors. Since 1997, they have been issued through the national interbank bond market and offered to institutional investors within and outside China. Issuers are typically policy banks, commercial banks, financial corporations, and financial asset management firms. Approval for issuance is required from the People's Bank of China.

Shares in Securities Investment Funds

Shares in securities investment funds are treated as securities under the Securities Law. In 2003, the Law on Securities Investment Funds was enacted to regulate their management and operations. Securities investment funds issue shares to public investors by indirectly investing in stocks and bonds traded on the stock exchange. These funds are managed by professionally qualified fund managers. The shares of such funds are held by a trustee acting in shareholders' benefit. In China, only a commercial bank may be a trustee.

A securities investment fund may be open or closed. An open fund allows investors to buy in or sell out freely during the term of the agreement. A closed fund is fixed and does not allow investors to divest or trade their shares during the term of the agreement. A securities investment fund can offer public or private issuance. Those offered to more than 200 specified investors are considered public, while those offered to fewer than 200 specified investors are private. A securities investment fund can be categorized as a stock, bond or currency fund, depending on the percentage of investment it holds in stocks, bonds or currency. A security investment fund must have at least 60 per cent of its assets in stocks to be considered a stock investment fund, 80 per cent in bonds to be considered a bond investment fund, and 100 per cent in currency to be considered a currency investment fund. The alternative is to be considered a mixed fund if investment ratios differ from the above prescribed percentages.

The current law, rules and regulations indicate that a securities investment fund can be organized as a corporation governed according to the principle of trust between fund managers, trustees and shareholders. Under the Law on Securities Investment Funds, a securities investment fund may be established as a corporation. In reality, however, such a fund seldom opts for a corporate structure.

3.3 Basic Principles of the Securities Law

As aforementioned, the first law related to securities since the founding of the People's Republic of China was enacted in 1998. In December 1998, the National People's Congress approved and promulgated the Securities Law, effective from July 1, 1999. The law was revised in 2005 with revisions effective from January 1, 2006. The revised law was inclusive of regulations governing securities issuance, securities trading, mergers and acquisitions of listed corporations, stock exchanges, securities firms, securities registration and clearing institutions, securities service institutions, associations of securities industry, administrative authorities of securities regulation and supervision and legal liabilities, and obligations and penalties. It stated its purpose as regulating securities issuance and trading, protecting lawful interests of investors, promoting an optimal socio-economic order and public interest, and enhancing the development of a socialist market economy. The law laid down basic guiding principles as equality, voluntary action, reasonable compensation, credibility, and integrity; the principle of compliance; the principle of division of securities business, management, and operations; the principle of unified governmental supervision; and the principle of a unity of self disciplinary management of securities trade, audits and supervision.

3.3.1 *The* San Gong *Principles*

The Securities Law provides for the *San Gong* Principles that aim to protect the interests of parties involved in the securities market. The *San Gong* Principles are openness, fairness and justice. *San* in Chinese means "three" and *Gong* refers to "openness, fairness, and justice". The law provides for the application of the *San Gong* Principles to securities issuance and trading.

3.3.1.1 Principle of Openness

Of the *San Gong* Principles, the principle of openness is the most essential. Openness is seen as the chief way of ensuring the prevention of securities fraud, just as the sun is known as the best disinfectant. In the Securities Law, the principle of openness is the foundation on which the principles of fairness and justice can be applied.

At the core of the principle of openness is information disclosure. Information disclosure is mandatory for securities issuers regarding material information as to any changes in the listed corporations, the financial activities and financial status of listed corporations, the transactions of mergers and acquisitions of listed corporations, and any other information that may impact the price of securities. Ideally, information disclosure should bring about a desired degree of transparency to the securities market, ensure a timely, full and accurate delivery of information to the investing public, and openly acquire information and knowledge regarding securities market investment.

3.3.1.2 Principle of Fairness

The principle of fairness is applied with the aim of developing an investment environment wherein concerned participants in the securities market are ensured equal status under the law, fair protection under the law, and equal opportunity for competition. This means that issuers, investors, securities dealers and securities service institutions will not receive differential treatment under law. The principle is interpreted to mean that securities issuers will have a fair opportunity in financing, securities management institutions will have a fair opportunity in securities market competition, and investors will have a fair opportunity in the securities market.

3.3.1.3 Principle of Justice

The principle of justice mandates just treatment by the state securities supervision and management institutions. It serves as a safeguard for the observance of the principles of openness and fairness. The legislature, in enacting laws, rules, and regulations, and the judiciary, in rendering resolutions of securities controversies, are urged to observe the principle of just treatment for all participants in the securities market.

3.3.2 Principles of Equality, Voluntary Action, Compensation, and Integrity

The principles of equality, voluntary action, compensation, and integrity are common principles of commercial law in China. The principles are established in the Securities Law as major public policies to regulate players in the securities market.

The principle of equality refers to a broad spectrum of equality inclusive of the rights of players in securities issuance and trading, equality between and among natural persons and between and among legal persons, and equality between natural persons and legal persons, equality during the course of trading and stock issuance, the right to independently make decisions, and the right to enjoy equal protection under the law.

Voluntary action refers to the right of those operating in securities trading or issuance activities to be free from unlawful interference. Those involved have the right to independently participate in stock trading or issuance, exercise lawful rights, and to be free from duress.

The principle of compensation is founded upon the principles of equality and voluntary action. Equality of status leads to equality of compensation. The securities law is designed to work against any act of deceit, fraud, the making of misleading statements or misrepresentation, or ill-performed promises.

3.3.3 Principle of Compliance and Anti-fraud Principle

The law mandates compliance of the securities law and administrative regulations by parties concerned. The law prohibits fraud, insider trading, and market manipulation.

3.3.4 Principle of Divided Management

The principle of divided management aims at maintaining divided management and operations of the securities, trust, banking, and insurance industries. Securities firms shall be separate from banks, insurance corporations, and trust institutions. The securities law provides an exception to the compliance of this provision for certain institutions if they are otherwise regulated by the state. To date, there have been no reports of this exemption having been put into practice.

Before 1993, China's financial industry has undergone a period of undivided management and operation. State financial regulation and supervision were relatively inept and the financial self-disciplinary mechanism inadequate to curb speculative activities in securities and real estate industries. After 1993, the State Council put forward the principle of divided management and operation that was subsequently established under the Securities Law. Article 43 of the Commercial Banking Law of 1995 forbids commercial banks from engaging in securities operations and management activities. It states that no commercial bank may undertake any trust investment, participate in securities management and operation, or invest in the real estate sector.

The state also imposed legal restrictions on the expenses of insurance funds by prohibiting their investment into certain prohibited sectors. The Insurance Law provides that insurance funds are limited to bank deposits and the trading of government bonds, financial bonds, and any other forms approved by the State Council. Insurance funds are prohibited from getting involved in the securities market and establishing securities firms.[1]

Since the promulgation of the Trust Law and the Securities Law, those in the trust industry have not been allowed to conduct mixed trust and securities operations. The Trust Law became effective on October 1, 2001, and has strictly prohibited the trust industry from undertaking business in non-trust industries. Together with the enactment of the Trust Investment Corporation Management Measures of 2002 and the Trust Investment Corporation Fund Trust Management Preliminary Measures of 2002, the legal foundations for the divided management and operation of the trust industry have been established. There has been a tendency to suggest that the finance industry has merged with the securities, banking, and insurance industries. Such a tendency has been gaining momentum especially before and after China's entry into the WTO and China's securities industry is facing ever increasing competition from foreign banks.

In August 1998, the People's Bank of China issued benchmark regulatory measures for fund management firms, namely the Regulatory Measures for the Entry of Fund Management Firms in the InterBank Market and Regulatory Measures for the Entry of Securities Firms into the Interbank Borrowing Market. These permit fund management firms may apply to the People's Bank of China to enter the interbank market to

[1] The Insurance Law of the People's Republic of China, article 105.

purchase securities on the primary market and trade on the secondary market. These measures have empowered securities firms to enter into the interbank market to conduct interbank borrowing and bond exchange subject to approval by the People's Bank of China and upon the recommendation of the CSRC. In October 1990, the State Council approved indirect entry into the secondary stock market by insurance corporations that purchase securities investment funds. In February 2000, the People's Bank of China and the CSRC jointly issued Regulatory Measures on Stock Pledges by Securities Firms, under which securities firms may apply for loans from commercial banks pledged by their own stocks and investment in securities fund firms. This serves to widen the financing avenue for securities firms.

3.3.5 Principles of Unitary Governmental Supervision and Regulation, Industrial Self-Disciplinary Regulation, and Audit Supervision

The combination of governmental supervision, industrial regulation, and trading self-discipline implied by the Gong San Principle has now been established in law. The State Council securities supervisory regulatory body shall regulate and supervise the national securities market on a unitary basis. Such a body may when needed establish agencies tasked with the delegated duties of supervision and regulation. Self-disciplinary regulation is largely viewed as a supplement to governmental supervision and regulation. The association of the securities industry is entrusted with the execution of self-disciplinary regulation which is premised upon governmental supervision and regulation. The third player in securities industry supervision and regulation is the state audit body authorized to audit stock exchanges, securities firms, securities registration and clearing institution, as well as securities supervision and regulation institutions.

3.4 Securities Issuance

3.4.1 General Introduction

The issuance of securities is governed by the framework of legal restrictions and issuance conditions that serve as the qualification requirements for issuers and conditions for securities issuance. Securities issuance needs to comply with legal procedures, issuance application procedures, and issuance examination requirements.

Frequently adopted types of issuances are direct issuance (*zhijie faxing*, 直接发行) and indirect issuance (*jianjie faxing*, 间接发行). Direct issuance refers to issuance by which the issuer takes unto itself the risks and obligations of securities issuance by selling securities directly to investors. Indirect issuance refers to issuance undertaken by one or more institutions as a medium or media between the issuer and investors. Such issuance is completed through an agency.

The issuance of securities may be by public offering (*gongkai faxing*,公开发行) or private placement (*si muo*私募). Public offerings reach investors via public means such as advertisements, public inducements, and other forms of public sale. They are directed towards undesignated investors or designated investors numbering over 200 persons. Public offerings are regularly conducted through indirect issuance. The law defines a public offering as: (1) an issuance to undesignated investors; (2) an issuance to more than 200 designated investors; or (3) any other kind of issuance as provided for under the law, rules and regulations.

A private placement is an issuance aimed at a few designated investors, including institutional investors, affiliated corporate investors, corporate staff and other persons within corporate associations such as shareholders, employees, staff members, and corporate counsels.

3.4.2 Establishment Issuance and New Share Issuance

An establishment issuance refers to the issuance of securities at the time of establishment of a corporation. According to the Corporation Law, the establishment of a joint stock limited liability corporation may either issue securities at the time of its establishment (*faqi sheli*, 发起设立) or subscribe to securities at the time of its establishment (*muji sheli*, 募集设立). An issuance of securities by promotion means that promoters shall subscribe to all the shares of the corporation upon its establishment. Subscription refers to an issuance by which promoters subscribe to a part of the shares of the corporation while issuing the rest to the public or designated investors at the establishment of the corporation. An issuance of new shares refers to a new issuance of securities by a corporation that needs further financing.

3.4.3 *Securities Issuance, Examination, and Approval System*

The Securities Law has adopted a system of examination and approval for the issuance of securities. The underlying principle is examination of the substance of the issuance. Under such a system, the issuer is required not only to fully and accurately disclose all important information necessary for investment purposes, but also satisfy the substantive conditions under the provisions of the law and rules. Upon approval being granted by the related government authorities, the issuer may initiate issuance. The securities authorities will examine in substance the truthfulness, accuracy, and entirety of the information disclosed by the issuer. Moreover, the examination authority will further examine in substance the investment value of the issuance in question. The government deems it necessary to step in to prevent the issuance of securities if regarded as unworthy of investment. However, insofar as risks involved in securities investment are concerned, an investor will be on their own.

3.4.4 *Conditions for Issuance*

Securities issuance is largely one of two kinds: establishment and new share issuance. The conditions and requirements for the two types of issuances are different. Establishment issuance (*sheli faxing*, 设立发行) does not include investment by the general public, and as such, it is not governed by the law. The Corporation Law is the proper governing sphere to cover the conditions and procedures for such an issuance. Insofar as promotion of establishment issuance is concerned (*muji sheli faxing*, 募集设立发行), it is governed by the appropriate laws, rules, and regulations related to the investing interest of the public. The law provides for the submission of the required documents and issuance applications for securities issuance of joint stock limited liability corporations to the securities regulatory and supervisory agency under the State Council. These include the articles of incorporation, a promoter's agreement, the names of promoters, the number of shares subscribed to by promoters, the types of contribution, the investment examination certificate, the prospectus, the names of the underwriting institutions and related agreements, a letter of sponsoring issuance, and approval documents for the establishment of the corporation, if any.

The securities law provides the necessary conditions for new share issuance. The basic requirements are that the company has a sound organizational structure, the capability for continued profitability, is in good financial shape, and that there have not been any fraudulent financial and accounting representations, statements or serious violations of the law in the last three years. The law leaves out a catch-all provision for any other kinds of conditions that the authorities concerned may prescribe in the future. Corporations aiming to issue new shares are required to submit an application and documentation for the subscription of new shares to the securities regulatory and supervisory agency. The required documents comprise the corporation's business license, shareholder meeting resolutions, prospectus, financial and accounting report, and the names of securities underwriting institutions.

3.5 Issuance of Corporate Bonds

3.5.1 New Issuance

The securities law provides for a set of detailed conditions for the new issuance of corporate bonds. The issuer should satisfy a number of conditions including that net assets of the joint stock limited liability corporation are no less than RMB 30 million and the accumulated balance of bonds are no more than 40 per cent of distributable profit over the last three years, leaving sufficient revenue to support interest payments for a year; that financing complies with state industrial policies; and that the interest yield on the bonds may not exceed limits prescribed by the State Council.

Issuers must provide their business license, articles of incorporation, corporate bonds subscription methods, asset evaluation report and examination report and any other documents required by the State Council.

3.5.2 New Share Issuance of Corporate Bonds

A new share issuance of corporate bonds should comply with provisions concerning the first issuance of bonds, as well as any other relevant provisions under the law. The law specifically prohibits new share issuance if the prior subscription is inadequate; if there has been a breach or a delay of corporate payment obligations and the situation has not been remedied; and if any event has occurred that changed the purpose of the subscription contrary to the law.

3.6 Application and Examination of Securities Issuance

3.6.1 *Application*

An application for securities issuance must comply with the requirements of the agencies or institutions that are entrusted with the examination with respect to the format and procedure of the submission. An issuer shall pledge accuracy, truthfulness and entirety of application to the State Council securities regulatory agency or any other agency with delegated authority. It is the legal duty of securities services institutions to guarantee the application's accuracy, truthfulness and entirety.

3.6.2 *Examination for Securities Issuance*

The examination authority for securities issuance is the State Council securities regulatory agency. The agency established that an issuance examination committee should consist of professionals from the State Council securities supervision and regulatory committee and external experts who cast votes to express their opinion with regard to securities issuance. The agency determines matters concerning the constitution, term, and working procedures of the issuance examination committee.

The examination procedures will be made public and be subject to supervision. The committee members may not be an interested party to the application, receive direct or indirect gifts, hold shares in the applicant corporation or be in private contact with the issuer.

The State Council agency or the authorized department should make a decision within three months of the date of application. If an application is rejected, reasons should be given.

Following approval, the subscription documents are required to be on designated public display before public issuance. No issuance may be timed for before this public display. No person may disclose relevant information before such information is made public.

The law prescribes that a correction of mistakes made in the interim of approval may bring the issuance to a halt if the correction is not completed. The agency may revoke approval even if securities have been issued but are outstanding, hold the issuer liable to return the issuance price plus interest to investors, hold the sponsors and issuer jointly and severally liable except where there is proof of innocence, and hold controlling shareholders of the issuer and person in actual control to be jointly and severally liable with the issuer if found at fault.

The law is cognizant that it is the issuer and issuance team members that shall be ultimately liable for any act that is not in compliance with the legal conditions or procedures of the issuance. However, with respect to the issue of degree of fault insofar as mental state is implicated in any wrongdoing that constitutes an act of violation of legal conditions and legal procedures, the law is silent. The law is also silent as to whether or not the entrusted administrative agency shall bear any responsibility or liability in that regard.

3.7 Securities Underwriting and Sponsorship

Securities underwriting is conducted through an underwriting agreement whereby the issuer sells their securities through an underwriter. An underwriting agreement is signed between issuer and underwriter. The agreement will typically include the following:

a) The name and domicile of the issuer and the name of the legal representative;
   The type, amount, quantity, and issuing price of the securities to be underwritten;
b) The terms of the underwriting including the starting date and ending dates;
c) The payment method of the underwriters;
d) The underwriting fees and methods of clearing;
e) Penalties for breach; and
f) The catch-all provisions that will deal with any other matters that are decided by the relevant Securities Regulatory Commission.

In practice there are two main kinds of underwriting. One is best effort underwriting (*jinli chengxiao*, 尽力承销), and the other is firm commitment underwriting (*baoxiao*, 包销).

Under a best effort underwriting arrangement, the underwriter will use its best efforts to conduct the sale of securities but return any unsold portion of securities to the issuer beyond the terms of the underwriting. The issuer and underwriter engage in an agency relationship whereby the issuer entrusts the underwriter to be the agent for the sale of its securities with the rights and obligations of the issuance remaining with the issuer.

Under a firm commitment underwriting, the underwriter agrees in the underwriting agreement to purchase total securities or buy back any securities that are yet to be sold at the end of the underwriting term. The underwriter may conduct standby underwriting whereby they will need to purchase all of the securities as a buyer from the issuer.

The issuer may consider using an underwriting syndicate for the underwriting if the size and amount of the issuance reaches a certain level. The issuance may use an underwriting syndicate if the face value of the securities issuance has reached RMB 50 million or more. The underwriting syndicate will consist of a lead underwriter and at least two or more underwriters. The non-lead underwriters work as sub-contractors who are directly responsible to the lead underwriter.

3.8 Duty of Securities Underwriters

3.8.1 Duty to Examine

Securities underwriters have the duty to professionally examine the truth, accuracy and entirety of documents, materials and information regarding the issuer, in accordance with customary professional standards and professional ethics. This is the duty of due diligence that securities firms in underwriting shall examine the truthfulness, accuracy, and entirety of the documents for public subscription and may not underwrite securities if any misleading or faulty statement or material omission is found. The law requires that remedial measures need to be immediately taken for any sold securities if the aforementioned situation occurs.

3.8.2 Duty to Make Diligent Efforts to Sell Underwritten Securities

A maximum of 90 days are allowed for underwriters to sell the securities concerned, and the underwriters are expected to work diligently during this sale period.

3.8.3 Duty to Return Securities

An underwriter has the affirmative duty to return securities to the issuer if upon the expiry of the consignment sale period, they fail to reach the required 70 per cent of public subscription. The issuer will pay the original issuing price plus any applicable bank interest to the stock subscribers.

3.8.4 Duty to Report

An underwriter has the duty to report for the record to China Securities Regulatory Commission within the legally stipulated timeframe after the subscription.

3.9 Sponsorship

The Securities Law has established the system of sponsorship by which a sponsor shall recommend issuance, direct the issuer to perform its legal duties consistently, and guarantee the truth, accuracy and entirety of the documents presented. The law makes sponsorship mandatory for the issuance of an IPO, new shares, and debt equity swaps. A sponsor may be held jointly and severally liable for any misleading and fraudulent statement and misrepresentation made by the issuer in conjunction with the issuance. The sponsor must be a qualified and licensed securities management firm.

3.10 The Stock Exchange

The stock exchange is a place where one may trade listed securities. One may be a person of full legal capacity, limited legal capacity, or without legal capacity so long as there is lawful representation and appropriate supervision. The law does not place any specific restrictions on personal trading capacity, but rather a qualification on those engaged in stock trading. These restrictions are there to help resolve problems in trading by interested parties who may be in possession of sensitive and useful market information that is not yet public. The law prohibits promoters of a joint stock limited liability corporation from transferring corporate stocks within the first year of a corporation's establishment. Senior managers, directors, or supervisors shall report any change in their shareholding of a corporation, may not transfer more than 25 per cent of their shareholding in the corporation during their term of office, and may not transfer corporate stocks within the first year of the corporation going public. Senior managers, directors, or supervisors may not transfer their corporate stocks within the first six months of their departure from office. Under the law, the articles of incorporation may further limit share transfer by senior management. The law also sets out another provision against the trading of shares by persons including the staff members of the stock exchanges, securities firms, securities registration clearing institutions, and securities supervision administrations. They may not within their tenure or term of office directly, under an alias, or by assuming the name of another person, hold and trade stocks and accept stocks as gifts.

One important restriction is that placed upon securities services institutions and their staff members. Specifically, the law prohibits auditors, asset evaluators or legal opinion providers that have provided documents relevant to stock trading and issuance from buying or selling the stocks within the period of stock underwriting and within six months of the expiry of the term of underwriting. In addition, such persons or institutions may not buy or sell stocks upon the date of acceptance of the agency of the issuing corporation until six working days following the release of relevant documents to the public.

The securities law also sets out restrictions of the trading of corporation stocks by a senior manager, supervisor, director, or any other person who holds more than 5 per cent of company shares within six months of owning them after IPO.

3.11 Going Public

3.11.1 Conditions for Securities Issuance

China has adopted a system of approval for the issuance of securities. The issuance must be approved by the approval authority (CSRC) or examined and approved by any other authorized agency under the State Council. Any unapproved issuance is void and illegal. The Securities Law sets forth conditions for securities issuance which vary between stocks, bonds, and other types of securities.

3.11.2 Stocks

Under the current legal regime, only joint stock limited liability corporations may issue stocks. General conditions apply to stock issuance upon establishment, for corporate restructuring, and new issuance.

3.11.2.1 Conditions for Stock Issuance Upon Establishment

A stock issuance upon establishment (*sheli faxing gupiao,* 设立发行股票) is generally referred to as an initial public offering (IPO). The corporation in question seeks to raise financing during an IPO and thereby establish itself as a joint stock limited liability corporation. The requisite conditions for stock issuance upon establishment are that (i) the operations and management of the corporation concerned are in line with state industrial policy requirements; (ii) only one type of common stock may be issued; (iii) the subscription of shares by promoters may not be below 35 per cent of the total stock issuance and may not be below RMB 30 million in proportion to the total stock issuance; (iv) the public issuance may not be below 25 per cent of the total stock issuance; the subscription by members of the corporation may not exceed 10 per cent of the public issuance; and in the event that the issuance exceeds RMB 400 million, the ratio of public issuance may be reduced but not to below 10 per cent of the total issuance, subject to approval by the securities supervision agency; (v) the promoters of the issuing corporation have not seriously violated the law within the last three years; and that (vi) the total equity of the corporation is no less than RMB 30 million.

3.11.2.2 Conditions for Stock Issuance Through Corporate Restructuring

A stock issuance through corporate restructuring must first satisfy the conditions for stock issuance upon establishment as described above. It must secondly satisfy certain other conditions. These are that (i) in the year before stock issuance, the ratio of corporate net assets to total assets was not below 30 per cent and the ratio of corporate intangible assets to net asset was not above 20 per cent (although this ratio may change subject to provisions of the Securities Regulatory Commission) and that (ii) the corporation concerned has been continuously profitable for the past three years. If the corporation concerned is state-owned, the decision with respect to the percentage of state-owned shareholdings in the corporation after stock issuance needs to be approved by the agency under the State Council or the relevant authorities.

*3.11.2.3 Conditions for New Share Issuance (*faxing xin gu*, 发行新股)*

A new share issuance is an issuance to raise further financing for a corporation after its establishment as a joint stock limited liability corporation. Not only must such issuance satisfy conditions required for a general stock issuance but it must also comply with special requirements for further financing. The Securities Law provides general conditions for these circumstances. The corporation should have a sound management mechanism in place and the capacity for consistent profitability and be in good financial shape. In addition, there must not have been any fraudulent financial and account reporting during the previous three years and not illegal act may have been committed. The corporation must show that funds received in previous rounds of stock issuance has not been diverted for any other use and moreover have been put to good use. The corporation must satisfy the rule that one year must have elapsed since the previous public issuance. The Securities Regulatory Commission may set further conditions from time to time.

3.12 Bonds

Bonds are securities issued for financing purposes bearing the promise to repay the principal and interest within an agreed period of time in accordance with the law. Corporations that may issue corporate bonds are joint stock limited liability corporations, wholly state-owned corporations, limited liability corporations invested by state investment entities or any other limited liability corporations.

3.12.1 Conditions for Initial Bond Issuance

The Securities Law allows joint stock limited liability corporations and limited liabilities corporations to issue bonds. The limitations imposed upon such issuances are that (i) net assets of a joint stock limited liability corporation may not be below RMB 30 million and for a limited liabilities corporation, RMB 60 million; (ii) the accumulated amount of bonds may not surpass 40 per cent of net assets of the issuing corporation; (iii) distributable profit over the previous three years should be sufficient to pay bond interest for a year; and (iv) the purpose for which the fund is to be raised is in line with state industrial policy. Interest on the bond may not exceed the limit set under provisions issued by the State Council. Financing raised from bond issuance may not be used to cover any loss or pay for non-operating expenses. The bonds will have a term of more than one year and the issuance of corporate bonds may not be below RMB 50 million.

3.12.2 *Conditions for New Issuance*

A new issuance is required to comply with the same terms applied to the initial issuance. In addition, the new issuance may not be approved if the initial subscription failed to meet the expected target amount or if there has been a default on the payment of interest and principle or a breach of debt obligations.

3.12.3 *Conditions for the Issuance of Debt Equity Swaps*

A corporation that issues a debt equity swap must comply with requirements for the issuance of bonds and stocks, subject to CSRC approval.

3.13 Procedures for Going Public

To be listed on the stock exchange, procedures include the application, examination, and execution of a listing agreement and notice. The issuing corporation initiates an application procedure, submits an application for the examination and approval of the stock exchange, and executes a listing agreement with the stock exchange. After the execution of the listing agreement, the issuer is required to put up a public notice of the listing within the prescribed period of time.

3.13.1 *Application and Examination*

An application for listing must be approved by the stock exchange. The law provides that the necessary documents should be submitted for approval. The documents include the application for listing, the shareholders meeting resolution for the listing application, the articles of incorporation, business license, audited financial and accounting reports for the last three years, legal opinion and letter of the listing sponsor, and the updated prospectus. Under the law, the stock exchange may request any other documents from the applicant.

3.13.2 *The Listing Agreement*

The issuing corporation and stock exchange are expected to agree to and execute a listing agreement with approval for listing from the stock exchange. This agreement normally takes the form of a document setting out the rights, duties and obligations of the stock exchange and the listing corporation. It should describe the types of securities to be listed, the date of issuance, their face value, the total amount of issuance, the accumulated amount of issuance, and associated expenses. As a regular matter, the issuing corporation will disclose in the listing agreement the financial and operating conditions and representations for compliance with the law, rules and regulations of the stock exchange.

3.13.3 The Listing Notice

The issuing corporation is required to put out a public notice of all listing-related documents having obtained approval for listing from the stock exchange. The issuing corporation is also required to disclose and put out a public notice of the date on which the stock is to be first traded, the names of the top ten stockholders of the corporation and their shareholding amount, the name of the person in actual control of the corporation, the names of directors, supervisors and senior managers and their ownership positions with regard to the stock and bond holdings of the corporation.

3.13.4 Bond Listing Procedures

The listing procedures for bonds are quite similar to those for stocks with respect to the application, examination, listing agreement, and public notice. With respect to the bond listing procedure, the law provides for the requisite documents to be submitted to the stock exchange for approval, and these mainly include the application for listing, the resolution of the board of directors for listing, the articles of incorporation, the business license, the description of the bond subscription, and the bond issuance amount. Bond listings also require a public notice.

3.13.4.1 The Issuance of Foreign Capital Stocks

Currently, B and H shares are two foreign capital stocks that concern foreign interests. B shares are foreign capital stocks issued by domestic issuers that are traded on the Shanghai or the Shenzhen Stock Exchange. H shares are foreign capital stocks issued by domestic issuers but traded on a foreign stock exchange. Chinese citizens residing in China may now also invest in B shares by virtue of a Notice on Certain Issues Concerning Investment in B Shares by Local Chinese Residents. This Notice was issued by the China Securities Regulatory Commission and State Administration of Industry and Commerce in 2001. From this date onwards, Chinese citizens residing in China have been accorded the same right to purchase B shares along with individuals, legal persons, and organizations from foreign countries, individuals, legal persons, and organizations of Hong Kong, Macau, and Taiwan and Chinese citizens residing abroad.

The conditions for B share issuance are quite similar to those required for A shares. The issuing corporation needs to submit an application subject to CSRC approval. Despite H shares being for the foreign market only, the issuing corporation is still required to satisfy certain conditions before a foreign issuance may proceed. Most of these conditions are formulated by the CSRC and other relevant regulatory agencies. The applicant is required to demonstrate that she acts in conformity with the law, regulations, and rules related to stocks traded on foreign stock markets. The applicant shall ensure that the funds raised are in line with state industrial policy, foreign exchange policies, and any other policies related to investment in fixed assets. The applicant should show that it has a sound corporate governance structure, internal control system, and stable senior management. The applicant should ensure a reliable source of foreign exchange for dividend payments to foreign shareholders. The applicant shall have minimum RMB 400 million in net assets and RMB 60 million minimum in after-tax profit in the preceding year of the operation, and must demonstrate growth potential and that the issuance will not fall below USD 50 million to the satisfaction of the approval authority.

Initial government approval for H share listings overseas for the issuer comes from the provincial government at the place of domicile of the issuer or directly from the State Council. Having obtained the necessary preliminary approvals, the issuing corporation will submit approval documentation to the CSRC at least three months in advance of the submission of the application to the securities regulatory agencies or the stock exchange where it aims to be listed on foreign territory. The CSRC will decide if the listing is in conformity with state industrial policy and foreign exchange and fixed asset investment policies. The CSRC will normally consult with the National Planning Commission and the Economic and Trade Commission on this matter. If the CSRC is satisfied with the application, the review committee will issue a written decision of approval. The issuer should then file a report naming the selected underwriter. The issuer will need to file the initial application to the CSRC at least five working days prior to submission to the foreign securities regulatory agencies or stock exchange and at least ten days prior to the submission of the final application to the foreign securities regulatory agencies or stock exchange. The issuer may not proceed with a foreign application without first obtaining approval from the CSRC. Usually, the issuer is required to submit for the relevant government approval shareholder meeting resolution, confirmation of asset appraisal by the state asset management agency if the issuing corporation has state-owned assets, confirmation by the state land resources management agency of land use rights, approval of the land use plan, articles of incorporation, any restructuring plan and relevant agreements, legal opinions, audit reports, asset appraisal reports, profit forecasts, and plan of public issuance, in addition to the listing plan.

3.13.4.2 Share Issuance in Securities Investment Funds

Securities investment funds are professionally managed by fund managers who act as fund trustees. Security investment funds are governed by the Trust Law, the Law on Securities Investment Funds, and the Securities Law. A fund manager may be either an individual or an institution. If the fund manager is an institution, the fund needs to be established according to legal procedures and is subject to CSRC approval.

The notable legal requirement for the establishment of a securities investment fund is the requirement for at least RMB 100 million in registered capital. It is required that shareholders must possess a sound professional reputation in securities operation, investment consultation, and trust asset management. There are also requirements for professionally qualified staff members, business premises, and securities protection facility installations that meet the particular demands of fund asset management.

The relevant authority approving the issuance of fund shares is the CSRC. The fund manager applies to the CSRC with the required materials including a written application, a draft contract for the purchase of fund shares, a draft contract for the custodianship of the capital, a draft prospectus, audited financial accounting reports of the fund manager and trustee for the preceding three years or since the year of establishment, and a statement certifying the qualifications of the fund manager and fund trustees as well as a letter of legal opinion. Approval from the CSRC greenlights publication of the prospectus by the fund manager. All documents for public viewing must be true, accurate, and complete without any false or misleading statements, representations or significant omissions. Moreover, the documents may not in any way promise any outcome of the investment or guarantee any profit-loss sharing contrary to the law.

3.14 Suspension or Termination of Stock Trading

The trading of stocks on the stock exchange is not a right but a privilege. This privilege may be terminated or suspended according to stock exchange instructions pursuant to the law, rules and regulations.

Suspension or termination of trading may generally occur if there has been any significant change in the total capitalization or equity structure of the corporation which has meant that it no longer satisfies listing requirements; if the operating performance or assets no longer satisfy listing requirements; if the corporation has lost its capacity for profitability due to asset disposal or poor financial conditions; or if the corporation commits any violative act of the law, rules or regulations.

The Securities Law provides that any one of the following circumstances may trigger a suspension of trading on the stock exchange, (1) signifiant changes have been effected in the equity structure that fail to satisfy the trading requirements of the stock exchange; (2) failure to disclose a financial status or refusal to correct a false presentation in the financial accounts; (3) the corporation has incurred losses in the preceding three years and has not been profitable in the subsequent three years; (4) the corporation has filed for bankruptcy; or (5) any other situations prescribed by the stock exchange.

3.14.1 Suspension and Termination of a Bond Listing

The privilege to trade bonds on the stock exchange may be suspended or terminated by the stock exchange on the grounds of malfeasance or for reasons associated with business operation difficulties rendering it unfit to satisfy requirements under stock exchange listing rules. It could be that the law has been violated; funds have been diverted for forbidden purposes; bond obligations have not been performed; a loss has occured in the preceding two years; or a change has rendered the corporation unfit to satisfy the listing requirements of the stock exchange. Termination of a bond listing may occur if the corporation fails to rectify such a problem within a period of time prescribed by the stock exchange or if the issue is severe. Dissolution or bankruptcy may also be a cause for termination.

The stock exchange has established a review committee to accept and review decisions made by the stock exchange as submitted by the corporation concerned so as to review and redress grievances.

3.15 Information Disclosure

A listed corporation is required to fulfill the duty of information disclosure under the law and stock exchange rules. The duty to perform information disclosure by a corporation is consistent throughout the period from becoming a public corporation until leaving the stock exchange. The duty of information disclosure is one of the fundemental principles of the law to protect public investors and allow for effective supervision and regulation of the stock exchanges by administrative agencies. The information to be disclosed is essential data concerning the assets and liabilities of the corporation, its financial condition, its profits and losses, business forecast, and shareholders' equity interests. This disclosure allows the investing public to make informed decisions regarding their investments. The legislature seems to be satisfied that investors are protected if investment decisions are made on an informed basis based upon the disclosure of requisite information.

3.15.1 Information

The fundemental requirement regarding information disclosure is that it must be accurate, complete and truthful. The information to be disclosed includes information contained in the stock or bond prospectus, the midterm report, the annual report, and the preliminary report for listed corporations.

3.15.1.1 The Prospectus for Stock Issuance

Drafted by promoters upon the establishment of a corporation, this prospectus contains information regarding major aspects of the corporation and subscription information, the amount of the subscription contributed to by promoters, the per share face value, the issuing price, the issuance of unregistered stocks, the objective of the issuance, and the rights and obligations of the subscribers.

3.15.1.2 The Prospectus for Bond Issuance

The main information in the prospectus is related to the objective of the issuance, the issuance amount, the face value of a bond, the yield, the payment terms, the guarantee, the issuing price, the dates related to the issuance and the expiry date, and the net assets of the corporation.

3.15.1.3 The Midterm Report

The securities law requires a corporation with stocks or bonds traded on the stock exchange to submit a midterm report to the CSRC and the stock exchange within two months of the end of the first half of each fiscal year. Such a report needs to be made public, and contains financial and accounting information, an operational report, a report regarding any major litigation, any change in the issued stocks and bonds, and any major events that are submitted for the resolution of the shareholder meeting.

3.15.1.4 The Annual Report

A listed corporation is required to submit an annual report to the CSRC and the stock exchange within four months of the end of each fiscal year. The annual report needs to be made public. The corporation shall state in its annual report a general description of the corporation, its financial and accounting conditions, its operating and management conditions, the shareholding positions taken by directors, supervisors, and senior management, the amount of issued stocks and bonds, a list of the names of the top ten shareholders and persons in actual control of the corporation and a report on their shareholding positions.

3.15.1.5 The Preliminary Report

A listed corporation is required to make a preliminary report to the CSRC and the stock exchange concerning any major event that may effect a significant change in the price of stocks, but is not yet known to investors. This report shall be made public. The public statement may provide causes for the occurence of the event, the present conditions, and any possible legal consequences. The law defines a significant event as any major change in the operational plan and business scope of the corporation, any major investment and asset purchase plan, any major contract to be entered into by the corporation that may effect in a material way its assets, liabilities, equities, interests and operations, any major debt obligations or breach, any major loss by the corporation, any relatively substantial change in the external environment of the operation of the corporation, any change in the directors, any change in the one-thirds of the supervisors and managers, any change in the shareholding position of the corporation or control of the corporation by 5 per cent shareholders or above or the person in actual control, any decision made by the corporation to decrease capital, merge, divest, dissolve or apply for bankruptcy, any major litigation involving the corporation, any revocation of the resolutions of shareholder meetings or of the board of directors under the law or declaration of nullity thereof, and any examination by a judicial institution into potential crime committed by the corporation or any injuntory measures taken against the directors, supervisors or senior management in the case of suspected crime.

3.15.2 Liabilities for the Breach of Duty of Information Disclosure

It is the affirmative duty of directors, supervisors and senior managers to ensure that the information disclosed about a listed company is truthful, accurate, and complete. Fixed term reports by the corporation must be confirmed by directors and senior managers in writing. The board of supervisors should examine fixed term reports and submit a written examination opinion thereof.

The corporation will bear liabilities for any misleading statements, misrepresentations, or material omissions that have resulted in a loss to investors. The directors, supervisors, senior managers, sponsors, and underwriters will be jointly and severally liable in conjunction with the issuing corporation excepting that the absence of fault is an available defence. If found at fault, the issuing corporation, controlling shareholders, and person in actual control of the corporation shall be severally and jointly liable in conjunction with the issuing corporation.

3.15.3 Supervision

The law empowers the CSRC to exercise supervision over annual reports, mid term reports, preliminary reports, statements of public notice, the issuance of new shares, and information disclosure of controlling shareholders and of any other person obligated to perform the duty of information disclosure under the law.

3.16 ACTIONS SANCTIONED UNDER THE SECURITIES LAW

Trading activities based upon the free will of investors are generally protected and indeed this protection is a main objective of the Securities Law. Any action that may endanger the achievement of such objective could become cause for legal sanction. Such actions include insider trading, market manipulation, making false and misleading statements and representations, commission of defrauding acts against customers and clients, and any other actions violative of the rules and regulations concerned.

3.16.1 *Insider Trading*

Insider trading (*neimu jiaoyi*, 内幕交易) is defined as a type of buying or selling of securities of a certain listed company conducted between or among persons with inside information or with illegally obtained information. It may be related to conduct that discloses such information or to suggestions given to other persons to buy or sell the securites concerned. Insider trading is a breach of fiduciary duty and a violation of the right to information held on the part of shareholders. The law specifically prohibits insider trading.

In the past decade, the securities regulator has been active in tackling various forms of securities fraud by applying penalties and filing criminal charges to protect investors as well as the integrity of the securities market. The 1993 Provisional Measures on the Prohibition of Securities Fraud was introduced specifically to deal with insider trading, market manipulation, false disclosure of information and other forms of share issuing and trading.

The Securities Law makes the 'prohibition of insider trading' a basic principle by postulating that any insider who has access to inside information or has unlawfully obtained insider information on securities being traded may not purchase or sell securities of the relevant corporation, divulge information, or advise any other person to purchase or sell such securities. Where insider trading incurs loss to investors, the person responsible shall be subject to compensation liabilities according to the law. These liabilities are not only limited to civil liabilities but may also result in criminal liabilities.

3.16.1.1 Criminal Liabilities of Insider Trading

According to the criminal law, any insider who possesses inside information about any stock exchange transaction or anyone who illegally obtains such information, prior to the publication of the information that concerns stock issuing or trading or that has a vital bearing on the stock price, buys or sells the stock or divulges the information, shall be subject to criminal detention and/or confiscation of any illegal gains. If the circumstances are serious, the wrongdoer may be sentenced to fixed-term imprisonment of no more than five years.[2]

3.16.1.2 Administrative Liabilities

Under the securities law, 'An insider who has access to insider information or securities trading, or any person who has obtained insider information or advises any other person to purchase or sell the securities before disclosure of the information regarding the issuance or trading of securities or any other information that may have any significant impact on the price of the securities, he or she shall be ordered to dispose the securities as illegally held according to the law. The illegal proceeds shall be confiscated and a fine of 1–5 times the illegal proceeds shall be imposed. Where there are no illegal proceeds or the illegal proceeds are less than RMB 30,000, a fine of between RMB 30,000 and RMB 60,000 shall be imposed. If an entity is involved in any insider trading, the person in charge and any other person directly responsible shall be given a warning, and a fine of RMB 30,000 to RMB 300,000 shall be imposed.'

Article 3 of the Supreme Court's Judicial Interpretation on Insider Trading Law in Criminal Cases provides guidance on when transactions may be considered 'obviously abnormal'. In making such determination, the judge takes into consideration the totality of the circumstances, including the degree of time matching, the degree of trading deviations and the degree of interest connectedness:

1. The time when an account was opened or closed, a fund account was activated or trading (custody) was designated or designated trading (custody transfer) revoked, and this was basically consistent with the time when the insider information was formed, changed or disclosed;

[2] The Criminal Law of the People's Republic of China, Article 180.

2. The time of funding change was basically consistent with the time when the insider information was formed, changed or disclosed;
3. The time when the securities or futures contract related to insider information was purchased or sold was basically consistent with the time when the insider information was formed, changed or disclosed;
4. The time when the securities or future contract related to insider information was purchased or sold was basically consistent with the time when the insider information was obtained;
5. The purchase or sale of a securities or futures contract was clearly different from normal trading habits;
6. The purchase or sale of a securities or futures contract, or the intensive holding of a securities or futures contract clearly deviates from the fundamentals reflected by the disclosed securities or futures information;
7. The withdrawal from and deposit in the account were relevant to or had interest relations with the person who had access to or illegally obtained such insider information, and
8. Any other obviously abnormal transactions.[3]

Article 4 of the Judicial Interpretation further endorses that a transaction conducted by a person in possession of inside information would not be treated as inside trading if the transaction is conducted according to a pre-existing written contract, plan or instruction, or based on other legal sources of information or other legal grounds.[4]

3.16.1.3 Insiders

Insiders are persons who acquire inside information about a listed corporation by virtue of their employment relationship with the corporation. Under the Securities Law, insiders in securities trading may include the directors, supervisors, or senior managers of the listed corporation, shareholders holding 5 per cent or more of the listed corporation, the person in actual control of the listed corporation, the directors, supervisors, or senior managers of a corporation in which the issuing corporation is a major shareholder, a person that may acquire inside information by virtue

[3] Judicial interpretation on Insider Trading Law in Criminal Cases, Article 3.
[4] Judicial interpretation on Insider Trading Law in Criminal Cases, Article 4.

of their position within the corporation and staff members of the securities supervisory institutions or persons entrusted to carry out their lawful obligations to regulate the issuance and trading of securities as well as staff members of the sponsoring corporation, underwriting firms, stock exchanges, securities registration and clearing institutions, and securities services institutions.

3.16.1.4 Inside Information

The law provides that inside information is any information that concerns the operating and financial conditions of the listed corporation or may effect a significant influence upon the stock price of a listed corporation. Examples of inside information would be any major event referred to under the law that must be disclosed in the preliminary report, a profit distribution plan or capital increase plan of the listed corporation, any major change in the equity structure of the corporation, any major change in the debt guarantee of the corporation, a mortgage or sale of major operating assets of the corporation that exceeds 30 per cent of the net value of such assets; any act by directors, supervisors, or senior management of a listed corporation that may bring about major damages or liabilities; and any projects regarding corporate acquisitions. The law provides that any person who causes a loss to an investor due to insider trading shall incur civil liability.

3.16.2 False or Misleading Statements

The securities law refers to the making of false statements as the making of statements by market participants, securities services institutions, and the staff members thereof that are false or misleading during the course of conduct of securities-related activities. The making of false or misleading statements directly violates the legal principles and the information disclosure system, runs counter to the basic legal principles of securities market law, and damages the investing public's interests. To a larger extent, it will disturb the normal order of the securities market. The law provides for a series of provisions against the making of false and misleading statements. For example, Article 20 of the law provides that issuers shall make accurate, truthful and complete statements and representations in their issuance documents, information disclosure reports and records to the State Council, the authorized government departments, and securities regulatory agencies. The law further provides that staff members of securities services institutions shall ensure the accuracy, entirety and truthfulness of the information and material presented for issuance. Article 31 further provides that the underwriters shall examine the truthfulness, accuracy, and entirety of the underwriting documents. Article 63 states that the information disclosed by the issuing corporation or the listed corporation shall be truthful, accurate and complete without false or misleading information or serious omissions. Article 69 pronounces that in the event that misleading or false information, misleading or false records, or material omissions are found in the prospectus, the issuing plan, financial or accounting reports, the annual report, the mid term report, the preliminary report or any other information disclosure material or reports that has already caused damage to investors during securities trading, the issuing corporation or the listed corporation shall bear liabilities for such damages. The directors, supervisors, senior management, or any other persons that are directly responsible shall bear liabilities and the underwriters and sponsors shall bear joint liabilites in conjunction with the issuers and the listed corporation unless no fault is found. Insofar as the liabilites of the controlling shareholders are concerned, the controlling shareholders or the person in actual control shall bear joint and several liabilities in conjunction with the issuer and the listed corporation.

Due to the nature of state ownership and the shareholding structure of the securities market and securities services institutions, Article 78 specifically prohibits acts violative of the Securities Law committed by state employees, media employees, and related personnel in touting false information and acts that may disrupt the securities market. The law specifically prohibits the making of false and misleading statements during the trading of securities over the stock exchange by securities corporations, securities registration and clearing institutions, securities services institutions and related personnel thereof, securities industry associations, and the CSRC and the related working staff thereof. It is imperative under the law that upon broadcasting and reporting any information regarding the securities market, the media shall observe the principle of truthfulness and objectivity. The law provides for the entirety, accuracy and truthfulness of reports made by securities services. The law specifically states that during the issuance, listing and trading, or any other securities related activities, securities services institutions are required to examine or verify the accuracy and truthfulness of the audit report, asset evaluation report, asset rating report, financial and accounting report, consultancy report, and the legal opinion. The duty imposed upon the institutions concerned is to observe the duty of due diligence. The personnel in charge of these institutions concerned will bear joint and several liabilities in conjunction with the issuer or the listed corporation for making or presenting misleading or false statements or material omissions.

3.16.3 *Civil Liabilities for False and Misleading Statements*

Under the securities law, a culprit who has made false statements regarding securities related activities bears civil, administrative and even criminal liabilities. On December 26, 2002, the Supreme People's Court announced that making false and misleading statements that have resulted in damages is the basis upon which a lawsuit may be grounded. The statement entitled, Several Provisons Regarding Civil Damage Claims Arising From False and Misleading Statements in the Securities Market, became effective on March 1 of the same year. The statement aimed to increase the operational capacity of the Securities Law with respect to securities related litigation. It describes in detail, among other things, the scope of the application of lawsuits, jurisprudence of court, litigation, affirmation of false statements, division of liabilities, exemption of liabilities, and determination of damages.

There is a statutory precondition imposed upon any civil lawsuit for damages resulting from false statements that must be satisfied before a case may go to court. An investor may not bring a claim of damages to court unless all other administrative remedies have been exhausted or they have received a judicial order in favour of the damages claim. This condition seeks to prevent or minimize abuse of the judicial process and is meant to facilitate investigation. It is meant to serve as a screening process before investors resort to filing their damages claims for judicial proceedings. This is quite unusual for the Chinese legal system which rarely sets up any precondition for contractual damage claims. In theory and practice, the requirement may prevent or minimize securities fraud-related abuses of the judicial process. For ordinary investors however, such a provision may turn out to be a double-edged sword.

A plaintiff may litigate singularly or jointly with other litigants. One thing to note is that to litigate jointly, a damage claim works differently from a class action lawsuit. A class action lawsuit is a popular concept under US securities law and the securities laws of other western countries. Here, to litigate jointly is a relatively simpler practice meaning that the court may merge or combine several lawsuits together if it comes to the decision that the lawsuits come from the same actions arising from the same sets of facts regarding false or misleading statements and having the same defendant or defendants.

3.16.4 Enforcement

To date, there has not been a universally accepted translation of the legal concept of "fiduciary duty". Many Chinese shareholders and managers are not fully aware of the necessity to avoid conflicts of interest. In the stock market, it has been estimated that about 80 per cent of all securities cases are connected with insider trading and about 80 per cent of transactions in securities cases are connected with insider trading. Being so widespread, it is no easy task to track down criminal activity and convict the perpetrators.

The development of the securities market has not been accompanied by sufficient legal enforcement. The Supreme People's Court issued a circular on September 21, 2001, instructing local courts to continue to ignore all civil compensation claims arising from insider trading, market manipulation, and other types of securities fraud. The reason rendered by the Supreme People's Court for not accepting such cases was that the courts do not have the necessary conditions to accept and hear such cases due to legislative and judicial limitations.

3.17 Mergers and Acquisitions

3.17.1 Acquisitions of Public Corporations

3.17.1.1 General Introduction

Corporations use mergers and acquisitions to achieve external expansions of their business. An acquisition is used to acquire an equity interest in a target corporation with the ultimate aim of attaining a share of the controlling interest of the target corporation. The concerned party to a merger or acqusition of a public corporation is the purchaser or the acquirer. The object of a merger or acquisition is the share interest of a target corporation. In the case of a public corporation, a shareholding of over 50 per cent of the corporation may help ensure control of the corporation. In practice, the circumstances surrounding the percentage of the shareholding for actual control of the corporation can be varied. A share percentage well below 50 per cent may still ensure control of the corporation.

If the purchaser is a legal person, that legal person status may be lost if the corporation concerned is merged with another. The corporation that has been merged into another corporation will transfer its rights, debts and obligations to the corporation into which it has merged.

The law does not impose restrictions on the capacity of the purchasing party. It simply provides that the purchaser must be of full capacity under the law. The merger or acquisition may be conducted solely or jointly by a natural or legal person.

There are three main ways in which an acquistion of a public corporation may take place. It may be done by executing a purchasing agreement entered into by the purchaser and shareholder of the target corporation. In this case, the shareholder would normally be the controlling shareholder of the target corporation, and the acquisition would be conducted over the stock exchange or any other public stock exchange market. Alternatively, the acquisition may be accomplished through a tender offer which is a type of purchasing offer made to the public. These types of acquisitions are in wide use by public corporations.

The tender offer stands as the most popular means of conducting a merger and acquisition in China, being conducted largely in public. As such, the public or parties concerned will know the extent of progress of the ongoing merger or acquisition.

The third way is by concentrated bidding over the stock exchange. Concentrated bidding is largely conducted in private until the reporting requirements need to be satisfied with respect to the acquired shares. A purchase conducted by way of concentrated bidding over the stock exchange will yield little information to public investors or even the target corporation regarding the intended purchase. At times, it will be difficult to tell from external circumstances as to whether the intent of the purchase is a takeover or simply a share transfer.

3.17.1.2 Disclosure of a Shareholding Interest

The disclosure of a shareholding interest is important to public investors. An acquisition by means of executing a purchasing agreement or a tender offer requires the purchaser to submit the purchasing report to the CSRC and make a report of the same to the public. The law requires that on attaining any level of share holding in a public corporation, an investor shall disclose this information. This disclosure requirement is fundemental as a supervisory and regulatory measure. In the meantime, it lends supervisory and regulatory room to move regarding any takeover actions of a public corporation.

The securities law provides that if an investor or a group of investors singularly or jointly acquires more than 5 per cent of the shares of a public corporation, they must submit a written report to the Securities Regulatory Commission and the stock exchange within three days, notify the parties concerned, and put out a public notice. Within this period, the investor may not buy or sell the shares of the corporation concerned. Investors who hold, singularly or jointly in agreement with others, more than 5 per cent of issued shares of a public corporation are requried to publish a report for every increase or decrease of 5 per cent in share ownership of the concerned corporation.

3.18 Tender Offer

3.18.1 General Concept

A tender offer (*yaoyue shougou*, 要约收购) is an offer to purchase the shares of a public corporation that is extended to undesignated persons through a public announcement outside the stock exchange. A tender offer is used to acquire shares of a public corporation by extending the offer to every and all shareholders of listed and non-listed shares of the target corporation. As those concerned are undesignated, the offeror may not know each and every shareholder as an offeree. Once the tender offer is publicized, any shareholder of the target corporation may commit their shares for transfer. The offer could extend to all shares or partial shares in a public corporation. It must be made on equal terms for all shareholders concerned. The offeror may not discriminate against any shareholder. The law provides for equality of terms and nondiscriminatory terms offered to all shareholders.

The tender offer is time-limited to no less than 30 days and no more than 60 days. This limit is to prevent an overextensive impact of the tender offer on the public market while giving the parties sufficient time to consider.

An extension of the tender offer during its term excludes other take-overs. The law provides that during the term of the tender offer the offeror may neither sell shares of the target corporation nor buy shares in the target corporation, as this would not be in compliance with the terms of the tender offer.

A tender offer will be set in motion if one of the circumstances described under the law occurs. The occurrence of such circumstances will trigger a tender offer if the investor extends to all the shares or the partial shares in the target corporation; if the investor holds or through agreement holds with other investors up to 30 per cent of issued shares of the public corporation; and if the investor continues to purchase shares. If the shares committed for selling by shareholders of the target corporation exceed the anticipated purchase quantity, the purchase will be conducted on a pro rata basis. In other words, the tender offer is the only permissible way to further acquire shares of the public corporation once the shareholding percentage of the purchaser in the target corporation has reached 30 per cent. A 30 per cent shareholding of a public corporation will, in the eyes of the law, ensure effective control over the corporation, as a 30 per cent shareholder may exercise control over the direction and operations of the corporation. This statutory tender offer requirement is seen as offering protection to minority investors to eliminate possible abuse by majority shareholders. The Securities Law was revised in 2014, which among other things, meant that approval of the securities regulatory agency before making a tender offer public was no longer needed. This was replaced by a clause permitting the offeror to extend their offer by way of direct public notification.

3.18.2 Disclosure Requirement

A disclosure by the purchasing corporation with regard to its holding of a percentage of shares of a public corporation is meant to serve as a mechanism to keep the purchaser, the target public corporation, the investors, the regulators and the securities market up to speed with the situation at the public corporation.

If the purchaser, singularly or jointly through agreements or arrangements, holds up to 30 per cent of the issued shares of a public company they are required to submit a report on the purchase to the CSRC and submit the same to any delegated authorities of the CSRC, copy the same to the stock exchange, notify the corporation concerned, and make a public notice thereof. Not fulfilling this requirement bars the purchaser from acquiring further shares of the public corporation concerned.

3.18.3 Report of the Tender and the Public Notice

As a tender offer is public in nature, the offeror is required to report the tender to the CSRC and the stock exchange before its submission. This requirement is testiment to the fact that the stock exchange in China is controlled and regulated by govermental institutions and agencies. These institutions and agencies exercise macro control over takeover activities related to public corporations.

The securities law provides for information disclosure with regard to tender offers of public corporations. The requisite documentary submission is a report of the tender of a public corporation to the CSRC and the stock exchange. Such a report should include the names and domiciles of the offerors, information about the decision to tender, the name of the target corporation, the objective of the tender, the amount of shares being offered for purchase, the terms of the offer, the funds for the tender, and the percentage of shares in the target corporation held by the offeror.

The offeror may proceed with publication of the offer 15 days after the submission of the above mentioned report to the authorities unless notified otherwise by the CSRC upon any finding of inappropriateness under the law or noncompliance of the law, rules and regulations.

3.18.4 Revocation and Changes

The general rule with respect to revocation of a tender offer is that, upon dispatch, a tender offer is irrevocable within the terms of the offer. Here, the legal effect of publication of a tender offer by the offeror is equivalent to that of a dispatch. The terms of the tender offer, however, may be subject to changes. The law generally provides that within the terms of the tender offer, the offeror may publize changes made thereto upon approval by the CSRC. Nonetheless, the pre-acceptance of the tender offer by an offeree could be revoked at any time before the expiry of the term. Pre-acceptance refers to a statement of preliminary intention to accept the tender offer by the shareholder offerees. It does not constitute an effective acceptance until the expiry of the term.

Upon the expiry of the term of the tender offer, the offeror shall purchase pre-accepted shares by shareholders in the target corporation on a pro rata basis according to the conditions of the offer. If the amount of the pre-accepted shares exceeds that of the offered amount, upon completion of the tender offer the purchaser shall report in writing to the CSRC regarding the tender offer, report the same to any delegated authorities of the CSRC where the public corporation resides and the stock exchange, notify the corporation concerned, and make a public announcement thereof.

3.18.5 The Agreement to Purchase

The law designates the agreement to purchase as a means to acquire the shares of a public corporation. An agreement to purchase (*xieyi shougou*, 协议收购) in the context of a merger and acquisition refers to one conducted by investors outside the stock exchange with the shareholders of the target corporation, and shareholders with larger shareholdings in particular, to negotiate privately with respect to the pricing and percentage of the acquisition of shares in the target corporation. This is done either to acquire a controlling interest in the target corporation or merge with the target corporation.

An agreement to purchase is usually conducted between interested parties and normally in private so as not to effect fluctuations in the share price of the target corporation. Contrary to a tender offer that treats shareholders equally, a merger or acquisition conducted by means of an agreement to purchase may discriminate against shareholders and classes of shareholders. An agreement to purchase is conducted between the offeror and designated offerees. The offeror and offeree freely negotiate the terms, and the course of negotiation is at parties' own volition. In addition, the agreement to purchase is nonexclusive with regard to other means of acquisitions. The offeror may also acquire shares in the target corporation over the stock exchange by such means as concentrated bidding. In the event that the investor wishes to continue to purchase shares of the corporation having already acquired 30 per cent, the investor is required to make any further purchase by way of a tender offer.

3.18.6 Rules Regarding an Agreement to Purchase

The securities law requires the purchaser to report in writing to the CSRC and the stock exchange within three days of executing an agreement to purchase and make any necessary public announcement. The agreement to purchase may become effective only after the public announcement is made and upon approval from the CSRC.

3.18.7 Compulsory Acquisition, Restriction and Other Requirements

Under the law, upon the completion of the tender offer acquisition, the minority shareholders have the right to request that majority shareholders buy their shares under the same terms. Majority shareholders are obligated to purchase these minority shares. However, this type of acquisition is not compulsory. Henceforth, it is still different from the compulsory acquisition requirement that poses as a protection mechanism for the benefit of minority shareholders that is widely practiced in common law countries and certain civil law countries.

After the tender offer purchase, the transferred shares may not be transferred within the first twelve months after purchase under the law. This is meant to stablize the shareholding structure within a period of time for the benefit of corporate operations.

The purchaser is required to report the purchase to the CSRC and the stock exchange within fifteen days of completion of the purchase. The purchaser is also required to obtain approval from departments concerned with share transfers.

3.19 The Stock Exchanges

The stock exchange is a platform where securities may be traded and exchanged. It provides securities traders and dealers with trading facilities, a venue, and related services. Using the stock exchange, traders may undertake their activities with greater efficiency and be better informed about movements in the securities market in a timely manner.

3.19.1 Organizational Structure

A stock exchange may take one of two organizational structures. The distinction is made upon differences in management style, risk management, and relationships between members and the stock exchange.

In China, there are currently two stock exchanges: the Shenzhen Stock Exchange and the Shanghai Stock Exchange. Both are organized as membership stock exchanges, which means they were set up with voluntary contributions from members. The members are nonprofit organizations providing concentrated bidding exchanges for the securities business. The law provides that a stock exchange may only be established as a legal person. Membership stock exchanges may be of legal person or non-legal person status. Despite being nonprofit institutitons, according to their charter, stock exchanges may collect membership fees, dues, annual trading fees, and listing fees from members, investors, and issuers to maintain regular operations and quality membership services.

Members are securities firms that may directly deal in securities over the stock exchange. A stock exchange is managed by self disciplinary acts bound by the charter rules and regulations by the members. They undertake no liabilities with regard to trading, and share no risks or losses with investors.

The establishment and dissolution of a stock exchange shall be made in compliance with a decision by the State Council. An interested party directly applies to the CSRC for establishment. The stock exchange charter must be stamped with approval from the State Council.

3.19.2 Membership

As they are membership organizations, stock exchanges have constituents as their members. These are lawfully established securities firms. The law requires that only members may deal in securities business over a stock exchange. Entry into a securities business association is a precondition to obtaining membership of a stock exchange for a securities firm.

3.19.3 Rights and Obligations

3.19.3.1 The Member Assembly

A member assembly is the highest authority of a stock exchange. Such an assembly is held once annually. A member will send a representative to attend the assembly.

3.19.3.2 Voting Rights

Members have the right to vote for members of the board or members of the supervisory and examination committee within the stock exchange and the right to serve on either of these two boards. The board of members and the supervisory and examination committee are the management and internal supervision arms of the stock exchange.

3.19.3.3 The Right to Make Propositions and Vote

Members enjoy an equal right to make propositions and vote irrespective of their contribution to the stock exchange.

3.19.3.4 The Right to Use Membership Seats

Members may acquire seats in the trading hall of a stock exchange, and dispatch agents to deal in securities, brokerage, and any other securities business, while enjoying services provided by the stock exchange. The right to use a seat in the stock exchange is exclusive to members. Non-members may not trade and deal on the trading floor.

3.19.3.5 The Right to Property

The Securities Law provides that any property and proprietary interest accumulated via membership of a stock exchange belongs to members and may not be distributed to members during the tenure of a stock exchange.

3.19.3.6 The Right to Supervise

Members enjoy the right to supervise the activities of the stock exchange and the activities of other members.

3.19.3.7 The Right to Transfer Seats

In accordance with the stock exchange charter and upon approval by the stock exchange, members may transfer their seats to exit the stock exchange.

3.19.4 Organizational Structure and Staffing

Under the law, the organization structure of the stock exchange includes the assembly of members, the board of members, the general manager, and the committee of supervisors as well as other special committees.

The assembly of members, constituted of all members, is the highest organ of authority of a stock exchange. Members of the board of members are elected by the assembly and serve as an executive business administration and decision-making organ when the assembly is not in session. The office of the general manager is directly under the board of members, accountable to the board of members and responsible for daily managerial functioning of the stock exchange.

The stock exchange has established a committee of supervision responsible for supervising the performance of the board of members and that of the general manager, professional staff members, and the accounting affairs of the stock exchange.

3.19.4.1 The Members Assembly

The members assembly is the highest authority of a stock exchange. The major rights of members include (i) formulation and amendment of the charter of the stock exchange which is subject to approval by the CSRC;

(ii) election and removal of members of the board; (iii) discussion and approval of the working report by the board of members and the general manager; (iv) and discussion and approval of the financial budget and final accounts of the stock exchange.

The assembly is held once annually. A preliminary meeting may be held if the number of members of the board of members present is below the quorum if at the request of one-thirds of members or as needed by the board of members. The members assembly shall have a two-thirds of the members present to consitute a quorum and resolutions need to be endorsed by more than half of members present at the meeting. The stock exchange will submit documents regarding the members assembly to the CSRC for filing.

3.19.4.2 The Board of Members

The law requires that the stock exchange establishes a board of members. The major responsibilities of the board include (i) resolution of how to execute member assembly decisions; (ii) the formulation and amendment of stock exchange business regulations; (iii) the examination and approval of the working report of the general manager; (iv) the examination and approval of the plan for a financial budget and final accounts by the general manager; (v) the examination and approval of the membership; (vi) the examination and approval of sanctions against members; and (vii) resolution as to whether or not to establish special committees.

The board of members of the stock exchange comprises of between seven and thirteen persons of whom non-members shall not comprise less than one-thirds of the total number of members and may not be over half of the total number of members of the board. Members of the board are elected by the member assembly. Non-members who sit on the board of members are appointed by the Securities Regulatory Commission. A term for board membership is three years and members may serve a maximum of two terms.

A board of members meeting is held once annually with quorum for resolutions being two-thirds of members present. The resolution of the board of members shall be filed with the Securities Regulatory Commission within two working days of the meeting.

A board of members has a chairperson and one or two vice chairpersons, and they are nominated and elected by the board. The general manager shall be a member of the board. The chairperson presides over the meetings. The chairperson may not concurrently hold the post of general manager of the stock exchange.

3.19.4.3 The General Manager

The stock exchange shall have one general manager and one to three deputy general managers. The general manager and deputy general managers may only be appointed and removed by the CSRC. A term for general manager and deputy general managers is three years for no more than two terms. The posts of the general manager and deputy general manager are full-time and may not be concurrently held by civil servants. The general manager is the legal representative of the stock exchange and in charge of daily operations under the leadership of the board of members.

3.19.4.4 The Board of Supervision and Examination

The board of members establishes the board of supervision and examination for a term of three years. The chairperson of the board of members is the chairperson of the board of supervision and examination. The board of supervision and examination is accountable for the supervision and examination of the compliance of senior management or staff members of the stock exchange, the execution of resolutions of the member assembly and that of the board of members, and for the financial conditions of the stock exchange.

3.19.4.5 Special Committees

The board of members, as needed, may set up special committees whose obligations, the tenure of the committee members, and the membership constitution are provided for under the charter.

3.19.4.6 The Senior Management and Professional Staff

The law forbids any person who has committed acts in violation of the law to undertake positions of responsibility at the stock exchange. Violaters forbidden to assume managerial responsibility are (i) those who were removed from positions in the stock exchange and securities registration and clearing institutions or were removed from directorship, supervisorship or senior management of securities firms and such removal has been less than five years since the date of the removal and (ii) the professional services members of law firms, registered accountant firms, investment consultancy institutions, financial consultancy institutions, asset evaluation corporations or other examination and licensure institutions who have been sanctioned for violations of the law and the revocation of their professional license. Such revocation of the requisite qualification has been less than five years.

3.20 Securities Registration and Clearing Institutions and Securities Services Institutions

3.20.1 Securities Registration and Clearing Institutions

3.20.1.1 General

The Securities Law provides that securities registration and clearing institutions are not-for-profit legal persons that offer concentrated registration custodial services and clearing services for stock exchanges. They are legal entities with independent funding, organizational structure and business premises that independently enjoy rights and undertake obligations under the law. Despite providing related services, they themselves neither participate in securities transactions nor act as security transaction agents.

3.20.1.2 The Establishment and Dissolution of Securities Registration and Clearing Institutions

Under the Securities Law, the conditions for the establishment of a securities registration and clearing institution are that (i) the applicant concerned should have capital of not less than RMB 200 million; (ii) the institution should have the necessary business premises and facilities for providing custodial and securities clearing services; and (iii) major members of the management and professional staff should be qualified to deal in securities business transactions. The CSRC is the approval authority in question.

As far as approval is concerned, China has adopted a system of establishment after approval. Under this system, an applicant may apply to the registration authority for a business license and a license to undertake securities registration business upon attainment of the requisite approval. Dissolution of a securities registration and clearing institution also needs to be approved by the CSRC.

Pursuant to the acquisition of the requisite licenses and approvals, a securities registration and clearing institution may open securities accounts and clearing accounts, manage securities custodial services, register the holders of securities, manage the clearing, delivery, and transfer of securities listed on the stock exchanges, dispatch securities dividends, and handle related enquiries.

3.20.1.3 The Business Scope of Securities Registration and Clearing Institutions

Securities registration and clearing institutions provide custodial services of securities, securities related material and information, the requisite business guarantee measures, and securities accounts. The law provides that securities traded over stock exchanges will be placed in a custodial depository with securities registration and clearing institutions so that no misuse of clients' securities may take place. The law provides that securities registration and clearing institutions shall provide securities issuers with a record of securities owners and related information, confirming all the relevant facts regarding the owners and guaranteeing the truthfulness, accuracy, and entirety of owner records, including registration and transfer information. They may not conceal, make changes thereto, nor destroy related information. The securities registration and clearing institutions are also required to provide the necessary service facilities, equipment, and data security protection installation, establish a regulatory system of business, financial and securities protection, and install a risk management system. The securities registration and clearing institutions are required to keep the original receipts and any related document of registration, custodial depository, and clearing services. The related documents should be kept for a minimum of 20 years.

The securities registration and clearing institutions are required to establish clearing risk funds to pay in advance or make up for nonpayment in the case of breach, technical failure, or force majeure.

The securities clearing fund refers to a fund established to prevent incidental loss to securities registration and clearing institutions. The fund may come from business income from securities registration and clearing institutions or be paid in proportion to business volume of securities transactions of clearing service users. The fund may not be used for any other purposes, however. The law requires that a special bank account must be set up for this depository purpose. The securities clearing risk fund must be separate from any other account in the securities registration and clearing institutions.

To deal in securities transactions, any investor entrusting a securities firm must open a securities account in their own name.

3.20.1.4 Securities Services Institutions

In China, securities services institutions refer to investment consulting institutions, financial consulting institutions, asset and reputation evaluation institutions and accounting firms. They are established to provide professional services for securities business. The governmental authority in charge is the CSRC. The law requires that professional staff members at securities services institutions have the necessary securities knowledge qualifications and a minimum of two years' practical experience. Securities investment consulting institutions may not undertake securities transaction business. Specifically, they may not (i) act as an agent to undertake securities investment; (ii) agree to share their investment profit or loss with the delegator; (iii) buy or sell the securities of the listed corporation for which the consulting institution has provided services; and (iv) disseminate or provide by way of the media or any other means false or misleading information to investors. Securities services institutions may charge for their services and are legally responsible for the services they provide.

The law imposes the duty of due care with respect to the listing, the trading of securities, the production of audit reports, asset evaluation reports, financial consulting reports or legal opinion letters. Services providers shall ensure the truthfulness, accuracy, and entirety of the information provided therein. Joint and several damage liability may be imposed for misleading statements, false statements, or material omissions in conjunction with the issuing corporation.

3.21 Supervision and Regulation of Securities Business

3.21.1 Securities Market Regulation

Securities market regulation refers to the supervision and regulation of the securities market by the securities regulatory agency and its authorized agencies. Such regulation includes securities related legislation, the guidance of the securities market by the rules and regulations, the examination and approval of qualifications for applicants of securities issuance, the examination and affirmation of qualifications for securities professional staff, the designation of the business scope of securities firms, and the restrictions upon and sanctions of prohibited securities trading.

The regulation of the securities market is a combination of administrative regulation and securities industry self-disciplinary regulation in China. Administrative regulation is established by the government or governmental agencies on behalf of the central government.

The securities law provides for a concentrated and unified supervision and regulation of the securities market on a nationwide basis. The main regulatory agency is the CSRC under the State Council. Under this national administrative regulation, the securities business association is the main body that performs self disciplinary regulation with the industry's self-disciplinary regulation as a supplement to governmental regulation. Such arrangement may help to ensure the efficacy and enhance the flexibility of securities supervision and regulation.

3.21.2 Securities Market Administrative Regulation

The authority in charge of administering supervision and regulation of the securities market is the CSRC. Before 1998, the authorities in charge were the State Council Securities Commission as the main agency and the State Planning Commission, the People's Bank of China, and the Ministry of Finance as agencies jointly responsible for supervision and regulation. After March 1998, the State Council underwent a structural reform to abolish the Securities Commission and the State Planning Commission. The establishment of the CSRC under the State Council was a result of reform of supervision and regulation of the securities market. The CSRC is virtually the only agency in charge of national market securities supervision and regulation.

Under the securities law, the CSRC functions to formulate securities regulatory legislation, execute and interpret the legislation concerned, and sanction any illegal acts. Specifically, the agency may carry out examination and approval, and exercise supervision and regulation of issuance, listing, transfer, registration custodial depositary business, and clearing activities. It may supervise the activities of securities issuers, listed corporations, securities firms, securities investment fund management corporations, securities services institutions, the stock exchanges, and securities registration and clearing institutions. It formulates qualification standards and rules of conduct for securities professionals, supervises and examines the disclosure of securities issuance, listing, and trading, guides and supervises the activities of securities industries associations, and sanctions against any illegal acts in violation of the relevant laws, rules and regulations.

The securities law confers upon the CSRC certain rights in performance of official duties. Such rights include (i) the right to carry out on-site examinations and checks of the securities issuer, listed corporation, securities firms, securities investment fund management corporations, securities service institutions, stock exchanges, securities registration and clearing institutions, and the right to enter premises to investigate for evidence of illegal activity; (ii) the right to make inquiries into matters and persons concerned and request the latter to make statements regarding the matter in investigation; (iii) the right to inspect and make copies of the documents and information related to the investigation and record communication related to the investigation; (iv) the right to inspect and copy any documents and information related to the record of securities transfer and registration transfer and to the record of financial and accounting information related to the investigation; (v) the right to seal any document and record that may be suspected of transfer, concealment, or destruction; (vi) the right to inspect the parties concerned and any bank accounts and securities accounts of persons or units under investigation; (vii) the right to freeze or seal up, upon approval by the person in charge at the CSRC, any illegal fund and securities that upon proof of evidence have already been transferred or are likely to be transferred; and (viii) the right to restrict the trading of securities by the parties under investigation that involve major securities violations such as market manipulation and insider trading.

The securities law, in addition, imposes duties upon the securities supervision and regulation agency and its staff members. The securities supervision and regulation agency and staff members shall observe the duties of loyalty, confidentiality, and to identify themselves as investigators. Moreover, the law upholds the principles of openness, justice, and fairness as fundamental law enforcement principles to be upheld by the securities regulation agency. The law provides that the CSRC shall publicize rules and regulations regarding the supervision and regulation of the securities market. The agency is required to publicize the results of investigations and impose sanctions against any violative acts.

3.21.3 Securities Market Self-Disciplinary Regulation

The securities market self-disciplinary regulatory body is principally a securities industry association of securities dealers. The securities industry association is self-disciplinary by nature. The organizational structure of the association comprises a member assembly and a board of members.

The member assembly holds the power of the association and shall produce a association charter which is then filed with the securities regulatory agency. The members of the board of members are elected in accordance with the charter.

The law provides that the association will educate members to comply with the law, rules, and regulations, provide securities related information to its members, refer any proposal and suggestion from members to the securities regulatory agency, formulate the rules of compliance for members, organize professional training and business exchange, mediate between and among members and their clients, and examine any violative acts by members, imposing sanctions accordingly. Most importantly, the association may share in carrying out securities supervision and regulation upon approval and under the authority of the securities regulatory agency.

3.22 Securities Firms

3.22.1 General

Securities firms are established under the relevant laws to engage in securities business. As important securities market participants, they act as financing channels in the securities issuance market and distribution market. In effect, securities firms are fundamental to the securities market. Under the law, securities firms are established as limited liability corporations or joint stock limited liability corporation.

Their scope of business spans securities underwriting, securities business, securities brokerage business, securities custodial business and any other securities related business.

3.22.2 Establishment

The securities law provides that a securities firm must satisfy certain conditions to be authorized before it can be established. Firstly, it shall provide articles of incorporation in compliance with the relevant law, rules and regulations. Secondly, major shareholder of securities firms should maintain profitability and a good business reputation without serious legal violations in the past three years. The net assets of any major shareholder should be no less than RMB 200 million. Thirdly, it should have the required registered capital. Fourthly, its directors, supervisors, and senior management should be qualified for their posts and the professional staff members should have securities business licenses. Fifthly, it should have established a sound risk management or internal control system. Finally, it should have a qualified business domicile and business facilities.

3.22.3 Establishment Procedures

The establishment of a securities firm shall be approved by the CSRC in accordance with the law. In China, approvals are by way of a licensing system. Within six months of receipt of an application for the establishment of a securities firm, the CSRC shall examine under the principle of due supervision in accordance with the statutory conditions and procedures to make a decision as to whether or not to approve the application and notify the applicant. It shall provide reasons if a decision of disapproval is issued. Upon approval, the applicant should, within the prescribed period of time, submit to the corporations registration agency an application for establishment and carry out the procedure to obtain a business license.

3.22.4 Registered Capital of Securities Firms

The registered capital requirement for a securities firm operates a tiered requirement system. The law has set up a minimum registration requirement for securities firms that engages in different types of business. Specifically, the minimum registered capital requirement is RMB 60 million for securities firms that engage in securities brokerage business, securities investment consultancy services, and related financial consultancy regarding securities trading and investment; the minimum required registered capital shall be RMB 100 million for security firms that engage in securities underwriting, sponsoring activities, securities asset management or other related securities business; and the minimum registered capital requirement shall be RMB 500 million for securities firms that engage in more than two of the aforementioned activities. The law also requires the registered capital of securities firms be paid-in capital.

3.22.5 Risk Control System

Securities investment is high risk, so the law requires securities firms to set up a system of internal risk control and management. The law has specifically provided for the ratio between net capital and liabilities, the ratio between net capital and net assets, the ratio between net capital and the scope of business of underwriting and asset management, the ratio between net assets and liabilities, and the ratio between cash flow and liabilities. These ratios are established by the CSRC.

Under the law, a security firm may not provide financing or other types of guarantees for its shareholders or persons affiliated with shareholders. The law also requires the establishment of a securities investment protection fund to be funded by securities firms. Securities firms are required to withhold the trading risk fund after distribution of annual net profits to make up any losses from securities trading.

3.22.6 *Major Changes*

The Securities Law provides that any major changes shall be approved by the CSRC. Major changes include changes relating to establishment, mergers, acquisitions, scope of business, increase or decrease in registered capital, shareholding of more than 5 per cent of the shares of securities firm, the actual controlling person, the articles of incorporation of the securities firm, the business registration of the securities firm, bankruptcy, suspension of business, or dissolution.

3.22.7 *Foreign Investment Interest in the Securities Industry and Asset Management*

Since the promulgation of the Securities Law of 1998, the government has gradually opened up the securities industry and asset management sectors to foreign investment. There are various administrative rules and regulations governing this sphere of investment which are subject to changes pursuant to public policies and industrial policy determinations. However, the trend of permitting foreign investment in the securities industry and asset management has been upward in recent decades. An increasing number of foreign firms and investors in the securities industry have taken advantage of the openness policy and built a foothold for future business prospects. Presently, foreign interests may invest in the share capital of domestic securities firms or companies by establishing foreign investment corporations limited by shares that may issue A shares or B shares over securities exchanges. Such firms or companies need to comply with foreign investment industrial policy set forth by the responsible governmental agency, i.e., MOFCOM, and requirements for a public issuance of shares. Foreign-invested shareholdings also need to observe a 10 per cent percentage in proportion to the total share investment of the company after the public issuance. The foreign-invested securities firm may engage in, among other things, the business of stocks including RMB-denominated stocks and foreign-invested shares and bonds and the brokerage business of foreign-invested shares and bonds. Shareholdings directly and indirectly owned by overseas investors or interests in foreign-invested securities firms may not exceed 49 per cent of the total share capital of such firms. This restriction may be removed in the near future awaiting the issuance of specific regulations. Foreign equity may invest in private equity asset management firms in the form of WFOEs or joint ventures for asset management related businesses. The supervisory agency is the Asset Management Association of China.

3.23 Transformation

3.23.1 Is the Installation of a Due Care Registration System the Answer?

Reform of the Securities Law has been subject to considerable thought for many years. Officially tabled for discussion and comment is a proposal to transform the administrative system for IPO approval to a due care registration system, thereby changing the function of the CSRC from substantive reviewer and examiner to due care reviewer and examiner. As such, the public issuance registration system will be based upon adequate information disclosure. The intention of the reform is to lessen the influence of governmental administration over the securities issuance market. The current approval mechanism has many defects. Despite the implementation of an approval system, securities fraud is still not uncommon. Moreover, the approval mechanism has been distorting supply and demand relations which may have resulted in an overrated P/E ratio, over-priced securities, and over-subscribed stock issuance, ultimately undermining the credibility of the CSRC. Even the CSRC has, from time to time, failed to abide by substantive review standards and has been accused of murky and ambiguous actions in granting approvals. One other major hurdle for the CSRC to overcome is that it needs to redress selective enforcement in the securities market and counteract local protectionism.

One chief objective is to change to a due care review system. This would comprise of due diligence, a due care review, and administrative examination of the veracity, legality, and entirety of application documents. Investors would be allowed to conduct an on-site investigation of the applicant corporation when in reasonable doubt. The proposed changes are meant to prevent the abuse of the IPO registration system, reinforce timely disclosure, and simplify information disclosure procedures.

Legal scholars have suggested the abolition of the current practice of mandatory sponsorship. Duties of sponsors should be owed to public investors, not to public corporations to help reduce related transactional stress if the law designates sponsor firms to be jointly and severally liable in conjunction with the defrauding public corporation to protect the interests of public investors.

Historically and over time, the government has been in favour of non-market means and administrative measures as approaches to solve practical problems in the securities market. In the presence of traditional planned-economy methodology and a less developed legal system and credit system, the implementation of reforms could be a long shot. The objective is switch from an external government-driven market to an internal-driven market, reform the issuance market and trading market, reduce the administrative licensing scheme, and create a service-oriented CSRC that will be acting in line with developments in the securities market.

3.23.2 *The Building of a Mechanism to Avoid Systemic Risks: A Postmortem on Recent Unregular Market Movements*

Since 2015, the Chinese stock market had experienced unanticipated movements that appeared to bear little relationship to actual performance of public corporations. The Shanghai securities index dropped from a high of 5100 to 4000, described by the media as a catastrophic shift. Several senior management members of securities firms and insurance companies were indicted on account of insider trading. The ex-chairman of the Insurance Regulatory Commission was reportedly involved in the stock market manipulation scandal.

Amidst such scandals, several questions were asked: Has the Securities Law has been effective in strengthening law enforcement in securities industry regulation? Do legal penalties need to be increased? Does the acquirer need to disclose their source of funding? Are provisions against securities market manipulation and for investor protection in need of further strengthening? At the core of these questions lies a fundamental concern that the securities market should do more to serve the real economy.

In early 2017 when the executive committee of the National People's Congress held the second round of its review session on revisions to the Securities Law, the proposed conversion to a registration system was absent from an agenda, that was more concerned with revisions that could help prevent stock market volatility and heighten the enforcement and regulatory powers of the CSRC in market supervision. It is expected that an all-round supervisory and regulatory measures would be in need to reduce systemic securities market risks. The establishment of a new financial regulatory body, the State Financial Stability and Development Committee, was announced. The intension was to calm a financial system that in recent years has endured, among other things, a stock market crash and a rapid accumulation of debt.[5] Whilst the establishment of this office has fallen short of expectations that it would create a financial super-regulator by combining the central bank with the agencies regulating securities, banking and insurance, it has nonetheless been a step forward toward building a mechanism to avert related systemic financial risks.

[5] The New York Times, November 10, 2017.

Appendix I: The Corporation Law of the People's Republic of China (2013 Amendment)

Chapter One General Provisions

Article 1 This Law is enacted in accordance with the Constitution in order to meet the needs of establishing a modern enterprise system to regulate the organization and conduct of corporations to protect the lawful rights and interests of corporations as well as the shareholders and creditors thereof to maintain social and economic order and to promote the development of the socialist market economy.

Article 2 A corporation referred to herein means a limited liability corporation or a joint stock limited corporation established within China in accordance herewith.

Article 3 Limited liability corporations and joint stock limited corporations are enterprise legal persons.

In the case of a limited liability corporation the shareholders are liable thereto to the extent of their capital contribution and the corporation is liable for its debts to the extent of all of its assets.

In the case of a joint stock limited corporation its total capital is divided into stocks of equal value and the shareholders are liable thereto to the extent of their share holdings and the Corporation is liable for its debts to the extent of all of its assets.

Article 4 As contributors of capital the shareholders of a corporation enjoy the rights of proprietors in proportion to their respective share of capital contributions to the corporation such as deriving benefits from its assets making major decisions and selecting its management.

D. Yu, *Chinese Business Law*, The Palgrave Series on Chinese Law,
https://doi.org/10.1007/978-981-13-0902-1

The corporation enjoys the full property rights of a legal person in respect of assets resulting from the investment by its shareholders and enjoys civil rights and bears civil liabilities in accordance with the law.

Title to the state-owned assets in the corporation shall vest in the State.

Article 5 A corporation with all of its assets owned by it as a legal person shall operate autonomously and be responsible for its own profit and loss in accordance with the law.

The corporation shall under the state's macro-regulation organize its production and operation autonomously in light of market demand with a view to improving economic return and productivity and accomplishing the preservation and increase of the value of its assets.

Article 6 A corporation shall adopt an internal management system which clearly sets out the rights and responsibilities of the relevant parties is conducive to scientific management and combines incentive with check and balance.

Article 7 If a state-owned enterprise is to be reorganized into a corporation it must in accordance with the conditions and requirements prescribed by national statutes and administrative regulations change its operating mechanism and orderly identify and verify its assets determine the respective owners of the property rights therein settle its creditor's rights and liabilities conduct assets appraisal and set up standard internal management organs.

Article 8 The establishment of a limited liability corporation or a joint stock limited corporation is subject to the requirements prescribed herein. An entity meeting the requirements prescribed herein may be registered as a limited liability corporation or a joint stock limited corporation as the case may be an entity failing to meet the requirements prescribed herein may not be registered as a limited liability corporation or a joint stock limited corporation as the case may be.

Where the establishment of a corporation is subject to examination and approval as required by the relevant national statutes or administrative regulations examination and approval procedure must be carried out in accordance with the law prior to its registration.

Article 9 The name of a limited liability corporation established in accordance herewith must contain the words limited liability corporation.

The name of a joint stock limited corporation established in accordance herewith must contain the words joint stock limited corporation.

Article 10 The Corporation shall be domiciled at the place where its principal executive office is located.

Article 11 In order to establish a corporation its articles of association must be prepared in accordance herewith. The articles of association of the corporation are binding upon the corporation and its shareholders, directors, supervisors and general manager.

The corporation's business scope shall be prescribed by its articles of association and be registered in accordance with the law. If an item in the Corporation's business scope is subject to any restriction prescribed by any national statute or administrative regulation approval for such item shall be obtained in accordance with the law.

The corporation shall conduct its business within its registered business scope. The Corporation may change its business scope by amending its articles of association in accordance with legally prescribed procedure and registering such amendment with the corporation registration authority.

Article 12 A Corporation may invest in another limited liability corporation or joint stock limited corporation and is liable to such corporation to the extent of its capital contribution.

Except for an investment corporation or a holding corporation stipulated by the State Council where a corporation is to invest in other limited liability corporations or joint stock limited corporations its cumulative investment may not exceed 50 percent of its net assets provided that if after the investment the capital is increased using profit distribution received from the corporation in which it invested the increased amount shall not be included.

Article 13 A corporation may establish branch corporations which do not have the status of enterprise legal persons and the civil liabilities thereof shall be borne by the corporation.

The corporation may establish subsidiary corporations which have the status of enterprise legal persons and bear civil liabilities independently in accordance with the law.

Article 14 In conducting its business a corporation must abide by the law observe industry ethics strengthen the development of socialist spiritual civilization and subject itself to supervision by the government and the public.

The corporation's lawful rights and interests are protected by law and shall not be infringed upon.

Article 15 A corporation must protect the lawful rights and interests of its workers strengthen labor protection and achieve workplace safety.

The corporation shall strengthen the professional education and on the job training of its workers in various forms so as to improve their quality.

Article 16 The workers of a corporation shall organize a labor union which shall conduct union activities and safeguard the lawful rights and interests of the workers in accordance with the law. The Corporation shall provide the necessary conditions for its labor union to conduct its activities.

In accordance with the Constitution and other relevant national statutes democratic management in the form of workers' assembly and other forms shall be adopted in a wholly state-owned corporation or a limited liability corporation established through investment by two or more state-owned enterprises or by two or more state-owned investment entities of other kinds.

Article 17 Activities of the elementary-level cell of the Chinese Communist Party in a corporation shall be conducted in accordance with the Charter of the Chinese Communist Party.

Article 18 Limited liability corporations with foreign investment are subject to this Law provided that where the provisions of national statutes governing Sino-foreign equity joint venture enterprises Sino-foreign cooperative joint venture enterprises and wholly foreign owned enterprises stipulate otherwise the stipulations therein shall prevail.

Chapter Two Establishment and Organs of a Limited Liability Corporation

Section One Establishment

Article 19 The establishment of a limited liability corporation is subject to the following conditions

i. The number of shareholders meets legal requirement
ii. The amount of shareholders' capital contribution reaches the minimum level prescribed by law
iii. The shareholders jointly prepare the articles of association
iv. There is a corporation name and the organs meeting the requirements for a limited liability corporation are established
v. There is a permanent place of business and there are necessary conditions for production and operation.

Article 20 A limited liability corporation shall be established through joint investment by not fewer than 2 but not more than 50 shareholders.

A state authorized investment entity or state authorized department may establish wholly state-owned limited liability corporations as the sole investor.

Article 21 In the case of a state-owned enterprise established before this Law becomes operative if it meets the conditions prescribed herein for the establishment of a limited liability corporation it may be reorganized into a wholly state-owned limited liability corporation in accordance herewith if it was established by a single investment entity or it may be reorganized into a limited liability corporation pursuant to Paragraph 1 of the previous Article if it was established by more than one investment entities.

The implementing procedures and detailed measures for reorganizing state-owned enterprises into corporations shall be separately prescribed by the State Council.

Article 22 The articles of association of a limited liability corporation shall set forth the following

i. its name and domicile
ii. its business scope
iii. its registered capital
iv. the names of its shareholders
v. the rights and obligations of its shareholders
vi. the forms and amounts of capital contribution made by shareholders
vii. the conditions under which the shareholders' shares of capital contribution may be assigned
viii. its organs the manners in which they are established and their respective powers and the rules governing their conduct of business
ix. its legal representative
x. the causes for its dissolution and the method for its liquidation
xi. other matters which shareholders deem necessary to provide for.

Shareholders shall sign or impress their chops on the articles of association.

Article 23 The registered capital of a limited liability corporation is the amount of capital contribution actually paid up by all shareholders and registered with the corporation registration authority.

The registered capital of a limited liability corporation shall not be less than

i. Renminbi 500,000 Yuan if it primarily engages in production
ii. Renminbi 500,000 Yuan if it primarily engages in commodity wholesale
iii. Renminbi 300,000 Yuan if it primarily engages in commodity retail
iv. Renminbi 100,000 Yuan if it engages in scientific and technical development consulting or service.

If for a specific industry the required minimum registered capital exceeds any of the minimum levels prescribed above such minimum requirement shall be separately prescribed by the relevant national statute or administrative regulations.

Article 24 Shareholders may contribute their capital in the form of cash as well as in the forms of tangible goods industrial property non-patented technology and land use rights at certain value. If any tangible goods industrial property non-patented technology or land use rights are contributed as capital they must be appraised and the property rights therein must be verified and the contributed items may not be over-valued or under-valued. Appraisal on land use rights shall be carried out in accordance with the provisions of the relevant national statute and administrative regulations.

Where industrial property or non-patented technology is contributed as capital at certain value its valuation shall not exceed 20 percent of the total registered capital except where the state makes special provisions for corporations utilizing high and new technologies.

Article 25 Each shareholder shall invest in full the capital contribution which he has subscribed for in accordance with the articles of association. If a shareholder makes his capital contribution in cash he shall deposit in full the amount of such cash capital contribution into a temporary bank account opened for the contemplated limited liability corporation If capital contribution is made in the form of tangible goods industrial property non-patented technology or land use rights the appropriate transfer procedure for the property rights therein shall be carried out in accordance with the law.

A shareholder who fails to invest the capital contribution which he has subscribed for in accordance with the previous Paragraph is liable for breach of contract to those shareholders who have invested in full the capital contribution they have subscribed for.

Article 26 Upon investment in full of their respective capital contribution by the shareholders a legally-prescribed capital verification institution must carry out capital verification procedure and issue a certificate.

Article 27 After a legally-prescribed capital verification institution has verified the shareholders' full capital contribution a representative designated by all shareholders or the agent appointed jointly thereby shall apply to the corporation registration authority for establishment registration and submit thereto documents such as the corporation registration application form the articles of association and the capital verification certificate etc.

Where approval by the relevant authority is required by the relevant national statute or administrative regulations the approval document shall be submitted at the time of applying for establishment registration.

The corporation registration authority shall grant registration to an applicant who meets the requirements prescribed herein and shall issue a corporation business license and shall not grant registration to an applicant who fails to meet the requirements prescribed herein.

The date of issuance of a corporation business license shall be the establishment date for a limited liability corporation.

Article 28 If after the establishment of a limited liability corporation it is discovered that the actual value of the tangible goods industrial property non-patented technology or land use rights contributed as capital is significantly below their value fixed in the articles of association the shareholder who contributed such item as capital shall contribute the difference in value and the other shareholders of the corporation at the time it was established shall be jointly and severally liable.

Article 29 Where a branch corporation is to be established contemporaneous with the establishment of a limited liability corporation an application for registration of such branch corporation shall be submitted to the corporation registration authority and it shall be issued a business license.

Where a branch corporation is to be established after the establishment of the limited liability corporation the corporation's legal representative shall apply to the corporation registration authority for registration of such branch corporation and it shall be issued a business license.

Article 30 Upon the establishment of a limited liability corporation each shareholder shall be issued a capital contribution certificate which shall set forth the following

i. the name of the corporation
ii. the date of registration of the corporation
iii. the corporation's registered capital
iv. the name of the shareholder the amount of his capital contribution and the date of capital contribution
v. the serial number and date of issuance of the capital contribution certificate.

The corporation's chop shall be impressed on each capital contribution certificate.

Article 31 A limited liability corporation shall maintain a record of shareholders which shall set forth the following

i. the name of each shareholder and the domicile thereof
ii. the amount of capital contribution invested by each shareholder
iii. the serial number of each capital contribution certificate.

Article 32 Shareholders are entitled to inspect the minutes of meetings of shareholder committee as well as the financial and accounting reports of the corporation.

Article 33 Shareholders shall share in the distribution of profits in proportion to their respective shares of capital contribution. Where the corporation is to increase its capital its shareholders have the preemptive right to subscribe for the increased amount.

Article 34 A shareholder may not withdraw its capital contribution after registration of the corporation.

Article 35 Shareholders may assign in whole or part their respective shares of capital contribution amongst themselves.

Transfer of his share of capital contribution by a shareholder to anyone other than another shareholder is subject to consent by a majority of all the shareholders who do not consent to the transfer shall purchase the share of capital contribution to be assigned and failure by those shareholders to make such purchase is deemed to be their consent to the assignment.

Where the shareholders consent to the assignment of share of capital contribution other shareholders have the preemptive right of purchase under the same conditions.

Article 36 Upon a shareholder's lawful assignment of his share of capital contribution the corporation shall record on the record of shareholders the name of the assignee the domicile thereof and the amount of capital assigned thereto.

Section Two Organs

Article 37 The shareholders' committee of a limited liability corporation consists of all the shareholders and the shareholders' committee is the corporation's organ of authority and shall exercise its powers in accordance herewith.

Article 38 The shareholders' committee shall exercise the following powers

i. determining the corporation's operational guidelines and investment plans
ii. electing and replacing directors and deciding upon matters relating to their remuneration
iii. electing and replacing supervisors who represent the shareholders and deciding upon matters relating to the remuneration of supervisors
iv. considering and approving reports by the board of directors
v. considering and approving reports by the board of supervisors or the supervisor as the case may be
vi. considering and approving annual financial budget plans and final accounting plans of the corporation
vii. considering and approving corporation profit distribution plans and plans to cover corporation losses
viii. adopting resolutions relating to increase or reduction of the corporation's registered capital
ix. adopting resolutions relating to issuance of corporation bonds
x. adopting resolutions relating to assignment of share of capital contribution by a shareholder to anyone other than a shareholder of the corporation
xi. adopting resolutions relating to merger division change of corporate form dissolution and liquidation of the corporation
xii. amending the articles of association.

Article 39 Unless otherwise provided herein the method for conducting business and voting procedure at a meeting of shareholders' committee shall be prescribed by the articles of association.

Any resolution adopted by the shareholders' committee relating to the corporation's increase or reduction of registered capital division merger dissolution or change of corporate form requires affirmative votes by shareholders representing two-thirds of the votes.

Article 40 A corporation may amend its articles of association. Adoption of a resolution to amend the articles of association requires affirmative votes by shareholders representing two-thirds of the votes.

Article 41 Shareholders shall exercise their voting rights at the meeting of shareholders' committee in proportion to their respective shares of capital contribution.

Article 42 The first meeting of shareholders committee shall be called and presided over by the shareholder with the largest share of capital contribution and shall exercise its powers in accordance herewith.

Article 43 Meetings of shareholders committee are classified as either regular meetings or interim meetings.

Regular meetings shall be timely held as prescribed in the articles of association. Shareholders representing one-fourth or more of the votes or one-third of the directors or supervisors may propose for an interim meeting.

Where a limited liability corporation has a board of directors a meeting of shareholders committee shall be called by the board and presided over by the chairman of the board where the chairman is unable to perform his duties due to any special reason the meeting shall be presided over by the vice-chairman or another director appointed by the chairman.

Article 44 In order to hold a meeting of shareholders committee notice shall be given to all shareholders 15 days in advance.

The shareholders' committee shall prepare minutes regarding the decisions on matters considered at the meeting of shareholders committee which shall be signed by the shareholders attending the meeting.

Article 45 A limited liability corporation shall have a board of directors which shall be composed of not fewer than 3 but not more than 13 directors.

Where a limited liability corporation has been established through investment by two or more state-owned enterprises or by two or more state-owned investment entities of other kinds there shall be representatives of the workers of the corporation on the board of directors. The representatives of the workers on the board shall be democratically elected by the workers of the corporation.

The board shall have one chairman and may have one to two vice-chairmen. The manner in which the chairman and vice-chairman are selected shall be prescribed by the articles of association.

The chairman is the legal representative of the corporation.

Article 46 The board of directors is accountable to the shareholders' committee and shall exercise the following powers

i. being responsible for calling meetings of shareholders committee and presenting reports thereto
ii. implementing resolutions adopted by the shareholders' committee
iii. determining the corporation's operational plans and investment programs
iv. preparing annual financial budget plans and final accounting plans of the corporation
v. preparing profit distribution plans and plans to cover corporation losses
vi. preparing plans for increasing or reducing registered capital of the corporation
vii. drafting plans for merger division change of corporate form or dissolution of the corporation
viii. determining the structure of the corporation's internal management
ix. appointing or removing the manager general manager Hereinafter referred to as the general manager of the corporation appointing or removing upon the general manager's recommendation deputy managers of the corporation and the officer in charge of finance and determining the remuneration for those officers
x. formulating the basic management scheme of the corporation.

Article 47 The term of the directors shall be prescribed by the articles of association provided that each term may not exceed 3 years. A director may continue to serve his post if he is re-elected upon the expiration of his term.

Prior to expiration of a director's term the shareholders' committee may not remove him without cause.

Article 48 A meeting of the board of directors shall be called and presided over by the chairman in the event that the chairman is unable to perform his duties due to any special reason the chairman shall appoint the vice-chairman or another director to call and preside over the meeting. One-third or more of the directors may propose for a meeting of the board.

Article 49 Unless otherwise provided herein the method for conducting business and voting procedure at the meeting of board of directors shall be prescribed by the articles of association.

In order to hold a board meeting notice shall be given to all directors 10 days in advance.

The board shall prepare minutes relating to the decisions on matters considered at the meeting which shall be signed by the directors attending the meeting.

Article 50 A limited liability corporation shall have a general manager to be appointed or removed by the board of directors. The general manager is accountable to the board and shall exercise the following powers

i. being in charge of the management of the corporation's production and operation and organizing the implementation of board resolutions
ii. organizing the implementation of annual operating plans and investment programs of the corporation preparing the plan for the structure of the corporation's internal management
iii. preparing the basic management scheme of the corporation
iv. formulating detailed corporation rules
v. recommending the appointment or removal of a deputy general manager and the officer in charge of finance
vi. appointing and removing officers of the corporation other than those to be appointed or removed by the board
vii. other powers prescribed by the articles of association or delegated by the board.

The general manager shall be present at board meetings.

Article 51 A small-scaled limited liability corporation with only a few shareholders may have an executive director without establishing a board of directors. The executive director may serve concurrently as the general manager of the corporation.

The powers of the executive director shall be prescribed in the articles of association by reference to the provisions of Article 46 hereof.

Absent a board of directors the executive director of a limited liability corporation shall be the legal representative thereof.

Article 52 A large-scaled limited liability corporation shall have a board of supervisors which shall be composed of not fewer than 3 members. The board of supervisors shall elect one of its members as the person responsible for calling meetings.

The board of supervisors shall be composed of shareholders' representatives and representatives of the workers' of the corporation at an appropriate ratio to be specifically prescribed in the articles of association. The workers' representatives on the board of supervisors shall be democratically elected by the workers of the corporation.

A small-scaled limited liability corporation with only a few shareholders may have one or two supervisors.

A director the general manager and the officer in charge of finance may not serve concurrently as a supervisor.

Article 53 Each term of a supervisor shall be 3 years and a supervisor may continue to serve his post upon expiration of his term if he is re-elected.

Article 54 The board of supervisors or the supervisor as the case may be shall exercise the following authorities

i. reviewing the financial affairs of the corporation
ii. monitoring the acts of the directors or the general manager to guard against violation of national statutes administrative regulations or the articles of association in the course of performance of their duties
iii. requiring the directors or the general manager to make rectification when any act thereof causes harm to corporation interests
iv. proposing for interim meetings of shareholders' committee
v. other authorities prescribed by the articles of association.

The supervisors shall be present at board meetings.

Article 55 When a corporation considers and decides upon matters which affect the personal interests of its workers such as their wages benefits production safety and labor protection or labor insurance it shall first hear the opinions of the labor union and the workers of the corporation and invite representatives of the labor union or the workers to be present at related meetings.

Article 56 When a corporation considers and decides upon major matters relating to its production and operation or formulates important rules and standards it shall hear the opinions and suggestions of the labor union and the workers.

Article 57 A person in any of the following categories may not serve as a director supervisor or the general manager of a corporation

i. without civil capacity or with limited civil capacity
ii. having been sentenced to prison for the following crimes and completion of the sentence being less than 5 years ago embezzlement bribery conversion of property misappropriation of property sabotage of social economic order or having been deprived of political rights as a result of a criminal conviction and completion of such sanction being less than 5 years ago
iii. having served as a director the factory chief or the general manager of a corporation or enterprise which underwent bankruptcy liquidation as a result of mismanagement and being personally responsible for such bankruptcy and completion of the bankruptcy liquidation being less than 3 years ago
iv. having served as the legal representative of a corporation or enterprise whose business license was revoked due to its violation of law and being personally responsible for such revocation and such revocation occurring less than 3 years ago in default of personal debt of a significant amount.

If the corporation elects or appoints a director or supervisor or employs the general manager in violation of the above Paragraph such election appointment or employment is invalid.

Article 58 No public servant may concurrently serve as a director supervisor or the general manager of a corporation.

Article 59 A directors supervisor or the general manager shall abide by the articles of association faithfully perform their duties and safeguard the interests of the corporation and may not abuse their positions and authorities at the corporation for private gain.

A directors supervisor or the general manager may not abuse their authorities by accepting bribes or generating other illegal income and may not convert corporation property.

Article 60 A director or the general manager may not misappropriate corporation funds or loan corporation funds to other people.

A director or the general manager may not deposit corporation assets into an account in his own name or in any other individual's name.

A director or the general manager may not give corporation assets as security for the debt of a shareholder or any other individual.

Article 61 A director or the general manager may not engage in the same business as the corporation in which he serves as a director or the general manager either for his own account or for any other person's account or engage in any activity detrimental to corporation interests. If a director or the general manager engages in any of the above mentioned business or activity any income so derived shall be turned over to the corporation.

Unless otherwise provided in the articles of association or otherwise agreed by the shareholders' committee a director or the general manager may not execute any contract or engage in any transaction with the corporation.

Article 62 Unless required by law or consented to by the shareholders' committee a director supervisor or the general manager may not disclose the corporation's confidential information.

Article 63 If a director supervisor or the general manager causes detriment to the corporation while performing his duties in violation of any national statute administrative regulation or the articles of association he shall be liable for the loss so caused.

Section Three Wholly State-Owned Corporations

Article 64 A wholly state-owned corporation referred to herein means a limited liability corporation established through sole investment by a state authorized investment entity or state authorized department.

Corporations designated by the State Council to produce special products or in special industries shall adopt the form of a wholly state-owned corporation.

Article 65 The articles of association of a wholly state-owned corporation may be formulated by the state authorized investment entity or state authorized department in accordance with the provisions hereof or may be prepared by its board of directors and submitted to the state authorized investment entity or state authorized department for approval.

Article 66 A wholly state-owned corporation shall not have a shareholders' committee and the state authorized investment entity or state authorized department shall authorize the board of directors to exercise part of the authorities of the shareholders' committee and to decide on major matters of the corporation provided that matters such as merger division or dissolution of the corporation capital increase or reduction by the corporation and issue of corporation bonds must be decided by the state authorized investment entity or state authorized department.

Article 67 Amended The Supervisory Committee of a wholly State-owned Corporation shall comprise personnel appointed by the State Council or agencies or departments and staff representatives. There shall be no fewer than three supervisors. The Supervisory Committee shall exercise the authorities enumerated in Items i and ii of Paragraph 1 of Article 54 hereof as well as other authorities granted by the State Council.

The supervisors shall be present at the meetings of board of directors.

A director the manager and the person in charge of finance shall not serve as a supervisor concurrently.

Article 68 A wholly state-owned corporation shall have a board of directors which shall perform its duties in accordance with the provisions of Article 46 and Article 66 hereof. Each term of the board of directors shall be 3 years.

There shall be not fewer than 3 but not more than 9 members on the board to be appointed or replaced by the state authorized investment entity or state authorized department according to the terms of the board. There shall be representatives of the workers on the board. The workers' representatives on the board shall be democratically elected by the workers.

The board of directors shall have a chairman and if needed a vice-chairman. The chairman and vice-chairman shall be appointed by the state authorized investment entity or state authorized department from the board members.

The chairman of the board is the legal representative of the corporation.

Article 69 A wholly state-owned corporation shall have a general manager to be appointed or removed by the board of directors. The general manager shall perform his duties in accordance with the provisions of Article 50 hereof.

If approved by the state authorized investment entity or state authorized department a board member may serve concurrently as the general manager.

Article 70 Absent approval by the state authorized investment entity or state authorized department the chairman vice-chairman a director or the general manager may not serve concurrently as the person in charge of any other limited liability corporation joint stock limited corporation or any other business organization.

Article 71 In the case of assignment of the assets of a wholly state-owned corporation the state authorized investment entity or state authorized department shall carry out examination and approval and the formalities for transfer of property rights shall be carried out in accordance with the relevant national statutes and administrative regulations.

Article 72 A large-scaled wholly state-owned corporation with sound operating and management system and good operating condition may be authorized by the State Council to exercise the proprietor's rights in respect of its assets.

Chapter Three Establishment and Organs of a Joint Stock Limited Corporation

Section One Establishment

Article 73 The establishment of a joint stock limited corporation is subject to the following conditions

i. The number of sponsors meets legal requirement
ii. The amount of capital stocks subscribed for by the sponsors and publicly placed reaches the legally-prescribed minimum capital level
iii. The issue of its shares and the preparation for its establishment comply with the law
iv. The sponsors prepare the articles of association and such articles of association are adopted by the establishment meeting
v. There is a corporation name and the organs complying with the requirements for a joint stock limited corporation are established
vi. There is a permanent place of business and there are necessary conditions for production and operation.

Article 74 A joint stock limited corporation may be established either by sponsorship or public share offer.

Establishment by sponsorship means establishment of the corporation through subscription by the sponsors for all the shares to be issued by the corporation.

Establishment by public share offer means establishment of the corporation through subscription by sponsors for part of the shares to be issued by the corporation and public placement of the remaining shares.

Article 75 In order to establish a joint stock limited corporation there shall be not fewer than 5 sponsors half of whom shall be domiciled in China.

In the case of reorganization of a state-owned enterprise into a joint stock limited corporation there may be fewer than 5 sponsors provided that such joint stock limited corporation shall be established by public share offer.

Article 76 Sponsors of a joint stock limited corporation must subscribe for the shares as required and conduct preparations for the establishment of the corporation in accordance herewith.

Article 77 Establishment of a joint stock limited corporation is subject to approval by the department authorized by the State Council or the People's Government at the provincial level.

Article 78 The registered capital of a joint stock limited corporation shall be the total amount of share capital which is paid in and registered with the corporation registration authority.

The minimum registered capital of a joint stock limited corporation may not be less than Renminbi 10,000,000 Yuan. Where the minimum level of registered capital required for a joint stock limited corporation exceeds the minimum level prescribed above such minimum level shall be separately prescribed by the relevant national statutes and administrative regulations.

Article 79 The articles of association of a joint stock limited corporation shall set forth the following

i. its name and domicile
ii. its business scope
iii. the method for its establishment
iv. the total number of shares of the corporation the value of each share and the registered capital of the corporation
v. the names of the sponsors and the number of shares they have subscribed for
vi. the rights and obligations of shareholders

vii. the composition of the board of directors its authorities term and rules of conducting business
viii. its legal representative
ix. the composition of the board of supervisors its authorities term and rules of conducting business
x. the method for corporation profit distribution
xi. the causes for its dissolution and the method for its liquidation
xii. the method for giving notice and making public announcement
xiii. other matters which the shareholders' general committee deems necessary to provide for.

Article 80 A sponsor may contribute his share capital in the form of cash or in the form of tangible goods industrial property non-patented technology or land use rights at certain value. If share capital is contributed in the form of tangible goods industrial property non-patented technology or land use rights they must be appraised and the property rights therein must be verified whereupon the value thereof shall be converted into shares. The contributed items may not be overvalued or undervalued. The appraisal of land use rights shall be carried out in accordance with the provisions of the relevant national statutes and administrative regulations.

The value of the industrial property and non-patented technology contributed as share capital by the sponsors shall not exceed 20 percent of the total registered capital.

Article 81 In the case of reorganizing a state-owned enterprise into a joint stock limited corporation conversion of state assets into shares through under-valuation sale of state assets at low price or distribution of state assets to individuals without compensation are strictly prohibited.

Article 82 In the case of establishing a joint stock limited corporation by sponsorship upon the sponsors' full subscription in writing for the shares to be issued as prescribed in the articles of association the sponsors shall promptly pay the share proceeds in full where tangible goods industrial property non-patented technology or land use rights are contributed in lieu of money the property rights therein shall be transferred in accordance with legally prescribed procedures.

Upon full contribution of the share capital which the sponsors have subscribed for they shall elect members to the board of directors and the board of supervisors and the board of directors shall apply for establishment registration by submitting the document approving the establishment of the corporation the articles of association and the capital verification certificate etc. to the corporation registration authority.

Article 83 In the case of establishing a joint stock limited corporation by public share offer the shares subscribed for by the sponsors shall be not less than 35 percent of the total number of shares of the corporation and the remaining shares shall be openly offered to the public.

Article 84 In offering shares to the public the sponsors shall deliver an application for public share offer to the securities regulatory authority under the State Council and submit thereto the following main documents

i. the document approving the establishment of the corporation
ii. the articles of association
iii. the operating forecast report
iv. the names of the sponsors the number of shares they have subscribed for the nature of their share capital contribution and the capital verification certificate
v. the prospectus
vi. the name and address of the depository bank for the share proceeds
vii. the name of the underwriter and related agreements.

Without approval by the securities regulatory authority under the State Council the sponsors my not offer shares to the public.

Article 85 Upon approval by the securities regulatory authority under the State Council a joint stock limited corporation may offer shares to the public overseas and the detailed procedure shall be specially prescribed by the State Council.

Article 86 The securities regulatory authority under the State Council shall approve an application for public share offer which meets the requirements prescribed herein and shall not approve any application for public share offer which fails to meet the requirements prescribed herein.

If it is discovered that an approval given is not in compliance with the requirements prescribed herein it shall be revoked. Where no share has been placed such share offer shall be terminated where shares have been placed the subscribers may demand that the sponsors return the share proceeds paid together with the interest thereon as if they have been deposited in a bank for a like period.

Article 87 The prospectus shall be accompanied with the articles of association prepared by the sponsors and shall set forth the following

i. the number of shares subscribed for by the sponsors
ii. the par value and issuing price of each share
iii. the total number of bearer share certificates issued
iv. the rights and obligations of the subscribers
v. the commencing time and expiration time of the share offer and a statement that in the event the shares have not be placed in full upon the expiration time the subscribers may revoke their share subscriptions.

Article 88 In a public share offer the sponsors shall make the prospectus available to the public and prepare the share subscription form. The share subscription form shall contain the items listed in the previous Article and a subscriber shall fill in the following the number of shares subscribed for the amount of share proceeds and his or her domicile and shall sign or impress his chop on the form. A subscriber shall pay the share proceeds according to the number of shares he has subscribed for.

Article 89 The sponsors' share offer to the public shall be underwritten by a securities underwriter established in accordance with the law and an underwriting agreement shall be executed.

Article 90 When conducting public share offer the sponsors shall execute an agreement with a bank for deposit of share proceeds.

The depository bank shall collect and hold the share proceeds in accordance with the agreement and issue receipts to subscribers who have paid their share proceeds and is obligated to provide to the relevant authority a certificate for receipt of share proceeds.

Article 91 After the proceeds from issue of the shares are paid in full the share capital must be verified by a legally-prescribed capital verification institution and a certificate shall be issued thereby. Within 30 days the sponsors shall hold and preside over the establishment meeting which is composed of the subscribers.

If the issued shares are not fully placed upon expiration of the time limit prescribed in the prospectus or the sponsors fail to hold the establishment meeting within 30 days of full payment of the proceeds from issue of the shares the subscribers may demand that the sponsors return the share proceeds paid together with the interest thereon as if they have been deposited in a bank for a like period.

Article 92 The sponsors shall notify each subscriber of the date of the establishment meeting or make a public announcement for such meeting 15 days in advance. The establishment meeting may not be held unless attended by subscribers representing at least half of the shares.

The establishment meeting shall exercise the following authorities

1. considering the report on pre-establishment activities prepared by the sponsors
2. adopting the articles of association
3. electing members of the board of directors
4. electing members of the board of supervisors
5. verifying expenses incurred for the establishment of the corporation
6. verifying the value of the assets contributed by the sponsors in lieu of share proceeds
7. where an event of force majeure or any material change in operating condition affecting the corporation's establishment has occurred a resolution not to establish the corporation may be adopted.

A resolution adopted at the establishment meeting on any of the matters mentioned in the previous Paragraph requires affirmative votes by subscribers representing at least half of the votes attending the meeting.

Article 93 Upon payment of the share proceeds or delivery of the items as contribution of share capital in lieu of share proceeds the sponsors and subscribers may not withdraw their share capital except where the shares issued are not fully placed in time the sponsors fail to hold the establishment meeting in time or the establishment meeting adopts a resolution not to establish the corporation.

Article 94 Within 30 days of the completion of the establishment meeting the board of directors shall apply for establishment registration by submitting to the corporation registration authority the following

i. the approval document issued by the relevant authority
ii. the minutes of the establishment meeting
iii. the articles of association
iv. the financial auditing report on pre-establishment activities
v. the capital verification certificate
vi. the names and domiciles of members of the board of directors and the board of supervisors
vii. the name and domicile of the legal representative.

Article 95 The corporation registration authority shall decide whether to grant registration to the joint stock limited corporation within 30 days of receipt of the application for establishment registration. Where the application meets the requirements prescribed herein registration shall be granted and the corporation shall be issued a business license where the application fails to meet the requirements prescribed herein registration shall not be granted.

The date on which the business license is issued shall be the date of the corporation's establishment. Upon establishment the corporation shall make a public announcement.

If established through public share offer upon establishment and registration the joint stock limited corporation shall submit to the securities regulatory authority under the State Council a report on the share offer activities for filing.

Article 96 Where a branch corporation is to be established contemporaneous with the establishment of a joint stock limited corporation an application for registration of such branch corporation shall be submitted to the corporation registration authority and it shall be issued a business license.

Where a branch corporation is to be established after the joint stock limited corporation's establishment the corporation's legal representative shall apply to the corporation registration authority for registration of such branch corporation and it shall be issued a business license.

Article 97 The sponsors of a joint stock limited corporation shall bear liabilities as follows

i. in the event of failure to establish the corporation being jointly and severally liable for the debts and expenses incurred as a result of the pre-establishment activities
ii. in the event of failure to establish the corporation being jointly and severally liable for the return of share proceeds paid by the subscribers together with the interest thereon as if they have been deposited in a bank for a like period.
iii. if the corporation's interest is harmed in the course of its establishment due to the negligence of the sponsors being liable to the corporation for damages.

Article 98 Where a limited liability corporation is to be converted into a joint stock limited corporation the requirements for establishing a joint stock limited corporation prescribed herein shall be met and the conversion shall be carried out in accordance with the procedure for the establishment of a joint stock limited corporation prescribed herein.

Article 99 Where conversion of a limited liability corporation to a joint stock limited corporation is approved in accordance with the law the total value of the converted shares shall be equivalent to the corporation's net assets value. Where conversion of a limited liability corporation to a joint stock limited corporation is approved in accordance with the law and its shares are offered to the public for the purpose of increasing capital such share offer shall be carried out in accordance with the provisions herein governing public share offer.

Article 100 Where conversion of a limited liability corporation to a joint stock limited corporation is approved in accordance with the law the creditor's rights and liabilities of the original corporation shall be assumed by the joint stock limited corporation resulting from the conversion.

Article 101 A joint stock limited corporation shall maintain its articles of association the record of shareholders the minutes of meetings of shareholders' general committee and its financial and accounting reports on the corporation's premises.

Section Two Shareholders' General Committee

Article 102 The shareholders' General Committee of a joint stock limited corporation is composed of all shareholders. The shareholders' general committee is the corporation's organ of authority and shall exercise its authorities in accordance herewith.

Article 103 The shareholder's general committee shall exercise the following authorities

i. determining the corporation's operational guidelines and investment plans
ii. electing and replacing members of the board of directors and deciding upon matters relating to their remuneration
iii. electing and replacing members of the board of supervisors who are the shareholders' representatives and deciding upon matters relating to the remuneration of the supervisors
iv. considering and approving reports by the board of directors
v. considering and approving reports by the board of supervisors
vi. considering and approving annual financial budget plans and final accounting plans of the corporation

vii. considering and approving profit distribution plans and plans to cover corporation losses
viii. adopting resolutions regarding increase or reduction of registered capital by the corporation
ix. adopting resolutions on the issue of bonds by the corporation
x. adopting resolutions on merger division change of corporate form dissolution and liquidation of the corporation
xi. amending the articles of association.

Article 104 The shareholders' general committee shall hold an annual meeting each year. An interim meeting of the shareholders' general committee shall be held within 2 months upon the occurrence of any of the following circumstances

i. The number of directors falls below the number prescribed herein or below two-thirds of the number prescribed in the articles of association
ii. The corporation's losses which are not covered have reached one-third of the total amount of the share capital
iii. Shareholders holding at least 10 percent of the corporation's stocks make a request
iv. The board of directors deems necessary
v. The board of supervisors proposes for such a meeting.

Article 105 A meeting of shareholders general committee shall be called by the board of directors in accordance with herewith and shall be presided over by the chairman of the board. Where the chairman is unable to perform his duties due to any special reason the meeting shall be presided over by the vice-chairman appointed by the chairman or another director appointed by the chairman. In order to hold a meeting of shareholders' general committee notice concerning the matters to be considered at the meeting shall be given to each shareholder 30 days in advance. An interim meeting of shareholders' general committee may not adopt any resolution on matters not stated in the notice.

Where the corporation has issued bearer share certificates a public notice concerning matters set forth in the previous Paragraph shall be made 45 days prior to the meeting.

When attending a meeting of shareholders' general committee holders of bearer share certificates shall deposit such certificates at the corporation from the 5th day prior to the meeting until the closing of the meeting.

Article 106 When a shareholder attends the meeting of shareholders' general committee each share he holds is entitled to one vote.

A resolution adopted by the shareholders' general committee requires affirmative votes by a majority of the votes held by shareholders attending the meeting. The shareholders' general committee's adoption of a resolution for merger division or dissolution of the corporation requires affirmative votes by at least two-thirds of the votes held by shareholders attending the meeting.

Article 107 An amendment to the articles of association requires affirmative votes by at least two-thirds of the votes held by shareholders attending the meeting of shareholders' general committee.

Article 108 A shareholder may attend a meeting of shareholders' general committee by proxy the proxy holder shall present the proxy statement issued by the shareholder to the corporation and shall exercise his voting rights to the extent authorized by the proxy.

Article 109 The shareholders' general committee shall prepare minutes regarding the decisions on matters considered at the meeting which shall be signed by the directors attending the meeting. The minutes shall be maintained together with the record containing signatures of the shareholders attending the meeting and the proxy statements.

Article 110 A shareholder is entitled to inspect the articles of association the minutes of meetings of shareholders' general committee and the financial and accounting reports of the corporation and is entitled to make a proposal or inquiry concerning the corporation's operation.

Article 111 Where a resolution adopted by the shareholders' general committee or the board of directors violates the relevant national statutes or administrative regulations or infringes on the rights and interests of the shareholders a shareholder is entitled to bring a suit to the People's Court to enjoin such illegal act or infringing act.

Section Three Board of Directors and General Manager

Article 112 A joint stock limited corporation shall have a board of directors which shall be composed of not fewer than 5 but not more than 19 members.

The board of directors is accountable to the shareholders' general committee and shall exercise the following authorities

i. being responsible for calling meetings of shareholders' general committee and presenting reports thereto

ii. implementing resolutions adopted by the shareholders' general committee
iii. determining the corporation's operating plans and investment programs
iv. preparing annual financial budget plans and final accounting plans of the corporation
v. preparing the corporation's profit distribution plans and plans to cover corporation losses
vi. preparing plans for increasing or reducing registered capital by the corporation and plans to issue corporation bonds
vii. drafting plans for merger division or dissolution of the corporation
viii. determining the structure of the corporation's internal management appointing or removing the general manager of the corporation appointing or removing upon the general manager's recommendation deputy general managers of the corporation and the officer in charge of finance and determining the remuneration for those officers
ix. formulating the corporation's basic management scheme.

Article 113 The board of directors shall have a chairman and may have one or two vice-chairmen. The chairman and vice-chairman shall be elected by the board of directors through affirmative votes by a majority of the directors.

The chairman is the legal representative of the corporation.

Article 114 The chairman shall exercise the following authorities

i. presiding over meetings of shareholders' general committee and calling and presiding over meetings of the board of directors
ii. supervising the implementation of resolutions adopted by the board of directors
iii. signing the share certificates and bond certificates of the corporation.

The vice-chairman shall assist the chairman in his work. Where the chairman is unable to exercise his authorities the vice-chairman appointed by the chairman shall exercise such authorities in his capacity.

Article 115 The term of directors shall be prescribed by the articles of association provided that each term shall not exceed 3 years. A director may continue to serve his post if he is re-elected upon the expiration of his term.

Prior to the expiration of a director's term the shareholders' general committee may not remove him without cause.

Article 116 The board of directors shall hold meetings at least twice a year and notice shall be given to all directors 10 days in advance.

Where an interim meeting of the board of directors is to be held the method and time limit for notification for calling the interim meeting may be prescribed separately.

Article 117 A meeting of the board of directors may not be held unless attended by at least half of the directors. A resolution adopted by the board of directors requires affirmative votes by a majority of all the directors.

Article 118 A meeting of the board of directors shall be attended by each director in person. Where a director is unable to attend the meeting for cause he may issue a written proxy entrusting another director to attend in his behalf and the proxy shall set forth the scope of authorization.

The board of directors shall prepare minutes regarding the decisions on matters considered at the meeting which shall be signed by the directors attending the meeting and the person preparing the minutes.

The directors shall be responsible for resolutions adopted by the board of directors. Where a resolution of the board violates any national statutes administrative regulations or the articles of association and causes the corporation to incur serious loss those directors participating in the adoption of the resolution are liable to the corporation for damages. Provided however if a director is proven to have dissented at the vote adopting such resolution and such dissension was noted in the minutes then the director may be exempt from liability.

Article 119 A joint stock limited corporation shall have a general manager to be appointed or removed by the board. The general manager is accountable to the board and shall exercise the following authorities

i. being in charge of managing the corporation's production and operation and organizing the implementation of resolutions adopted by the board
ii. organizing the implementation of annual operating plans and investment programs of the corporation
iii. drafting the plan for the structure of the corporation's internal management
iv. drafting the basic management scheme of the corporation

v. formulating detailed rules of the corporation
vi. recommending for appointment or removal of the deputy general managers and the officer in charge of finance
vii. appointing and removing officers of the corporation other than those to be appointed or removed by the board
viii. other authorities prescribed by the articles of association and delegated by the board.

The general manager shall be present at board meetings.

Article 120 In light of the needs of the corporation the board of directors may authorize the chairman to exercise part of the authorities of the board when it is not in session.

The board of directors of the corporation may decide that a board member is to serve concurrently as the general manager.

Article 121 When a corporation considers and decides upon matters which affect the personal interests of its workers such as workers' wages benefits production safety and labor protection or labor insurance it shall first hear the opinions of the labor union and the workers of the corporation and invite representatives of the labor union or the workers to be present at related meetings.

Article 122 When a corporation considers and decides upon major matters relating to its production and operation or formulates important rules and standards it shall hear the opinions and suggestions of the labor union and the workers.

Article 123 The directors and the general manager shall abide by the articles of association faithfully perform their duties and safeguard the interests of the corporation and may not abuse their positions and authorities at the corporation for private gain.

The provisions from Article 57 to Article 63 hereof setting forth the circumstances in which a person may not serve as a director or the general manager and the obligations and responsibilities of the directors and the general manager shall apply to the directors and general manager of a joint stock limited corporation.

Section Four Board of Supervisors

Article 124 A joint stock limited corporation shall have a board of supervisors which shall be composed of not fewer than 3 members. The board of supervisors shall elect one member to serve as the person responsible for calling meetings.

The board of supervisors shall be composed of the shareholders' representatives and representatives of the workers of the corporation in an appropriate ratio to be prescribed by the articles of association. The workers' representatives on the board of supervisors shall be democratically elected by the workers of the corporation.

A director the general manager and the officer in charge of finance may not serve concurrently as a supervisor.

Article 125 Each term of a supervisor shall be three years and a supervisor may continue to serve his post at the expiration of his term if he is re-elected.

Article 126 The board of supervisors shall exercise the following authorities

i. reviewing the financial affairs of the corporation
ii. monitoring the acts of the directors or the general manager to guard against violation of national statutes administrative regulations or the articles of association in the course their performance of duties
iii. requiring the directors or the general manager to make rectification when any act thereof harms corporation interests
iv. proposing for interim meetings of shareholders' general committee.
v. other authorities prescribed by the articles of association.

The supervisors shall be present at board meetings.

Article 127 The method for conducting business and voting procedure for the board of supervisors shall be prescribed by the articles of association.

Article 128 A supervisor shall perform his supervisory duties faithfully in accordance with the provisions of national statutes administrative regulations and the articles of association.

The provisions from Article 57 to Article 59 hereof and from Article 62 to Article 63 hereof setting forth the circumstances in which a person may not serve as a supervisor and the obligations and responsibilities of supervisors shall apply to the supervisors of a joint stock limited corporation.

Chapter Four Issue and Transfer of Shares of a Joint Stock Limited Corporation

Section One Issue of Shares

Article 129 The capital of a joint stock limited corporation shall be divided into shares and all the shares shall be of equal value.

Shares of the corporation are represented by share certificates. A share certificate is a certificate issued by the corporation certifying the share held by a shareholder.

Article 130 When shares are issued the principles of openness fairness and equity shall be followed and each share in the same class must have the same rights and receive the same interests.

For shares issued at the same time each share shall be issued on the same conditions and at the same price. All entities or individuals subscribing for shares shall pay the same price for each share.

Article 131 The issuing price per share may be at par value or above par value but may not be below par value.

The pricing of shares issued at above par value is subject to approval by the securities regulatory authority under the State Council.

The premium resulting from issuance of shares at a price above par value shall be allocated to the corporation's capital reserve fund.

The detailed regulatory measures concerning issuance of shares at a premium shall be prescribed by the State Council separately.

Article 132 A share certificate shall be in paper form or in other forms prescribed by the securities regulatory authority under the State Council.

A share certificate shall set forth the following major items

i. the name of the corporation
ii. the corporation's date of registration and establishment
iii. the class and par value of the shares and the number of shares represented
iv. the serial number of the share certificate.

The share certificate shall be signed by the chairman of the board and the corporation's chop shall be impressed thereon.

Share certificates held by the sponsors shall be marked with the words Sponsors' Share.

Article 133 Share certificates issued by the corporation to its sponsors state authorized investment institutions or legal persons shall be registered share certificates bearing the names of such sponsors institutions or legal persons and may not be registered under any other names or in the names of their legal representatives.

Share certificates issued to the public may be in the form of either registered share certificates or bearer share certificates.

Article 134 A corporation issuing registered share certificates shall maintain a record of shareholders which shall set forth the following

i. the name and domicile of each shareholder
ii. the number of shares held by each shareholder
iii. the serial numbers of share certificates held by each shareholder
iv. the date on which each shareholder acquired his shares.

A corporation issuing bearer share certificates shall record the number of such share certificates their serial numbers and their issuing dates.

Article 135 The State Council may make separate stipulations relating to a corporation's issuance of shares of classes other than those prescribed herein.

Article 136 Upon registration and establishment a joint stock limited corporation shall promptly deliver the share certificates to its shareholders officially. Prior to registration and establishment the corporation may not deliver any share certificate to its shareholders.

Article 137 Issuance of new shares by a corporation is subject to the following conditions

i. Previously issued shares have been fully subscribed for and at least one year has passed since the previous share issue
ii. The corporation has been profitable consecutively for the most recent three years and is able to pay dividends to its shareholders
iii. The financial and accounting documents of the corporation contain no misrepresentation for the most recent three years
iv. the corporation's projected profit rate reaches the interest rate of bank deposits for a like period.

Where the corporation distributes its current year profit in the form of new shares issuance of such shares are exempt from the restriction prescribed in Item ii of the previous Paragraph.

Article 138 Where a corporation is to issue new shares the shareholder's general committee shall adopt a resolution concerning the following

i. the classes and number of the new shares
ii. the issuing price of the new shares
iii. the commencing and ending dates of issuance of the new shares
iv. the classes and number of new shares issued to the existing shareholders.

Article 139 Upon adoption of a resolution by the shareholders' general committee to issue new shares the board of directors shall apply to the department authorized by the State Council or the People's Government at the provincial level for approval. Where the new shares are offered to the public approval by the securities regulatory authority is required.

Article 140 When a corporation is approved to issue new shares to the public it shall make public the prospectus for the issue of new shares its financial and accounting statements and subsidiary statements and shall prepare the subscription form.

If the corporation offers new shares to the public such share offer shall be underwritten by a lawfully established securities underwriter and the corporation shall execute an underwriting agreement therewith.

Article 141 In issuing new shares a corporation may determine the pricing scheme in light of the sustainable profitability of the corporation and the appreciation of the corporation's assets.

Article 142 Upon full receipt of the share proceeds from the corporation's newly issued shares the corporation shall carry out amendment registration with the corporation registration authority and shall make a public announcement.

Section Two Assignment of Shares

Article 143 Shares held by a shareholder may be assigned in accordance with the law.

Article 144 Assignment of shares by a shareholder must be carried out at a lawfully established securities exchange.

Article 145 Assignment of registered share certificates is effected by the shareholder's endorsement thereof or by other methods prescribed by the relevant national statutes or administrative regulations.

In the case of assignment of registered share certificates the corporation shall record the assignee's name and domicile on the record of shareholders.

Recording change of shareholders on the record of shareholders referred to in the previous Paragraph may not be carried out for a period of 30 days prior to the holding of a meeting of shareholders' general committee or 5 days prior to the record date for the purpose of dividend distribution determined by the corporation.

Article 146 Assignment of bearer share certificates takes effect upon delivery thereof by the shareholder to the assignee at a lawfully established securities exchange.

Article 147 Shares of a corporation held by its sponsors may not be assigned for a period of 3 years commencing from the date of the corporation's establishment.

The directors supervisors and general manager of the corporation shall report to the corporation the number of the corporation's shares held thereby and may not assign such shares while they are in office.

Article 148 A state authorized investment institution may assign shares held by it in accordance with the law and may also purchase shares held by other shareholders. The authority of approval for and regulatory measures concerning such assignment or purchase of shares shall be separately prescribed by the relevant national statutes or administrative regulations.

Article 149 A corporation may not purchase its own shares except in the case of share cancellation for the purpose of reducing the corporation's capital or in the case of merger with another corporation holding shares of the corporation.

Upon repurchase of its shares pursuant to the previous Paragraph the corporation shall cancel such shares within 10 days and carry out amendment registration in accordance with the relevant national statutes or administrative regulations and shall make a public announcement.

The corporation may not accept its own shares as the collateral under a security arrangement.

Article 150 If a registered share certificate is stolen lost or destroyed the shareholder may petition a People's Court for the invalidation thereof through the public notice procedure prescribed in the Civil Procedural Law of the People's Republic of China.

After the People's Court has invalidated such share certificate through the public notice procedure the shareholder may apply to the corporation for re-issuance of a certificate for the share.

Section Three Listed Corporations

Article 151 A Listed corporation referred to herein means a joint stock limited corporation whose issued shares have been approved by the State

Council or the securities regulatory authority authorized by the State Council to be listed and traded on a securities exchange.

Article 152 A joint stock limited corporation applying for listing of its shares shall meet the following requirements

i. The corporation's shares have been issued to the public with approval by the securities regulatory authority under the State Council
ii. The amount of total share capital of the corporation is at least Renminbi 50,000,000 Yuan
iii. The corporation has been in operation for at least three years and has been profitable consecutively for the most recent three years where the corporation is reorganized from a former state-owned enterprise in accordance with the law or newly established after the implementation hereof with its principal sponsor being a large-scaled or medium-scaled state-owned enterprise the required period may be counted continuously
iv. There are at least 1000 shareholders each of whom holds shares with face value of not less than Renminbi 1000 Yuan and the shares issued to the public amount to at least 25 percent of the total number of shares of the corporation and where the amount of total share capital of the corporation exceeds Renminbi 400,000,000 Yuan the shares issued to the public amount to at least 15 percent of the total number of shares of the corporation
v. The corporation has not engaged in any material illegal act for the most recent three consecutive years and the financial and accounting reports thereof contain no misrepresentation
vi. Other requirements prescribed by the State Council.

Article 153 The application by a joint stock limited corporation for listing of its shares shall be submitted to the State Council or the securities regulatory authority authorized thereby for approval and the relevant documents shall be submitted in accordance with the applicable national statutes and administrations regulations.

The State Council or the securities regulatory authority authorized thereby shall approve an application for listing of shares which meets the requirements prescribed herein and shall not approve any application which fails to meet the requirements prescribed herein.

Upon approval of its application for listing of shares the corporation approved for listing shall make public its share listing report and shall maintain its application documents at a designated place for inspection by the public.

Article 154 The shares of a corporation approved for listing shall be listed in accordance with the provisions of applicable national statutes and administrative regulations.

Article 155 Upon approval by the securities regulatory authority under the State Council the shares of a corporation may be listed abroad and the detailed measures shall be specially prescribed by the State Council.

Article 156 A listed corporation shall make public its financial conditions and operating conditions at regular intervals in accordance with the relevant national statutes and administrative regulations and shall make public its financial and accounting reports semiannually in each fiscal year.

Article 157 The securities regulatory authority under the State Council shall suspend the trading of a listed corporation in any of the following circumstances

i. Matters such as the total share capital or the composition of equity ownership of the corporation have changed so that the corporation no longer meets the requirements for listing
ii. The corporation fails to make public its financial condition as required or has made misrepresentations in its financial and accounting reports
iii. The corporation has engaged in material illegal act
iv. The corporation has been suffering losses for the most recent three consecutive years.

Article 158 Where a listed corporation is in a circumstance set forth in either Item ii or iii of the previous Article and after investigation it is confirmed that the circumstance is serious or the listed corporation is in a circumstance set forth in either Item i or iv and has not been able to eliminate such circumstance within a prescribed time limit and hence no longer meets the requirements for listing the securities regulatory authority under the State Council shall issue a decision to de-list its shares.

Where the corporation is to be dissolved pursuant to a resolution is ordered to cease its operation by the relevant authority in charge in accordance with the law or is declared bankrupt the securities regulatory authority under the State Council shall issue a decision to de-list its shares.

Chapter Five Corporation Bonds

Article 159 For the purpose of financing production and operation a joint stock limited corporation a wholly state-owned corporation or a limited liability corporation established through investment by two or more state-owned enterprises or two or more state authorized investment entities may issue corporation bonds in accordance herewith.

Article 160 Corporation bonds referred to herein means a form of security which is issued by a corporation in accordance with legally prescribed procedure and which provides that the principal thereof and interest thereon shall be paid at specified times.

Article 161 In order to issue corporation bonds the following requirements must be met

i. The net assets of the corporation shall be not less than Renminbi 30,000,000 Yuan in the case of a joint stock limited corporation and not less than Renminbi 60,000,000 Yuan in the case of a limited liability corporation
ii. The cumulative value of corporation bonds shall not exceed 40 percent of the corporation's net assets
iii. The average distributable profit for the most recent three years is sufficient to pay one year's interest on the corporation bonds
iv. The proceeds received shall be invested in a manner consistent with state industrial policy
v. The interest rate on the bonds shall not exceed the level of interest rate set by the State Council
vi. Other requirements prescribed by the State Council.

The proceeds from issuance of corporation bonds shall be used for the purpose approved by the approval authority and may not be used to cover losses and non-operating expenditures.

Article 162 No additional corporation bonds may be issued in any of the following circumstances

i. Corporation bonds previously issued have not been fully subscribed for
ii. The fact that the corporation is in default of any of the previously issued corporation bonds or corporation debt or is late in payment of principal and interest has occurred and is currently existing.

Article 163 Where a joint stock limited corporation or limited liability corporation is to issue corporation bonds its board of directors shall prepare a plan and the shareholders' committee shall adopt a resolution on such matter.

Where a wholly state-owned corporation is to issue corporation bonds the decision shall be made by the state authorized investment entity or state authorized department.

After a resolution has been adopted or a decision has been made pursuant to the previous two Paragraphs the corporation shall apply to the securities regulatory authority under the State Council for approval.

Article 164 The overall volume of corporation bonds issue shall be determined by the State Council. In examining and approving application for corporation bonds issue the securities regulatory authority under the State Council may not extend its approval beyond the volume set by the State Council.

The securities regulatory authority under the State Council shall approve an application for corporation bonds issue which complies with the provisions hereof and shall not approve an application which fails to comply with the provisions hereof.

Where it has been discovered that an approval given for corporation bonds issue is not in compliance with the provisions hereof such approval shall be revoked. If the corporation bonds have not been issued the issue shall be terminated if the corporation bonds have been issued the issuing corporation shall return the proceeds paid by the subscribers together with the interest thereon as if they have been deposited in a bank for a like period.

Article 165 For an application to the securities regulatory authority under the State Council for corporation bonds issue the following documents shall be submitted

i. the corporation's registration certificate
ii. the articles of association of the corporation
iii. the plan for corporation bonds offer
iv. the assets appraisal report and capital verification report.

Article 166 Upon approval of an application for corporation bonds issue the plan for corporation bonds offer shall be made public.

The plan for corporation bonds offer shall set forth the following major items

i. the name of the corporation
ii. the total value of the bonds and the par value of each bond
iii. the rate of interest on the bonds
iv. the time limit and method for payment of the principal of and interest on the bonds
v. the commencing and ending date of the bonds issue
vi. the net assets value of the corporation
vii. the total value of issued and outstanding corporation bonds
viii. the underwriter of the corporation bonds.

Article 167 In the case of corporation bonds issue a corporation must state on each bond certificate the name of the corporation the par value of the bond interest rate and repayment period and the bond certificate shall be signed by the chairman of the board and the corporation's chop shall be impressed thereon.

Article 168 corporation bonds may be classified as either registered bonds or bearer bonds.

Article 169 If a corporation has issued bonds it shall maintain a record of bondholders.

If registered bonds are issued the following shall be recorded on the corporation's record of bondholders

i. the name and domicile of each bondholder
ii. the dates on which the bondholders acquired the bonds and the serial numbers of the bond certificates
iii. the total value of the bonds the par value of each bond the interest thereon the term thereof and method for payment of principal and interest
iv. the date of issue of the bonds.

If bearer corporation bonds are issued the corporation's record of bondholders shall record the total value of such bonds the interest rate thereon the term thereof and the method for repayment and the date of issue and the serial numbers of the bond certificates.

Article 170 Corporation bonds may be assigned. Assignment of corporation bonds shall be carried out at a lawfully established securities exchange.

The assignment price of corporation bonds shall be agreed upon between the assignor and the assignee.

Article 171 Assignment of registered bonds is effected by the bondholder's endorsement of the bonds or by other methods prescribed by the relevant national statutes or administrative regulations.

In the case of assignment of registered bonds the corporation shall record the assignee's name and domicile on the record of bondholders.

Assignment of bearer bonds takes effect upon delivery thereof by the bondholder to the assignee at a lawfully established securities exchange.

Article 172 Upon adoption of a resolution by the shareholders' general committee a listed corporation may issue bonds which are convertible to its shares and it shall prescribe the specific method for such conversion in the plan for corporation bonds offer.

In order to issue convertible corporation bonds an application shall be submitted to the securities regulatory authority under the State Council for approval. In order to issue convertible corporation bonds in addition to meeting the requirements for issue of bonds the corporation shall also meet the requirements for issue of shares.

In the case of issue of convertible corporation bonds the face of the bond certificate shall be marked with the word Convertible and the number of convertible corporation bonds shall be specified in the corporation's record of bondholders.

Article 173 Where convertible corporation bonds are issued the corporation shall exchange its shares for the bonds held by the bondholders using the prescribed method of conversion provided that the bondholders have the option on whether or not to convert their bonds.

Chapter Six Financial and Accounting Affairs of Corporation

Article 174 A corporation shall establish its financial and accounting system in accordance with the relevant national statutes administrative regulations and the stipulations of the finance authority under the State Council.

Article 175 A corporation shall prepare its financial and accounting reports at the end of each fiscal year which shall be reviewed and verified in accordance with the law.

The financial and accounting reports shall include the following financial and accounting statements and subsidiary statements

i. balance sheet
ii. income statement

iii. statement of cash flow
iv. explanation of financial conditions
v. statement of profit distribution

Article 176 A limited liability corporation shall deliver its financial and accounting reports to each shareholder within the time limit prescribed by the articles of association.

The financial and accounting reports of a joint stock limited corporation shall be available at the corporation's premises for shareholders' inspection as from the 20th day prior to the annual meeting of shareholders' general committee.

A joint stock limited corporation established through public share offer shall make public its financial and accounting reports.

Article 177 In distribution of its current year after-tax profit a corporation shall allocate 10 percent to its statutory reserve fund 5–10 percent to its statutory welfare fund. Allocation to the corporation's statutory reserve fund may be waived once the cumulative amount of funds therein exceeds 50 percent of the corporation's registered capital.

Where the statutory reserve fund is not sufficient to cover the corporation's loss from the previous year the current year profit shall be used to cover such loss before allocation is made to the statutory reserve fund and the statutory welfare fund pursuant to the previous Paragraph.

After allocation to the statutory reserve fund has been made from the after-tax profit of the corporation and upon adoption of a resolution by the shareholders' committee allocation may be made to the discretionary reserve fund.

After the corporation has covered its losses and made allocation to the reserve funds and statutory welfare fund the remainder of the profit shall be distributed to the shareholders in proportion to their capital contribution in the case of a limited liability corporation and in proportion to their share holdings in the case of a joint stock limited corporation.

If the shareholders' committee or the board of directors in violation of the previous Paragraph distributes profit to the shareholders before covering corporation losses and making allocation to corporation statutory reserve fund and statutory welfare fund the profit so distributed must be returned to the corporation.

Article 178 The premium received by a joint stock limited corporation through issuance of shares at prices above par value in accordance herewith as well as other incomes to be allocated to the capital reserve fund as stipulated by the finance authority under the State Council shall be allocated to the capital reserve fund.

Article 179 The reserve funds of the corporation shall be used to cover corporation losses expand its production and operation or be converted to the corporation's increased capital.

Where a joint stock limited corporation upon adoption of a resolution by the shareholders' general committee is to convert the reserve funds into corporation capital new shares shall be distributed to the shareholders in proportion to their original share holdings or the par value of each share shall be increased. Provided however upon conversion of statutory reserve fund into capital the amount remaining in the statutory reserve fund may not fall below 25 percent of the registered capital.

Article 180 The statutory welfare fund allocated by the corporation shall be used for the collective welfare of the workers thereof.

Article 181 The corporation may not establish any separate accounting book besides the accounting books prescribed by law. The corporation's assets may not be deposited into any account established under an individual's name.

Chapter Seven Merger and Division of Corporation

Article 182 If a corporation is to undergo merger or division its shareholders' committee shall adopt a resolution.

Article 183 The merger or division of a joint stock limited corporation is subject to approval by the department authorized by the State Council or the People's Government at the provincial level.

Article 184 Corporations may be merged in two forms i.e. merger by absorption and merger by consolidation.

One corporation absorbing another corporation is merger by absorption and the corporation being absorbed shall be dissolved. Merger of two or more Corporations through establishment of a new corporation is a consolidation and the corporations being consolidated shall be dissolved.

In a merger of corporations the corporations shall execute a merger agreement and prepare their respective balance sheets and schedules of assets. The corporations shall notify their creditors within 10 days of adoption of merger resolutions and shall publish a notice at least 3 times in a newspaper within 30 days. Creditors are entitled to claim full payment of the debts of the corporations or require the provision of appropriate assurances within 30 days of receipt of the notice or within 90 days of publication of the first notice if such creditors did not receive the notice. The corporations may not be merged unless debts are fully paid or appropriate assurances are provided.

Once the corporations are merged the creditor's rights and debtor's liabilities of the merged corporations shall be assumed by the surviving corporation or the newly formed corporation after merger.

Article 185 Where a corporation is to undergo division its assets shall be divided accordingly.

In dividing the corporation a balance sheet and a schedule of assets shall be prepared. The corporation shall notify its creditors within 10 days of adoption of a division resolution and shall publish a notice at least 3 times in a newspaper within 30 days. Creditors are entitled to claim full payment of the corporation's debts or require the provision of appropriate assurances within 30 days of receipt of the notice or within 90 days of publication of the first notice if such creditors did not receive the notice. The corporation may not be divided unless debts are fully paid or appropriate assurances are provided.

The liabilities of the corporation prior to its division shall be assumed by the corporations resulting from the division according to the agreement reached among them.

Article 186 Where a corporation needs to reduce its registered capital a balance sheet and a schedule of assets must be prepared.

The corporation shall notify its creditors within 10 days of adoption of a resolution to reduce its registered capital and shall publish a notice at least 3 times in a newspaper within 30 days. Creditors are entitled to claim full payment of the corporation's debts or require the provision of appropriate assurances within 30 days of receipt of the notice or within 90 days of publication of the first notice if such creditors did not receive the notice.

After capital reduction the corporation's registered capital may not fall below the statutory minimum capital level.

Article 187 When a limited liability corporation is to increase its registered capital after subscription for the newly increased capital the shareholders shall make capital contribution in accordance with the provisions hereof concerning capital contribution for the establishment of a limited liability corporation.

When a joint stock limited corporation is to issue new shares for the purpose of increasing its registered capital the shareholders' subscription for the new shares shall be carried out in accordance with the provisions hereof concerning payment of share proceeds for the establishment of a joint stock limited corporation.

Article 188 In the case of merger or division of a corporation where any registered item requires change amendment registration shall be carried out with the corporation registration authority in accordance with the law where the corporation is dissolved corporation de-registration shall be carried out in accordance with the law where a new corporation is established establishment registration shall be carried out in accordance with the law.

Where a corporation is to increase or reduce its registered capital an amendment registration shall be carried out with the corporation registration authority in accordance with the law.

Chapter Eight Bankruptcy Dissolution and Liquidation of Corporation

Article 189 Where a corporation is adjudged bankrupt in accordance with the law due to its failure to repay debts when due the People's Court shall organize the shareholders the relevant authorities and professionals to establish a liquidating committee to carry out the corporation's bankruptcy liquidation in accordance with the provisions of the applicable laws.

Article 190 A corporation may be dissolved in any of the following circumstances

i. the term of operation prescribed by the corporation's articles of association has expired or any other cause for dissolution prescribed by the corporation's articles of association has occurred
ii. the shareholders' committee has adopted a resolution for dissolution
iii. dissolution is required due to merger or division of the corporation.

Article 191 Where a corporation is to be dissolved pursuant to Item i or ii of the previous Article a liquidating committee shall be formed within 15 days the liquidating committee of a limited liability corporation shall be composed of its shareholders and members of the liquidating committee of a joint stock limited corporation shall be determined by the shareholders' general committee where the corporation fails to form a liquidating committee to carry out liquidation within the prescribed time limit its creditors may petition the People's Court to appoint the relevant persons to form a liquidating committee to carry out liquidation. The People's Court shall accept such petition and promptly appoint members of the liquidating committee to carry out liquidation.

Article 192 Where the corporation is ordered to terminate due to its violation of law or administrative regulations the corporation shall be dissolved and the relevant department in charge shall organize the shareholders the relevant authority and related professionals to form a liquidating committee to carry out liquidation.

Article 193 The liquidating committee shall exercise the following authorities in the course of liquidation

i. identifying the corporation's assets and preparing a balance sheet and a schedule of assets respectively
ii. notifying creditors through notice or public announcement
iii. handling the corporation's ongoing businesses which are related to liquidation
iv. making full payment of taxes owed
v. identifying the corporation's creditor's rights and debtor's liabilities
vi. disposing of the remaining assets after full payment of corporation debts
vii. participating in civil actions on behalf of the corporation.

Article 194 The liquidating committee shall notify creditors within 10 days of its establishment and shall make a public announcement in a newspaper at least 3 times within 60 days. Creditors shall file their creditor's rights with the liquidating committee within 30 days of receipt of the notice and within 90 days of publication of the first notice if such creditors did not receive the notice.

In filing for creditor's rights the creditors shall state the relevant matters relating to the creditor's rights and provide supporting materials. The liquidating committee shall record such creditor's rights.

Article 195 After identifying the corporation's assets and preparing the balance sheet and schedule of assets the liquidating committee shall prepare a liquidating plan which shall be submitted to the shareholders' committee or the relevant authority for ratification.

Where the corporation's assets are sufficient for payment of corporation debts such assets shall be paid out in the following order payment of liquidating expenses payment of wages and expenses for labor insurance of the workers payment of taxes owed and payment of corporation debts.

After payments have been made in accordance with the previous Paragraph the remaining assets shall be distributed to the shareholders in proportion to their shares of capital contribution in the case of a limited liability corporation and in proportion to their share holdings in the case of a joint stock limited corporation.

In the course of liquidation the corporation may not conduct new business. Before payments have been made in accordance with Paragraph 2 above the assets of the corporation may not be distributed to the shareholders.

Article 196 Where a corporation commences liquidation due to its dissolution and after identification of corporation assets and preparation of the balance sheet and schedule of assets the liquidating committee discovers that the corporation does not have sufficient assets to fully repay corporation debts the liquidating committee shall immediately file a bankruptcy application with the People's Court.

Once the corporation is adjudged bankrupt by a ruling of the People's Court the liquidating committee shall transfer the liquidating affairs to the People's Court.

Article 197 Upon completion of a corporation's liquidation the liquidating committee shall prepare a liquidating report which shall be submitted to the shareholders' committee or the relevant authority for ratification and upon ratification the liquidating committee shall submit such report to the corporation registration authority to apply for corporation de-registration and make a public announcement of the corporation's termination. Where the corporation fails to apply for corporation de-registration the corporation registration authority shall revoke its business license and make a public announcement.

Article 198 Members of the liquidating committee shall faithfully perform their duties and carry out their liquidating obligations in accordance with the law.

Members of the liquidating committee may not abuse their authorities by accepting bribes or receiving other illegal income and may not misappropriate corporation assets.

A committee member who causes loss to the corporation or its creditors due to his intentional misconduct or gross negligence shall be liable for damages.

Chapter Nine Branch of Foreign Corporation

Article 199 Foreign corporations may establish branches within China to conduct business in accordance herewith.

A foreign corporation referred to herein means a corporation registered and established outside China under foreign laws.

Article 200 In order to establish a branch within China a foreign corporation must submit an application to the Chinese authority in charge together with the relevant documents such as its articles of association the corporation registration certificate issued in its home country etc. Upon approval it shall carry out registration with the corporation registration authority and be issued a business license.

The examination and approval procedure for branches of foreign corporations shall be separately prescribed by the State Council.

Article 201 In order to establish a branch within China a foreign corporation must appoint a representative or agent in charge of such branch within China and fund its branch as appropriate in light of the nature of its intended business.

Where operation of certain branches of foreign corporations is subject to a minimum level of funding such level shall be prescribed by the State Council separately.

Article 202 The branch of a foreign corporation shall identify the nationality and form of liability in its name.

The branch of a foreign corporation shall maintain the articles of association of such foreign corporation on its premises.

Article 203 A foreign corporation is a foreign legal person and its branch established within China does not have the status of a Chinese legal person.

A foreign corporation shall bear civil liabilities in respect of the business conducted by its branch within China.

Article 204 While conducting business within China the branch of a foreign corporation established after approval must abide by Chines law and may not harm the public interest of China and its lawful rights and interests are protected by Chinese law.

Article 205 When a foreign corporation cancels its branch within China such corporation must fully repay the debts thereof in accordance with the law and carry out liquidation in accordance with the provisions hereof concerning corporation liquidation procedure. The corporation may not transfer the assets of such branch abroad prior to full repayment of its debts.

Chapter Ten Legal Liabilities

Article 206 In the case of corporation registration where an applicant obtains corporation registration in violation hereof by making false statement of registered capital submitting false certificates or by concealing material facts through other fraudulent means the corporation shall be ordered to make rectification and in case false statement of registered capital was made the corporation shall be fined not less than 5 percent but not more than 10 percent of the amount of registered capital falsely stated the corporation submitting false certificates or concealing material facts shall be fined not less than 10,000 Yuan but not more than 100,000 Yuan where the circumstances are serious the corporation registration shall be revoked. Where such action constitutes a crime criminal liability shall be imposed in accordance with the law.

Article 207 In the case of issue of corporation shares or bonds where the prospectus subscription form or plan for corporation bonds offer is falsely prepared the issuing activities shall be ordered to cease and an order shall be issued for the return of the proceeds received together with interest thereon and a fine of not less than 1 percent but not more than 5 percent of the proceeds illegally received shall be imposed. Where such action constitutes a crime criminal liability shall be imposed in accordance with the law.

Article 208 In the case of capital contribution where the sponsors or shareholders falsify capital contribution by failing to pay money to deliver tangible goods or to transfer property rights thus defrauding the creditors or the public rectification shall be ordered and such persons shall be fined not less than 5 percent but not more than 10 percent of the amount of capital contribution falsified. Where such action constitutes a crime criminal liability shall be imposed in accordance with the law.

Article 209 Where the sponsors or shareholders of a corporation withdraw their capital contribution after the establishment of the corporation they shall be ordered to make rectification and such persons shall be fined not less than 5 percent but not more than 10 percent of the amount of capital contribution withdrawn. Where such action constitutes a crime criminal liability shall be imposed in accordance with the law.

Article 210 Where a corporation issues corporation shares or bonds on its own without approval by the appropriate authorities provided for herein the issuing activities shall be ordered to cease and the proceeds received together with interest thereon shall be returned and a fine of not less than 1 percent but not more than 5 percent of the proceeds illegally received shall be imposed. Where such action constitutes a crime criminal liability shall be imposed in accordance with the law.

Article 211 Where a corporation in violation hereof establishes another set of accounting books besides those prescribed by law it shall be ordered to make rectification and the corporation shall be fined not less than 10,000 Yuan but not more than 100,000 Yuan. Where such action constitutes a crime criminal liability shall be imposed in accordance with the law.

Where corporation assets are deposited into an account established under an individual's name the illegal gain shall be confiscated and a fine of not less than 2 times but not more than 5 times of the illegal gain shall be imposed. Where such action constitutes a crime criminal liability shall be imposed in accordance with the law.

Article 212 Where a corporation provides to its shareholders and the public financial and accounting reports which are false or which conceal material facts a fine of not less than 10,000 Yuan but not more than 100,000 Yuan shall be imposed on the supervisor directly in charge and the other persons directly responsible. Where such action constitutes a crime criminal liability shall be imposed in accordance with the law.

Article 213 Where in violation hereof state-owned assets are converted into shares at low prices or sold to individuals at low prices or distributed to individuals without compensation administrative penalty shall be imposed on the supervisor directly in charge and the other persons directly responsible. Where such action constitutes a crime criminal liability shall be imposed in accordance with the law.

Article 214 Where the directors supervisors or the general manager abuse their authorities by accepting bribes or receiving other illegal income or convert corporation assets any such illegal gain shall be confiscated and they shall be ordered to return the corporation assets and shall be disciplined by the corporation. Where such action constitutes a crime criminal liability shall be imposed in accordance with the law.

Where a director or the general manager misappropriates corporation funds or loan corporation funds to third parties he shall be ordered to return the corporation funds and shall be disciplined by the corporation and the income derived from such transaction shall be turned over to the corporation. Where such action constitutes a crime criminal liability shall be imposed in accordance with the law.

Where in violation hereof the directors or the general manager gives corporation assets as security for the personal debts of any director of the corporation or any other person the security arrangement shall be ordered to be canceled and such persons shall be held liable for damages in accordance with the law and the income derived from the illegal provision of security shall be turned over to the corporation. Where the circumstance is serious such persons shall be disciplined by the corporation.

Article 215 Where in violation hereof a director or the general manager engages in the same business as the corporation either for his own account or for another person's account in addition to turning over any income so derived to the corporation such person may also be disciplined by the corporation.

Article 216 Where a corporation fails to make allocation to the statutory reserve fund and statutory welfare fund in accordance herewith such corporation shall be ordered to make full allocation to the required funds and a fine of not less than 10,000 Yuan but not more than 100,000 Yuan may be levied on the corporation.

Article 217 Where a corporation fails to notify creditors through notice or public announcement in accordance herewith while carrying out merger division reduction of registered capital or liquidation it shall be ordered to make rectification and the corporation shall be fined not less than 10,000 Yuan but not more than 100,000 Yuan.

Where in the course of liquidation the corporation conceals its assets makes false statements in its balance sheet or schedule of assets or distributes corporation assets prior to full repayment of corporation debts it shall be ordered to make rectification and the corporation shall be fined not less than 1 percent but not more than 5 percent of the value of the concealed assets or the value of the assets distributed prior to full repayment of corporation debts. A fine of not less than 10,000 Yuan but not more than 100,000 Yuan shall be imposed on the supervisor directly in charge and the other persons directly responsible. Where such action constitutes a crime criminal liability shall be imposed in accordance with the law.

Article 218 Where the liquidating committee fails to submit the liquidating report to the corporation registration authority in accordance herewith or conceals any material fact or makes any material omission in the liquidating report submitted it shall be ordered to make rectification.

Where a member of the liquidating committee abuses his authority to engage in fraudulent activity for private gain to obtain illegal income or convert corporation assets such member shall be ordered to return the corporation assets and the illegal income shall be confiscated and such member may be fined not less than 2 times but not more than 5 times the illegal income. Where such action constitutes a crime criminal liability shall be imposed in accordance with the law.

Article 219 Where an institution conducting assets appraisal capital verification or testing and verification provides a false certificate the illegal income so derived shall be confiscated and a fine of not less than 2 times but not more than 5 times the illegal income shall be imposed and the relevant authority in charge may order such institution to cease operation and revoke the qualification certificates of the persons directly responsible. Where such action constitutes a crime criminal liability shall be imposed in accordance with the law.

Where an institution conducting assets appraisal capital verification or testing and verification provides a report with material omission due to its negligence it shall be ordered to make rectification and where the circumstance is relatively serious a fine of not less than 2 times but not more than 3 times the income so derived shall be imposed and the relevant authority in charge may order such institution to cease operation and revoke the qualification certificates of the persons directly responsible.

Article 220 Where the relevant authority in charge authorized by the State Council approves an application for the establishment of a corporation which fails to meet the requirements prescribed herein or approves an application for issue of shares which fails to meet the requirements prescribed herein and the circumstance is serious administrative penalty shall be imposed on the supervisor directly in charge and the other persons directly responsible in accordance with the law. Where such action constitutes a crime criminal liability shall be imposed in accordance with the law.

Article 221 Where the securities regulatory authority under the State Council approves an application for share offer share listing or bonds issue which fails to meet the requirements prescribed herein and the circumstance is serious administrative penalty shall be imposed on the supervisor directly in charge and the other persons directly responsible in accordance with the law. Where such action constitutes a crime criminal liability shall be imposed in accordance with the law.

Article 222 Where the corporation registration authority grants registration to an application which fails to meet the requirements prescribed herein and the circumstance is serious administrative penalty shall be imposed on the supervisor directly in charge and the other persons directly responsible in accordance with the law. Where such action constitutes a crime criminal liability shall be imposed in accordance with the law.

Article 223 Where the department in charge of the corporation registration authority compels it to grant registration to an application which fails to meet the requirements prescribed herein or engages in cover up for an illegal registration administrative penalty shall be imposed on the supervisor directly in charge and the other persons directly responsible in accordance with the law. Where such action constitutes a crime criminal liability shall be imposed in accordance with the law.

Article 224 Where an entity passes itself off as a limited liability corporation or joint stock limited corporation while not registered as such in accordance with the law it shall be ordered to make rectification or such entity shall be closed down and a fine of not less than 10,000 Yuan but not more than 100,000 Yuan may be imposed. Where such action constitutes a crime criminal liability shall be imposed in accordance with the law.

Article 225 Where a corporation fails to commence operation for more than 6 months without proper cause or suspends operation on its own without proper cause for more than 6 consecutive months after commencement of operation the corporation registration authority shall revoke its corporation business license.

Where the corporation fails to carry out amendment registration in accordance herewith when a registered item of the corporation has changed it shall be ordered to register within a prescribed time limit and where the corporation has not carried out registration after expiration of the time limit a fine of not less than 10,000 Yuan but not more than 100,000 Yuan shall be imposed.

Article 226 Where in violation hereof a foreign corporation establishes a branch within China without approval it shall be ordered to make rectification or such branch shall be ordered to terminate and a fine of not less than 10,000 Yuan but not more than 100,000 Yuan may be imposed.

Article 227 Where a relevant authority performing approval function hereunder fails to approve an application which meets conditions prescribed by law or the corporation registration authority fails to grant registration to an application which meets conditions prescribed by law the affected party may apply for administrative review or institute an administrative action in accordance with the law.

Article 228 Where a corporation violates of this Law and is therefore liable for civil damages as well as for an administrative fine or criminal fine and its assets are not sufficient to cover both its assets shall first be used to cover the civil liability for damages.

Chapter Eleven Supplementary Provisions

Article 229 Amended Corporations registered and established prior to the implementation of this Law in accordance with law administrative regulations local regulations and the Standard Opinions Concerning Limited Liability Corporations and the Standard Opinions Concerning Joint Stock Limited Corporations formulated by the relevant authority in charge under the State Council shall remain in existence provided that those corporations which do not meet all the conditions prescribed herein shall meet such conditions within the time limit prescribed. Detailed implementing measures shall be formulated by the State Council separately.

In the case of a Joint Stock Limited Liability Corporation in the high and new technology category the ratio of capital contribution in the form of industrial technology and non-patented proprietary technology by sponsors as a percentage of registered capital the conditions for issuance of new shares or initial public offering shall be separately stipulated by the State Council.

Article 230 This Law shall become operative as of July 1 1994.

Appendix II: The Law of the People's Republic of China on Sino-foreign Equity Joint Ventures (2016 Amendment)

Article 1 With a view to expanding international economic co-operation and technical exchange, the People's Republic of China permits foreign corporations, enterprises, other economic organizations or individuals (hereafter referred to as "foreign joint venturers") to joint with Chinese corporations, enterprise or other economic organizations (hereafter referred to as "Chinese joint ventures") in establishing joint ventures in the People's Republic of China in accordance with the principle of equality and mutual benefit and subject to approval by the Chinese Government.

Article 2 The Chinese Government protects, in accordance with the law, the investment of foreign joint ventures, the profits due to them and their other lawful rights and interest in a joint venture, pursuant to the agreement, contract and articles of association approved by the Chinese Government.

Joint ventures shall follow the provisions of the laws and regulations of the People's Republic of China in all their activities.

The state does not practise nationalization and expropriation of a joint venture; under special circumstances, the state, in accordance with the needs of social public interest, expropriates a joint venture pursuant to legal procedures and offers corresponding compensations.

Article 3 The joint venture agreement, contract and articles of association signed by the parties to the venture shall be submitted to the competent authorities of foreign economic relations and trade (hereafter referred to as approval authorities), and the approval authorities shall, within three

D. Yu, *Chinese Business Law*, The Palgrave Series on Chinese Law,
https://doi.org/10.1007/978-981-13-0902-1

months, decide whether to approve or disapprove them. After approval, the joint venture shall register with the state competent authorities of administration for industry and commerce to obtain a licence to do business and start operations.

Article 4 A joint venture shall take the form of a limited liability corporation.

The proportion of the investment contributed by the foreign joint venturer(s) shall generally not be less than 25% of the registered capital of a joint venture.

The parties to the venture shall share the profits, risks and losses in proportion to their respective contributions to the registered capital.

No assignment of the registered capital of a joint venturer shall be made without the consent of the other parties to the venture.

Article 5 Each party to a joint venture may make its investment in cash, in kind or in industrial property rights, etc.

The technology and the equipment that serve as a foreign joint venturer's investment must be advanced technology and equipment that actually suit our country's needs. If the foreign joint venturer causes losses by deception through the intentional use of backward technology and equipment, it shall pay compensation for the losses.

The investment of a Chinese joint venturer may include the right to the use of a site provided for the joint venture during the period of its operation. If the right to the use of the site does not constitute a part of a Chinese joint venturer's investment, the joint venture shall pay the Chinese Government a fee for its use.

The various investments referred to above shall be specified in the joint venture contract and articles of association, and the value of each (excluding that of the site) shall be jointly assessed by the parties to the venture.

Article 6 A joint venture shall have a board of directors, which shall have its size and composition stipulated in the contract and the articles of association after consultation between the parties to the venture, and the directors shall be appointed and replaced by the parties to the venture. The Chairman and the vice-chairman are determined by the parties to the venture or elected by the board of directors. Either party of the Chinese-foreign joint venturers may be the chairman and the other shall assume the office of vice-chairman. In handling major problems, the board of directors shall reach a decision through consultation by the parties to the venture, in accordance with the principle of equality and mutual benefit.

The board of directors is empowered, pursuant to the provisions of the articles of association of the joint venture, to discuss and decide all major problems of the venture: expansion programmes, proposals for production and operating activities, the budget for revenues and expenditures, distribution of profits, plans concerning manpower and pay scales, the termination of business and the appointment or employment of the president, the vice-president(s), the chief engineer, the treasurer and the auditors, as well as their powers and terms of employment, etc.

The offices of president and vice-president(s) (or factory manager) and deputy manager(s) shall be assumed by the respective parties to the venture.

Contracts shall be entered into in accordance with the law to prescribe the recruitment, dismissal, remuneration, welfare, labor protection, labor insurance, etc.

Article 7 The staff employees of the joint venture may establish trade unions in accordance with the law, carry out the activities of the trade union and defend the lawful rights and interests of the employees.

Joint ventures shall provide necessary conditions for the activities of the trade unions thereof.

Article 8 After payment, pursuant to the provisions of the tax laws of the People's Republic of China, of the joint venture income tax on the gross profit earned by the joint venture and after deduction from the gross profit of a reserve fund, a bonus and welfare fund for staff and workers, and a venture expansion fund, as provided in the articles of association of the joint venture, the net profit shall be distributed to the parties to the joint venture in proportion to their respective contributions to the registered capital.

A joint venture may enjoy the preferential treatment of reduction of or exemption from tax pursuant to relevant state taxation laws or administrative decrees.

A foreign joint venturer that reinvests in China its share of the net profit may apply for refund of a part of the income taxes already paid.

Article 9 A joint venture shall, with its business licence, open a foreign exchange account at the banks or other financial organizations approved by the state foreign exchange control administrative organs to handle foreign exchange business.

The pertinent foreign exchange transactions of a joint venture shall be conducted in accordance with the regulations on foreign exchange control of the People's Republic of China. In its operating activities a joint venture may directly raise funds from foreign banks.

All insurances of joint ventures shall be procured at the insurance corporations within the territory of the People's Republic of China.

Article 10 The Joint venture may purchase the materials such as raw materials, fuels, etc. as needed within the approved scope of business either on the domestic or international market according to the principle of fairness and reasonableness.

A joint venture is encouraged to market its products outside China. Export products may be distributed to foreign markets through the joint venture directly or through associated agencies, and they may also be distributed through China's foreign trade agencies. Products of the joint venture may also be distributed in the Chinese market.

Whenever necessary, a joint venture may establish branches outside China.

Article 11 The net profit that a foreign joint venturer receives after fulfilling its obligations under the laws and the agreement and the contract, the funds it receives at the time of the joint venture's scheduled expiration or early termination, and its other funds may be remitted abroad in accordance with the foreign exchange regulations and in the currency specified in the joint venture contract.

A foreign joint venturer shall be encouraged to deposit in the Bank of China foreign exchange that it is entitled to remit abroad.

Article 12 The wages, salaries and other legitimate income earned by the foreign staff and workers of a joint venture, after payment of the individual income tax under the tax laws of the People's Republic of China, may be remitted abroad in accordance with the foreign exchange regulations.

Article 13 The contract period of a joint venture may be decided differently according to its particular line of business and circumstance. The joint ventures of some trades should decide the contract period; and other may or may not decide the contract period. A joint venture that has set a contract period should, if the parties to the joint venture agree to extend the contract period, apply to the approval authorities six months ahead of the expiration of the contract period. The latter should make the decision of approval or disapproval within one month as of the date of application.

Article 14 In case of heavy losses, failure of a party to fulfil the obligations prescribed by the contract and the articles of association, force majeure, etc., the contract may be terminated through consultation and agreement by the parties to the venture, subject to approval by the approval authorities and to registration with the state competent authorities of administration for industry and commerce. In cases of losses caused by a breach of contract, the financial responsibility shall be borne by the party that has violated the contract.

Article 15 Where a joint venture does not involve the implementation of special administrative measures for the entry into the country according to the provisions of the State, it shall apply the filing management to the examination and approval items stipulated in Articles 3, 13 and 14 of this Law. The special administrative measures for the admission as prescribed by the state shall be promulgated or approved by the State Council for publication.

Article 16 Disputes arising between the parties to a joint venture that the board of directors cannot settle through consultation may be settled through mediation or arbitration by a Chinese arbitration agency or through arbitration by another arbitration agency agreed upon by the parties to the venture.

Where no arbitration clauses have been included in the joint venture contract or no written arbitration agreement have been reached after a dispute arises, any party may bring a suit with the people's court.

Article 17 This Law shall come into force on the date of its promulgation.

The Law of the People's Republic of China on Sino-foreign Contractual Joint Ventures (2017 Amendment)

Article 1 This Law is formulated to expand economic cooperation and technological exchange with foreign countries and to promote the joint establishment, on the principles of equality and mutual benefit, by foreign enterprises and other economic organizations or individuals (hereinafter referred to as the foreign party) and Chinese enterprises or other economic organizations (hereinafter referred to as the Chinese party) of Chinese-Foreign Contractual Joint Ventures (hereinafter referred to as contractual joint ventures) within the territory of the People's Republic of China.

Article 2 In establishing a contractual joint venture, the Chinese and foreign parties shall, in accordance with the provisions of this Law, prescribe in their contractual joint venture contract such matters as the investment or conditions for cooperation, the distribution of earnings or products, the sharing of risks and losses, the manners of operation and management and the ownership of the property at the time of the termination of the contractual joint venture.

A contractual joint venture, which meets the conditions for being considered a legal person under Chinese law, shall acquire the status of a Chinese legal person in accordance with law.

Article 3 The State shall, according to law, protect the lawful rights and interests of the contractual joint ventures and of the Chinese and foreign parties.

A contractual joint venture shall abide by Chinese laws and regulations and may not injure the public interests of China.

The relevant State authority shall exercise supervision over the contractual joint ventures according to law.

Article 4 The State shall encourage the establishment of productive contractual joint ventures that are export-oriented or technologically advanced.

Article 5 For the purpose of applying for the establishment of a contractual joint venture, such documents as the agreement, the contract and the articles of association signed by the Chinese and foreign parties shall be submitted for examination and approval to the department in charge of foreign economic relations and trade under the State Council or to the department or Local government authorized by the State Council (hereinafter referred to as the examination and approval authority). The examination and approval authority shall, within 45 days from the date of receiving the application, decide whether or not to grant approval.

Article 6 When the application for the establishment of a contractual joint venture is approved, the parties shall, within 30 days from the date of receiving the certificate of approval, apply to the administrative department for industry and commerce for registration in order to obtain a business license. The date of issue of the business license of contractual joint venture shall be the date of its establishment.

A contractual joint venture shall, within 30 days of its establishment, carry out tax registration with the tax authorities.

Article 7 If the Chinese and foreign parties, during the period of operation of their contractual joint venture, agree through consultation to make major modifications to the contractual joint venture contract, they shall report to the examination and approval authority for approval; if the modifications include items involving statutory industry and commerce registration or tax registration, they shall register the modifications with the administrative department for industry and commerce and with the tax authorities.

Article 8 The investment or conditions for cooperation contributed by the Chinese and foreign parties may be provided in cash or in kind, or may include the right to the use of land, industrial property rights, non-patent technology or other property rights.

Article 9 The Chinese and foreign parties shall, in accordance with the provisions of the laws and regulations and the agreements in the contractual joint venture contract, duly fulfill their obligations of contributing full investment and providing the conditions for cooperation. In case of failure to do so within the prescribed time, the administrative department for industry and commerce shall set another time limit for the fulfillment of such obligations; if such obligations are still not fulfilled by the new time limit, the matter shall be handled by the examination and approval authority and the administrative department for industry and commerce according to relevant State regulations.

The investments or conditions for cooperation provided by the Chinese and foreign parties shall be verified by an accountant registered in China or the relevant authorities, who shall provide a certificate after verification.

Article 10 If a Chinese or foreign party wishes to make an assignment of all or part of its rights and obligations prescribed in the contractual joint venture contract, it shall be subject to consent of the other party or parties and report to the examination and approval authority for approval.

Article 11 A contractual joint venture shall conduct its operational and managerial activities in accordance with the approved contract and articles of association for the contractual joint venture. The right of a contractual joint venture to make its own operational and managerial decisions shall not be free from any interference.

Article 12 A contractual joint venture shall establish a board of directors or a joint managerial institution, which shall, according to the contract or the articles of association for the contractual joint venture, decide on the major issues concerning the venture. If the Chinese or foreign party assumes the chairmanship of the board of directors or the directorship of the joint managerial institution, the other party shall assume the vice-chairmanship of the board or the deputy directorship of the joint managerial institution. The board of directors or the joint managerial institution may decide on the appointment or employment of a general manager, who shall take charge of the daily operation and management of the contractual joint venture. The general manager shall be accountable to the board of directors or the joint managerial institution.

If a contractual joint venture, after its establishment, chooses to entrust a third party with its operation and management, it shall be subject to the unanimous consent of the board of directors or the joint managerial institution, and register the change with the administrative department for industry and commerce.

Article 13 The employment, dismissal, remuneration, welfare benefits, occupational protection, labour insurance, etc. of the staff members and workers of a contractual joint venture shall be specified in contracts concluded in accordance with law.

Article 14 The staff and workers of a contractual joint venture shall, in accordance with law, establish their trade union organization to carry out trade union activities and protect their lawful rights and interests.

A contractual joint venture shall provide the necessary conditions for the venture's trade union to carry out its activities.

Article 15 A contractual joint venture shall establish its account books within the territory of China, file its accounting statements according to relevant regulations and accept supervision by the financial and tax authorities.

If a contractual joint venture, in violation of the provisions prescribed in the preceding paragraph, does not establish its account books within the territory of China, the financial and tax authorities may impose a fine on it, and the administrative department for industry and commerce may order it to suspend its business operation or may revoke its business license.

Article 16 A contractual joint venture shall, by presenting its business license, open a foreign exchange account with a bank or any other financial institution, which is permitted by the exchange control authorities of the State to conduct transactions in foreign exchange.

A contractual joint venture shall handle its foreign exchange transactions in accordance with the State regulations on foreign exchange control.

Article 17 A contractual joint venture may obtain loans from financial institutions within the territory of China and may also obtain loans outside the territory of China.

Loans to be used by the Chinese and foreign parties as investment or conditions for cooperation, and their guarantees shall be provided by each party on its own.

Article 18 The various kinds of insurance coverage of a contractual joint venture shall be furnished by insurance institutions within the territory of China.

Article 19 A contractual joint venture may, within its scope of operation approved, import materials it needs and export products it produces. A contractual joint venture may, in adherence to the principles of fairness and rationality, purchase on both the Chinese and the world market the raw and semi processed materials, fuels and other materials it needs within the approved scope of operation.

Article 20 A contractual joint venture shall, in accordance with State regulations on tax, pay taxes and may enjoy the preferential treatment of tax reduction or exemption.

Article 21 The Chinese and foreign parties shall share earnings or products, undertake risks and losses in accordance with the agreements prescribed in the contractual joint venture contract.

If, upon the expiration of the period of a venture's operation, all the fixed assets of the contractual joint venture, as agreed upon by the Chinese and foreign parties in the contractual joint venture contract, are to belong to the Chinese party, the Chinese and foreign parties may prescribe in the contractual joint venture contract the ways for the foreign party to recover its investment ahead of time during the period of the venture's operation.

If, according to the provisions of the preceding paragraph, the foreign party is to recover its investment ahead of time during the period of the venture's operation, the Chinese and foreign parties shall, as stipulated by the relevant laws and agreed in the contractual joint venture contract, be liable for the debts of the venture.

Article 22 After the foreign party has fulfilled its obligations under the law and the contractual joint venture contract, the profits it receives as its share, its other legitimate income and the funds it receives as its share upon the termination of the venture, may be remitted abroad according to law.

The wages, salaries or other legitimate income earned by the foreign staff and workers of contractual joint ventures, after the payment of the individual income tax according to law, may be remitted abroad.

Article 23 Upon the expiration or termination in advance of the term of a contractual joint venture, its assets, claims and debts shall be liquidated according to legal procedures. The Chinese and foreign parties shall, in accordance with the agreement specified in the contractual joint venture contract, determine the ownership of the venture's property.

A contractual joint venture shall, upon the expiration or termination in advance of its term, cancel its registration with the administrative department for industry and commerce and the tax authorities.

Article 24 The period of operation of a contractual joint venture shall be determined through consultation by the Chinese and foreign parties and shall be clearly specified in the contractual joint venture contract. If the Chinese and foreign parties agree to extend the period of operation, they shall apply to the examination and approval authority 180 days prior to the expiration of the venture's term. The examination and approval authority shall decide whether or not to grant approval within 30 days from the date of receiving the application.

Article 25 Where a joint venture does not involve the implementation of special administrative measures for the entry into the country according to the provisions of the State, it shall apply the filing management to the examination and approval items stipulated in Articles 3, 13 and 14 of this Law. The special administrative measures for the admission as prescribed by the state shall be promulgated or approved by the State Council for publication.

Article 26 Any dispute between the Chinese and foreign parties arising from the execution of the contract or the articles of association for a contractual joint venture shall be settled through consultation or mediation. In case of a dispute which the Chinese or foreign parties is unwilling to settle through consultation or mediation, or of a dispute which they have failed to settle through consultation or mediation, the Chinese and foreign parties may submit it to a Chinese arbitration agency or any other arbitration agency for arbitration in accordance with the arbitration clause in the contractual joint venture contract or a written agreement on arbitration concluded afterwards.

The Chinese or foreign party may bring a suit in a Chinese court, if no arbitration clause is provided in the contractual joint venture contract and if no written agreement is concluded afterwards.

Article 27 The detailed rules for the implementation of this Law shall be formulated by the department in charge of foreign economic relations and trade under the State Council and reported to the State Council for approval before implementation.

Article 28 This Law shall come into force as of the date of its promulgation.

The Law of the People's Republic of China on Wholly Foreign-Owned Enterprises (2017 Amendment)

Article 1 With a view to expanding economic cooperation and technical exchange with foreign countries and promoting the development of China's national economy, the People's Republic of China permits foreign enterprises, other foreign economic organizations and individuals (hereinafter collectively referred to as "foreign investors") to set up enterprises with foreign capital in China and protects the lawful rights and interests of such enterprises.

Article 2 As mentioned in this Law, "enterprises with foreign capital" refers to those enterprises established in China by foreign investors, exclusively with their own capital, in accordance with relevant Chinese laws. The term does not include branches.

Article 3 The establishment of foreign-funded enterprises must be conducive to the development of China's national economy. The state encourages the export of products or advanced foreign-funded enterprises.

Provisions shall be made by the State Council regarding the lines of business which the state forbids enterprises with foreign capital to engage in or on which it places certain restrictions.

Article 4 The investments of a foreign investor in China, the profits it earns and its other lawful rights and interests are protected by Chinese law.

Enterprises with foreign capital must abide by Chinese laws and regulations and must not engage in any activities detrimental to China's public interest.

Article 5 The state shall not nationalize or requisition any enterprise with foreign capital. Under special circumstances, when public interest requires, enterprises with foreign capital may be requisitioned by legal procedures and appropriate compensation shall be made.

Article 6 The application to establish an enterprise with foreign capital shall be submitted for examination and approval to the department under the State Council which is in charge of foreign economic relations and trade, or to another agency authorized by the State Council.

The authorities in charge of examination and approval shall, within 90 days from the date they receive such application, decide whether or not to grant approval.

Article 7 After an application for the establishment of an enterprise with foreign capital has been approved, the foreign investor shall, within 30 days from the date of receiving a certificate of approval, apply to the industry and commerce administration authorities for registration and obtain a business licence.

The date of issue of the business licence shall be the date of the establishment of the enterprise.

Article 8 An enterprise with foreign capital which meets the conditions for being considered a legal person under Chinese law shall acquire the status of a Chinese legal person, in accordance with the law.

Article 9 An enterprise with foreign capital shall make investments in China within the period approved by the authorities in charge of examination and approval. If it fails to do so, the industry and commerce administration authorities may cancel its business license.

The industry and commerce administration authorities shall inspect and supervise the investment situation of an enterprise with foreign capital.

Article 10 In the event of a separation, merger or other major change, an enterprise with foreign capital shall report to and seek approval from the authorities in charge of examination and approval, and register the change with the industry and commerce administration authorities.

Article 11 Enterprises with foreign capital shall conduct their operations and management in accordance with the approved articles of association, and shall be free from any interference.

Article 12 When employing Chinese workers and staff, an enterprise with foreign capital shall conclude contracts with them according to law, in which matters concerning employment, dismissal, remuneration, welfare benefits, labour protection and labour insurance shall be clearly prescribed.

Article 13 Workers and staff of enterprises with foreign capital may organize trade unions in accordance with the law, in order to conduct trade union activities and protect their lawful rights and interests.

The enterprises shall provide the necessary conditions for the activities of the trade unions in their respective enterprises.

Article 14 An enterprise with foreign capital must set up account books in China, conduct independent accounting, submit the fiscal reports and statements as required and accept supervision by the financial and tax authorities.

If an enterprise with foreign capital refuses to maintain account books in China, the financial and tax authorities may impose a fine on it, and the industry and commerce administration authorities may order it to suspend operations or may revoke its business license.

Article 15 The raw materials, fuels and other materials required by a foreign-funded enterprise within the approved business scope can be purchased in the domestic market or in the international market according to the principle of fairness and reasonableness.

Article 16 Enterprises with foreign capital shall apply to insurance corporations in China for such kinds of insurance coverage as are needed.

Article 17 Enterprises with foreign capital shall pay taxes in accordance with relevant state provisions for tax payment, and may enjoy preferential treatment for reduction of or exemption from taxes.

An enterprise that reinvests its profits in China after paying the income tax, may, in accordance with relevant state provisions, apply for refund of a part of the income tax already paid on the reinvested amount.

Article 18 Enterprises with foreign capital shall handle their foreign exchange transactions in accordance with the state provisions for foreign exchange control.

Enterprises with foreign capital shall open an account with the Bank of China or with a bank designated by the state agency exercising foreign exchange control.

Article 19 The foreign investor may remit abroad profits that are lawfully earned from an enterprise with foreign capital, as well as other lawful earnings and any funds remaining after the enterprise is liquidated.

Wages, salaries and other legitimate income earned by foreign employees in an enterprise with foreign capital may be remitted abroad after the payment of individual income tax in accordance with the law.

Article 20 With respect to the period of operations of an enterprise with foreign capital, the foreign investor shall report to and secure approval from the authorities in charge of examination and approval.

For an extension of the period of operations, an application shall be submitted to the said authorities 180 days before the expiration of the period.

The authorities in charge of examination and approval shall, within 30 days from the date such application is received, decide whether or not to grant the extension.

Article 21 When terminating its operations, an enterprise with foreign capital shall promptly issue a public notice and proceed with liquidation in accordance with legal procedure.

Pending the completion of liquidation, a foreign investor may not dispose of the assets of the enterprise except for the purpose of liquidation.

Article 22 At the termination of operations, the enterprise with foreign capital shall nullify its registration with the industry and commerce administration authorities and hand in its business licence for cancellation.

Article 23 Where a foreign-funded enterprise does not engage in any special administrative measures for the entry into or exercise of the state's provisions, it shall apply the record-keeping management to the examination and approval items stipulated in Articles 6, 10 and 20 of this Law. The special administrative measures for the admission as prescribed by the state shall be promulgated or approved by the State Council for publication.

Article 24 The department under the State Council which is in charge of foreign economic relations and trade shall, in accordance with this Law, formulate rules for its implementation, which shall go into effect after being submitted to and approved by the State Council.

Article 25 This Law shall go into effect on the day of its promulgation.

Interim Measures for the Recordation Administration of the Formation and Modification of Foreign-Funded Enterprises [Revised]

Order of the Ministry of Commerce, (No. 3 [2016])

Chapter I General Provisions

Article 1 For the purposes of further expanding opening up, promoting the reform of the foreign investment management system, and improving the lawful, international, and convenient business environment, these Measures are developed in accordance with the Law of the People's Republic of China on Chinese-Foreign Equity Joint Ventures, the Law of the People's Republic of China on Chinese-Foreign Contractual Joint Ventures, the Law of the People's Republic of China on Wholly Foreign-Owned Enterprises, the Company Law of the People's Republic of China, relevant laws and administrative regulations, and the decision of the State Council.

Article 2 These Measures shall apply to the formation and modification of foreign-funded enterprises that do not involve the implementation of special administrative measures for access as prescribed by the state.

Article 3 The competent department of commerce under the State Council shall be responsible for coordinating and directing the recordation administration of the formation and modification of foreign-funded enterprises nationwide.

The competent departments of commerce of all provinces, autonomous regions, municipalities directly under the Central Government, cities under separate state planning, the Xinjiang Production and Construction Corps, and sub-provincial cities, and relevant institutions in the pilot free trade zones and the state-level economic and technological development zones, as the recordation authorities for the formation and modification of foreign-funded enterprises, shall be responsible for the recordation administration of the formation and modification of foreign-funded enterprises within their jurisdictions.

A recordation authority shall carry out the work of recordation through the integrated foreign investment management information system (hereinafter referred to as the "integrated management system").

Article 4 Foreign-funded enterprises or their investors shall, in accordance with these Measures, truthfully, accurately and completely provide the recordation information, and fill out the letter of undertaking for recordation application, without any false record, misleading statement or material omission. Foreign-funded enterprises or their investors shall appropriately keep the certification materials relevant to the recordation information submitted.

Chapter II Recordation Procedures

Article 5 For the formation of a foreign-funded enterprise which is subject to recordation as prescribed in these Measures, after obtainment of pre-approval of the enterprise name, the representative designated by or the agent jointly entrusted by all investors (or all promoters in the case of a foreign-funded joint stock company, hereinafter referred to as "all promoters") shall, before the issuance of the business license, or the representative designated by or the agent entrusted by the foreign-funded enterprise shall, within 30 days after the issuance of the business license, fill out and submit online the Application Form for the Recordation of the Formation of Foreign-Funded Enterprises (hereinafter referred to as the "Application Form for Formation") and relevant documents through the integrated management system, and undergo the recordation formalities for formation.

Article 6 Where a foreign-funded enterprise which is subject to recordation as prescribed in these Measures undergoes any of the following modifications, the representative designated by or the agent entrusted by the foreign-funded enterprise shall, within 30 days after the occurrence of the modification, fill out and submit online the Application Form for the Recordation of Modification of Foreign-Funded Enterprises (hereinafter referred to as the "Application Form for Modification") and relevant documents through the integrated management system, and undergo the recordation formalities for modification.

(1) Modification of the basic information of the foreign-funded enterprise, including the name, registered address, type of enterprise, business period, investment industry, business type, scope of business, whether it falls within the scope of tax reduction or exemption for imported equipment as prescribed by the state, registered capital, total investment, organizational structure, legal representative, and information, contact person, and contact way of the ultimate actual controller of the foreign-funded enterprise.
(2) Modification of the basic information of any investors of the foreign-funded enterprise, including name, nationality / region or address (place of registration or registered address), type and number of certificate, amount of capital contribution subscribed, way of investment, duration of capital contribution, source of capital, and investor type.
(3) Modification of the equity (shares) and cooperation interests.
(4) Merger, division and termination.
(5) Mortgage or transfer of the property or rights and interests of the wholly foreign-owned enterprise.
(6) Advanced recovery of investment by the foreign party to a Chinese-foreign contractual joint venture.
(7) Entrusted business management of a Chinese-foreign contractual joint venture.

Where merger, division, capital reduction and other matters shall be announced in accordance with relevant laws and regulations, the information on undergoing the formalities of announcement shall be given when undergoing the formalities of modification recordation.

Where any of the aforesaid modifications involves a resolution of the highest authority, the time when the highest authority of the foreign-funded enterprise makes the resolution shall be taken as the time of occurrence of the modification; and where it is otherwise prescribed in the laws and regulations with respect to the conditions for the entry into force of any modification of a foreign-funded enterprise, the time when the corresponding requirements are met shall be the time of occurrence of the modification.

A listed foreign-funded company and a company quoted in the National Equities Exchange and Quotations may, when the change of foreign investors' shareholding ratio accumulatively exceeds 5% and the controlling or relatively controlling status changes, undergo the formalities for recordation of the modification of investors' basic information or share change.

Article 7 To undergo the formalities for the recordation of formation or modification of a foreign-funded enterprise, the foreign-funded enterprise or its investors shall, through the integrated management system, upload and submit the following documents:

(1) The materials on the pre-approval of the name of the foreign-funded enterprise or the business license of the foreign-funded enterprise.
(2) The Letter of Undertaking for the Application for Recordation of the Formation of Foreign-Funded Enterprises signed by all investors (or all promoters) of the foreign-funded enterprise or their authorized representative or the Letter of Undertaking for the Application for Recordation of the Modification of Foreign-Funded Enterprises signed by the legal representative of the foreign-funded enterprise or the representative authorized by him or her.
(3) The certifications on the issue that all investors (or all promoters) or the foreign-funded enterprise designate representative or jointly entrust agent, including the power of attorney and the identity certificate of the entrusted person.
(4) The certifications on the issue that the investor or legal representative of the foreign-funded enterprise authorizes any other person to sign relevant documents, including the power of attorney and the identity certificate of the authorized person (not required, if the investor or legal representative of the foreign-funded enterprise does not authorize any other person to sign relevant documents).
(5) The certifications on eligibility status or natural person identity certificates of investors (not required, if the modification does not involve the modification of investors' basic information).

(6) The natural person identity certificate of the legal representative (not required, if the modification does not involve the modification of the legal representative).

Where any of the aforesaid documents is in foreign language, a Chinese translation shall also be uploaded and submitted at the same time. The foreign-funded enterprise or its investors shall ensure that the content of the Chinese translation is consistent with that of the original document in foreign language.

Article 8 Where the investors of a foreign-funded enterprise have submitted the recordation information prior to the issuance of the business license and the actual situation of the investment undergoes any change, they shall, within 30 days after the issuance of the business license, undergo the formalities for modification recordation with the recordation authority with respect to the change.

Article 9 Where a foreign-funded enterprise formed upon approval undergoes any modification and the foreign-funded enterprise after modification does not involve the implementation of special administrative measures for access as prescribed by the state, recordation formalities shall be undergone; and where recordation is completed, its Approval Certificate for a Foreign-Funded Enterprise shall concurrently become invalid.

Article 10 Where any modification of a foreign-funded enterprise subject to recordation administration involves the implementation of special administrative measures for access as prescribed by the state, the approval formalities shall be undergone under relevant laws and regulations on foreign investment.

Article 11 After a foreign-funded enterprise or its investors submit the Application Form for Formation or the Application Form for Modification and relevant documents online, the recordation authority shall check the completeness and accuracy of the form of the information submitted, and whether the matter under application falls within the scope of recordation. Where the matter falls within the scope of recordation as prescribed by these Measures, the recordation authority shall, within three working days, complete the recordation. Where the matter falls outside the scope of recordation, the recordation authority shall, within three working days, notify the foreign-funded enterprise or its investors online to undergo relevant formalities in accordance with relevant provisions and notify relevant departments to handle the matter according to the law.

Where the recordation authority finds that the information submitted by the foreign-funded enterprise or its investors is incomplete or inaccurate in form or the foreign-funded enterprise's business scope needs to be further explained, the recordation authority shall, within 15 working days, notify the foreign-funded enterprise online at one time to submit relevant supplementary information online. The time for submitting supplementary information shall not be included in the time limit for recordation. Where the foreign-funded enterprise or its investors fail to supplement relevant information within 15 working days, the recordation authority will notify the foreign-funded enterprise or its investors online of failure to complete recordation. The foreign-funded enterprise or its investors may file another application for recordation for the same formation or modification matter, and where the formation or modification matter has been carried out, an application shall be separately filed within five working days.

A recordation authority shall issue the recordation results through the integrated management system and a foreign-funded enterprise or its investors may inquire about the recordation results in the integrated management system.

Article 12 After the completion of recordation, a foreign-funded enterprise or its investors may, upon strength of the materials (photocopy) on pre-approval of the name of the foreign-funded enterprise or its business license (photocopy), obtain a Recordation Receipt for the Formation of a Foreign-Funded Enterprise or a Recordation Receipt for the Modification of a Foreign-Funded Enterprise (hereinafter referred to as the "Recordation Receipt") from the recordation authority.

Article 13 A Recordation Receipt issued by a recordation authority shall specify the following contents:

(1) The foreign-funded enterprise or its investors have submitted application materials for recordation of formation or modification and these materials comply with the formal requirements.
(2) The formation or modification matter of the foreign-funded enterprise that undergoes the recordation formalities shall be specified.
(3) The formation or modification of the foreign-funded enterprise falls within the recordation scope.
(4) Whether it falls within the scope of tax reduction or exemption for imported equipment as prescribed by the state.

Chapter III Supervision and Administration

Article 14 Competent departments of commerce shall supervise and inspect the compliance with these Measures by foreign-funded enterprises and their investors.

Competent departments of commerce may conduct supervision and inspection by random inspection, inspection according to tip-offs, inspection according to the suggestions of or information provided by relevant departments or the judicial organs, launching inspection ex officio, and other methods.

Competent departments of commerce shall closely cooperate with public security, state-owned assets, customs, taxation, industry and commerce, securities, foreign exchange and other relevant administrative departments and strengthen information sharing. A competent department of commerce shall, when finding during the process of supervision and inspection that a foreign-funded enterprise or its investors have any violation of any law or regulation beyond its management responsibility, notify relevant department in a timely manner.

Article 15 Competent departments of commerce shall, according to the requirements of fairness and standardization, the recordation number of foreign-funded enterprises, and other information, randomly select and determine inspection objects, and randomly appoint inspectors to conduct supervision and inspection of foreign-funded enterprises and their investors. The results of random inspection shall be published by competent departments of commerce through the foreign investment information publication platform of the Ministry of Commerce.

Article 16 A citizen, a legal person, or any other organization finding that a foreign-funded enterprise or its investors have any acts in violation of these Measures may report to the competent department of commerce. Where a report is made in writing against a specific person and relevant facts and evidence are provided, the competent department of commerce shall conduct necessary inspection upon receipt of the report.

Article 17 Other relevant departments or judicial organs finding in the course of performing their duties that foreign-funded enterprises or their investors have any acts in violation of these Measures may offer suggestions of supervision and inspection to the competent departments of commerce, and the competent departments of commerce shall conduct inspection in a timely manner upon receipt of relevant suggestions.

Article 18 Where a foreign-funded enterprise or its investors fail to undergo recordation formalities under the provisions of these Measures or have records of false recordation, refusal to cooperate with supervision and inspection, and refusal to implement the decision of administrative penalty made by a competent department of commerce, the competent department of commerce may, according to its powers, conduct inspection thereof.

Article 19 The supervision and inspection conducted by a competent department of commerce on a foreign-funded enterprise and its investors shall cover:

(1) whether the recordation formalities are undergone under the provisions of these Measures;
(2) whether the recordation information submitted by the foreign-funded enterprise or its investors is true, accurate and complete;
(3) whether investment and management activities are carried out in the prohibited investment areas as listed in the special administrative measures for access as prescribed by the state;
(4) whether investment and management activities are carried out in the restricted investment areas as listed in the special administrative measures for access as prescribed by the state without approval;
(5) whether there is circumstance that triggers a national security review;
(6) whether a Recordation Receipt is forged, altered, leased, lent, or transferred; and
(7) whether a decision of administrative penalty made by the competent department of commerce is implemented.

Article 20 In the course of inspection, a competent department of commerce may consult or require the inspected party to provide relevant materials according to the law, and the inspected party shall truthfully provide the materials.

Article 21 When implementing inspection, a competent department of commerce shall not hinder the normal production or business activities of the inspected party, or accept any property or services provided by the inspected party, or seek other illegal interests.

Article 22 Information on the credit of foreign-funded enterprises or their investors obtained by competent departments of commerce or other competent departments in supervision and inspection shall be recorded in the foreign investment credit file system of the Ministry of Commerce. Where a foreign-funded enterprise or its investors fail to undergo the recordation formalities under the provisions of these Measures, involve false recordation, forge, alter, lease, lend, or transfer the Recordation Receipt, refuse to cooperate with the supervision and inspection or refuse to implement a decision of administrative penalty made by a competent department of commerce, the competent department of commerce shall publish relevant credit information through the foreign investment information publication platform of the Ministry of Commerce.

The Ministry of Commerce shall share the credit information of foreign-funded enterprises and their investors with relevant departments.

The credit information published or shared by a competent department of commerce according to the preceding two paragraphs shall not contain any personal privacy, or trade secrets of a foreign-funded enterprise or its investors, or any state secrets.

Article 23 A foreign-funded enterprise and its investors may consult their own credit information in the foreign investment credit file system of the Ministry of Commerce, and may provide relevant supporting materials and apply to the competent department of commerce for correction if they believe that relevant information records are incomplete or inaccurate. If verified to be true, correction shall be made.

As to any records of dishonesty generated from the violation of these Measures, where the foreign-funded enterprise or its investors no longer have any acts in violation of these Measures within three years after correcting the violations and performing the obligations, the competent department of commerce shall remove the record of dishonesty.

Chapter IV Legal Liability

Article 24 A foreign-funded enterprise or its investors that, in violation of the provisions of these Measures, fail to perform the obligations of recordation within the prescribed time limit, or have any material omission in the course of recordation shall be ordered to take corrective action within a prescribed time limit by the competent department of commerce; and where they fail to take corrective action within the prescribed time limit or the circumstances are serious, a fine of not more than 30,000 yuan shall be imposed.

A foreign-funded enterprise or its investors that, in violation of the provisions of these Measures, evade the obligations of recordation, conceal the true situation when undergoing the recordation formalities, provide misleading or false information, or forge, alter, lease, lend, or transfer the Recordation Receipt shall be ordered to take corrective action within a prescribed time limit and be fined not more than 30,000 yuan by a competent department of commerce. Those who violate other laws and regulations shall be held liable by relevant departments.

Article 25 A foreign-funded enterprise or its investors that carry out investment and management activities in the restricted investment fields as listed in the special administrative measures for access as prescribed by the state without approval shall be ordered to take corrective action within a prescribed time limit and be fined not more than 30,000 yuan by the competent department of commerce. Those who violate other laws and regulations shall be held liable by relevant departments.

Article 26 A foreign-funded enterprise or its investors that carry out investment and management activities in the prohibited investment fields as listed in the special administrative measures for access as prescribed by the state shall be ordered to take corrective action within a prescribed time limit and be fined not more than 30,000 yuan by the competent department of commerce. Those who violate other laws and regulations shall be held liable by relevant departments.

Article 27 A foreign-funded enterprise or its investors that evade, refuse or otherwise obstruct the supervision and inspection of the competent department of commerce shall be ordered to take corrective action and may be fined not more than 10,000 yuan by the competent department of commerce.

Article 28 Relevant staff members that abuse powers, neglect duties, practice favoritism or make falsification, or seek or accept bribes in the course of recordation or supervision and administration shall be given administrative sanctions according to the law; and where a crime is constituted, relevant staff members shall be held criminally liable in accordance with the law.

Chapter V Supplementary Provisions

Article 29 Where the formation or modification matter of a foreign-funded enterprise accepted by the competent department of commerce prior to the entry into force of these Measures has not been approved and falls within the scope of recordation, the approval procedures shall be terminated and the foreign-funded enterprise or its investors shall undergo the recordation formalities under these Measures.

Article 30 Foreign investment matters involving anti-monopoly review shall be handled in accordance with the relevant provisions.

Article 31 Foreign investment matters involving national security review shall be handled in accordance with the relevant provisions. Where a recordation authority deems that a foreign investment matter may fall within the scope of national security review when handling the formalities of recordation or conducting supervision and inspection and the investors of the foreign-funded enterprise fail to file an application to the Ministry of Commerce for national security review, the recordation authority shall notify the investors to file an application to the Ministry of Commerce for national security review in a timely manner, temporarily suspend the handling of relevant formalities, and concurrently report relevant information to the Ministry of Commerce.

Article 32 Foreign-funded enterprises of investment type (including investment companies and venture capital enterprises) shall be deemed as foreign investors, and be governed by these Measures.

Article 33 These Measures shall apply, mutatis mutandis, to investment made by investors in the Hong Kong Special Administrative Region, the Macao Special Administrative Region or the Taiwan Region that does not involve the implementation of the special administrative measures for access as prescribed by the state.

Article 34 Where Hong Kong service suppliers invest only in the service trade areas in the mainland which are open to Hong Kong as prescribed in the Agreement on Trade in Services to the Mainland and Hong Kong Closer Economic Partnership Arrangement, and Macao service suppliers invest only in the service trade areas in the mainland which are open to Macao as prescribed in the Agreement on Trade in Services to the Mainland and Macao Closer Economic Partnership Arrangement, the recordation of their formation and modification shall be governed by the Measures for the Administration of Recordation of Investments by Hong Kong and Macao Service Suppliers in the Mainland (for Trial Implementation).

Article 35 In the case of any discrepancy between the departmental rules and relevant documents issued by the Ministry of Commerce before these Measures come into force and these Measures, these Measures shall prevail.

Article 37 These Measures shall come into force on the date of issuance. The Measures for the Recordation Administration of Foreign Investment in Pilot Free Trade Zones (for Trial Implementation, Announcement No. 12 [2015], MOC) shall be concurrently repealed.

Decision of the Ministry of Commerce to Amend the Interim Measures for the Recordation Administration of the Formation and Modification of Foreign-Funded Enterprises (2017) [Effective]

Order of the Ministry of Commerce, (No. 2 [2017])

For the purposes of promoting the reform of the foreign investment administrative system and reflecting the reform orientation of simplifying administrative procedures, decentralizing powers, combining decentralization with appropriate control, and optimizing services, recordation administration shall apply to foreign investors' mergers and acquisitions of domestic non-foreign-funded enterprises and strategic investments in listed companies, provided that they do not involve special administrative measures and mergers and acquisitions of affiliates. The Ministry of Commerce hereby decides to amend the Interim Measures for the Recordation Administration of the Formation and Modification of Foreign-Funded Enterprises (Order No. 3 [2016, MOF]) as follows:

I. One paragraph is added in Article 5 as paragraph 2: "Where a non-foreign-funded enterprise changes into a foreign-funded enterprise by acquisition, merger, or any other means, falling within the scope of recordation as prescribed in these Measures, it shall, in accordance with the preceding paragraph, undergo the formation recordation formalities, and complete and submit the Formation Application Form."

II. One item is added to paragraph 1 of Article 6 as item (3): "Modification of the basic information on transactions for the formation of the foreign-funded enterprise by acquisition or merger."

III. One article is added as Article 7: "Where a foreign investor makes strategic investment in a non-foreign-funded listed company, falling within the scope of recordation as prescribed in these Measures, it shall, before or within 30 days after securities registration with the securities depository and clearing institution, undergo the recordation formalities, and complete and submit the Formation Application Form.

"Where a foreign-funded listed company introduces any new strategic investment from a foreign investor, falling within the scope of recordation, it shall, before or within 30 days after securities registration with the securities depository and clearing institution, undergo the modification recordation formalities, and complete and submit the Modification Application Form.

"Where, after the completion of recordation, any recorded information on strategic investment changes, the modification recordation formalities shall be undergone within five days of the information disclosure obligator's fulfillment of its information disclosure obligation as required by the securities law and relevant provisions."

IV. One item is added to paragraph 1 of Article 7 as item (7): "The equity structure chart of the final actual controller of the foreign-funded enterprise (not required if the modification does not involve the modification of the final actual controller of the foreign-funded enterprise)," and the material required in this item is added to the "Materials Submitted Online" in the Annexes.

V. One item is added to paragraph 1 of Article 7 as item (8): "In the case of payment by a foreign investor with equities of an overseas company, the Certificate of Outbound Investment by an Enterprise held by the domestic enterprise which obtains the equities of the overseas company, and the material required in this item is added to the "Materials Submitted Online" in the Annexes.

VI. In Annex 1, "Application Form for the Formation Recordation of a Foreign-Funded Enterprise" in the "Application Materials for the Formation Recordation of a Foreign-Funded Enterprise" is deleted, and in Annex 2, "Application Form for the Modification Recordation of a Foreign-Funded Enterprise" in the "Application Materials for the Modification Recordation of a Foreign-Funded Enterprise" is deleted.

In addition, the numbering of relevant clauses shall be adjusted accordingly.

Appendix III: The Securities Law of the People's Republic of China (2014 Amendment)

Chapter I General Provisions

Article 1 The present Law is formulated in order to standardize the issuance and trading of securities, protect the legitimate rights and interests of investors, safeguard the economic order and public interests of the society and promote the development of the socialist market economy.

Article 2 The present Law shall apply to the issuance and trading of stocks, corporate bonds as well as any other securities as lawfully recognized by the State Council within the territory of the People's Republic of China. Where there is no such provision in the present Law, the provisions of the Corporation Law of the People's Republic of China and other relevant laws and administrative regulations shall apply.

Any listed trading of government bonds and share of securities investment funds shall be governed by the present Law. In case there is any special provision in any other law or administrative Regulation, such special provision shall prevail.

The measures for the administration of issuance and trading of securities derivatives shall be prescribed by the State Council according to the principles of the Present Law.

Article 3 The issuance and trading of securities shall be carried out according to the principles of openness, fairness and impartiality.

Article 4 The parties involved in any issuance or transaction of securities shall have equal legal status and shall uphold the principles of free will, compensation, and uprightness and creditworthiness.

D. Yu, *Chinese Business Law*, The Palgrave Series on Chinese Law,
https://doi.org/10.1007/978-981-13-0902-1

Article 5 The issuance and trading of securities shall abide by laws and administrative regulations. Any fraud, insider trading or manipulation of the securities market shall be prohibited.

Article 6 The divided operation and management shall be applied to the industries of securities, banking, trust and insurance. The securities companies and the business organs of banks, trust, and insurance shall be separately established, unless it is otherwise provided for by the state.

Article 7 The securities regulatory authority under the State Council shall carry out centralized and unified supervision and administration of the national securities market.

The securities regulatory authority under the State Council may, according to the relevant requirements, establish dispatched offices, which shall perform their duties and functions of supervision and administration according to their authorization.

Article 8 Under the centralized and unified supervision and administration of the state regarding the issuance and trading of securities, a securities industrial association shall be established according to law, which shall adopt the self-regulating administration.

Article 9 The auditing organs of the state shall carry out auditing supervision of the securities exchanges, securities companies, securities registration and clearing institutions, and securities regulatory bodies.

Chapter II Issuance of Securities

Article 10 A public issuance of securities shall meet the requirements of the relevant laws and administrative regulations, and shall be reported to the securities regulatory authority under the State Council or any department as authorized by the State Council for examination and approval according to law. Without any examination and approval according to law, no entity or individual may make a public issuance of any securities.

It shall be deemed as a public issuance under any of the following circumstances:

(1) Making a public issuance of securities towards unspecified objects;
(2) Making a public issuance of securities to accumulatively more than 200 specified objects;
(3) Making a public issuance as prescribed by any law or administrative regulation.

For any securities that are not issued in a public manner, the means of advertising, public inducement or public issuance in any disguised form shall not be adopted thereto.

Article 11 An issuer that applies for the public issuance of stocks or convertible corporate bonds by means of underwriting according to law or for the public issuance of any other securities, which is subject to recommendation as is prescribed by any law or administrative regulation, shall hire an institution with the qualification of recommendation as its recommender.

A recommender shall observe the operational rules and industrial norms and, based on the principles of being honesty, creditworthy, diligent and accountable, carry out a prudent examination of the application documents and information disclosure materials of its issuers as well as supervise and urge its issuers to operate in a regulative manner.

The qualification requirements of the recommender as well as the relevant measures for administration shall be formulated by the securities regulatory authority under the State Council.

Article 12 A public offer of stocks for establishing a joint stock limited company shall meet the requirements as prescribed in the Corporation Law of the People's Republic of China as well as any other requirements as prescribed by the securities regulatory authority under the State Council which have been approved by the State Council. An application for public offer of stocks as well as the following documents shall be reported to the securities regulatory authority under the State Council:

(1) The constitution of the company;
(2) The promoter's agreement;
(3) The name or title of the promoter, the amount of shares as subscribed to by the promoters, the category of contributed capital as well as the capital verification certification;
(4) The prospectus;
(5) The name and address of the bank that receives the funds as generated from the issuance of stocks on the behalf of the company; and
(6) The name of the underwriting organization as well as the relevant agreements.

Where a recommender shall be hired, as is prescribed by the present Law, a Recommendation Letter of Issuance as produced by the recommender shall be submitted as well.

Where the establishment of a company shall be reported for approval, as is prescribed by any law or administrative regulation, the relevant approval documents shall be submitted as well.

Article 13 An initial public offer (IPO) of stocks of a company shall meet the following requirements:

(1) Having a complete and well-operated organization;
(2) Having the capability of making profits continuously and a sound financial status;
(3) Having no false record in its financial statements over the latest 3 years and having no other major irregularity; and
(4) Meeting any other requirements as prescribed by the securities regulatory authority under the State Council which have been approved by the State Council.

A listed company that makes any initial non-public offer of stocks shall meet the requirements as prescribed by the securities regulatory authority under the State Council, which have been approved by the State Council and shall be reported to the securities regulatory authority under the State Council for examination and approval.

Article 14 A company that makes an IPO of stocks shall file an application for public offer of stocks and submit the following documents to the securities regulatory authority under the State Council:

(1) The business license of the company;
(2) The constitution of the company;
(3) The resolution of the general assembly of shareholders;
(4) The prospectus;
(5) The financial statements;
(6) The name and address of the bank that receives the funds as generated from the public offer of stocks on the behalf of the company; and
(7) The name of the underwriting institution as well as the relevant agreements.

Where a recommender shall be hired, as is prescribed by the present Law, the Recommendation Letter of Issuance as produced by the recommender shall be submitted as well.

Article 15 The funds as raised through public offer of stocks made by a company shall be used according to the purpose as prescribed in the prospectus. Any alteration of the use of funds as prescribed in the prospectus shall be subject to a resolution of the general assembly of shareholders. Where the company fails to correct any unlawful alteration of its use of funds or where any alteration of its use of funds fails to be adopted by the general assembly of shareholders, the relevant company shall not make any IPO of stocks. In the foregoing circumstance, a company shall not make any non-public offer of stocks.

Article 16 A public issuance of corporate bonds shall meet the following requirements:

(1) The net asset of a joint stock limited company is no less than RMB 30 million yuan and the net asset of a limited-liability company is no less than RMB 60 million yuan;
(2) The accumulated bond balance constitutes no more than 40% of the net asset of a company;
(3) The average distributable profits over the latest 3 years are sufficient to pay the 1-year interests of corporate bonds;
(4) The investment of raised funds complies with the industrial policies of the state;
(5) yield rate of bonds does not surpass the level of interest rate as set by the State Council; and
(6) Any other requirements as prescribed by the State Council.

The funds as raised through public issuance of corporate bonds shall be used for the verified purposes and shall not be used for covering any deficit or non-production expenditure.

The public issuance of convertible corporate bonds as made by a listed company shall not only meet the requirements as provided for in paragraph 1 herein but also meet the requirements of the present Law on the public offer of stocks, and shall be reported to the securities regulatory authority under the State Council for examination and approval.

Article 17 As to an application for public issuance of corporate bonds, the following documents shall be reported to the department as authorized by the State Council or the securities regulatory authority under the State Council:

(1) The business license of the company;
(2) The constitution of the company;
(3) The procedures for issuing corporate bonds;

(4) An assent appraisal report and an asset verification report; and
(5) Any other document as prescribed by the department as authorized by the State Council or by the securities regulatory authority under the State Council.

Where a recommender shall be hired, as is prescribed by the present Law, the Recommendation Letter of Issuance as produced by the recommender shall be submitted as well.

Article 18 Under any of the following circumstances, no more public issuance of corporate bonds may be carried out:

(1) Where the corporate bonds as issued in the previous public issuance haven't been fully subscribed;
(2) Where a company has any breach relating to the corporate bonds as publicly issued or any other debts, or has postponed the payment of the relevant principal plus interests, and such situation still exists; or
(3) Where a company violates the present Law by altering the purpose of use of the funds raised through public issuance of corporate bonds.

Article 19 The formats and ways of submitting application documents as reported by an issuer for examination and approval of securities issuance according to law shall be prescribed by the competent organ or department in charge of examination and approval.

Article 20 The application documents for securities issuance as reported by an issuer to the securities regulatory authority under the State Council or the department as authorized by the State Council shall be authentic, accurate and complete.

A securities trading service institution and its staff that produces the relevant documents for securities issuance shall strictly perform its/his statutory functions and duties and guarantee the authenticity, accuracy and integrity of the documents as produced thereby.

Article 21 Where an issuer applies for an IPO of stocks, it shall, after submitting the application documents, disclose the relevant application documents in advance according to the provisions of the securities regulatory authority under the State Council.

Article 22 The securities regulatory authority under the State Council shall establish an issuance examination committee, which shall examine the applications for stock issuance according to law.

The issuance examination committee shall be composed of professionals from the securities regulatory authority under the State Council and other relevant experts from outside the said authority, cast votes to decide on the applications for stock issuance and give its examination opinions.

The specific formulation measures, tenure of members as well as work procedures of the issuance examination committee shall be formulated by the securities regulatory authority under the State Council.

Article 23 The securities regulatory authority under the State Council shall take charge of the examination and approval of the applications for stock issuance according to the statutory requirements. The procedures for examination and approval shall be publicized and shall be subject to supervision according to law.

The personnel participating in the examination and verification of stock issuance shall not have any interest relationship with an issuance applicant, shall not directly or indirectly accept any present of the issuance applicant, not hold any stock as verified for issuance, and shall not have any private contact with an issuance applicant.

The department as authorized by the State Council shall carry out the examination and approval of applications for issuance of corporate bonds by referring to the preceding 2 paragraphs herein.

Article 24 The securities regulatory authority under the State Council or the department as authorized by the State Council shall, within 3 months as of accepting an application for securities issuance, make an decision on approval or disapproval according to the statutory requirements and procedures, but the time for an issuer to supplement or correct its application documents for issuance according to the relevant requirements shall not be calculated in the aforesaid term for examination and approval. In the case of disapproval, an explanation shall be given.

Article 25 Where an application for securities issuance has been approved, the relevant issuer shall, according to the provisions of the relevant laws and administrative regulations, announce the relevant financing documents of public issuance before publicly issuing any securities and shall make the aforesaid documents available for public reference in a designated place.

Before the information of securities issuance is publicized according to law, no insider may publicize or divulge relevant information.

An issuer shall not issue any securities before making an announcement of the relevant financing documents of public issuance.

Article 26 The securities regulatory authority under the State council or the department as authorized by the State Council shall, where finding any decision on approving securities issuance fails to comply with the relevant statutory requirements and procedures and if the relevant securities haven't been issued, revoke the decision on approval and terminate the issuance. For any securities that have been issued but haven't been listed, the relevant decision on approval for issuance shall be revoked. The relevant issuer shall, according to the issuing price plus interests as calculated at the bank deposit rate for the corresponding period of time, refund the securities holders. A recommender shall bear several and joint liabilities together with the relevant issuer, except for one who is able to prove that he has no fault therein. Where any controlling shareholder or actual controller has any fault, he shall bear several and joint liabilities together with the relevant issuer.

Article 27 After a legal offer of stocks, an issuer shall be responsible for any flux in its operations or profits by itself. The investment risk as incurred therefrom shall be borne by investors themselves.

Article 28 Where an issuer issues any securities to any non-specified object and if the said securities shall be underwritten by a securities company, as is provided for by any law or administrative regulation, the issuer shall conclude an underwriting agreement with a securities company. The forms of "sale by proxy" or "exclusive sale" shall be adopted for the underwriting of securities.

The term "sale by proxy" refers to an underwriting form, whereby a securities company sells securities as a proxy of the relevant issuer and, upon the end of the underwriting period, returns all the securities unsold to the relevant issuer.

The term "exclusive sale" refers to an underwriting form, whereby a securities company purchases all of the securities of an issuer according to the agreement there between or purchases all of the remaining unsold securities by itself upon the end of the underwriting period.

Article 29 An issuer that makes public issuance of securities has the right to select a securities company for underwriting according to law at its own will. A securities company shall not canvass any securities underwriting business by any unjust competition means.

Article 30 Where a securities company underwrites any securities, it shall conclude an agreement with the relevant issuer on sale by proxy or exclusive sale, which shall indicate the following items:

(1) The name, domicile as well as the name of the legal representative of the parties concerned;
(2) The classes, quantity, amount as well as issuing prices of the securities under sale by proxy or exclusive sale;
(3) The term of sale by proxy or exclusive sale as well as the start-stop date;
(4) The ways and date of payment for sale by proxy or exclusive sale;
(5) The expenses for and settlement methods of sale by proxy or exclusive sale;
(6) The liabilities for breach; and
(7) Any other matter as prescribed by the securities regulatory authority under the State Council.

Article 31 A securities company that engages in the underwriting of securities shall carry out verification on the authenticity, accuracy and integrity of the financing documents of public issuance. Where any false record, misleading statement or major omission is found, no sales activity may be carried out. Where any securities have been sold out under the foregoing circumstances, the relevant sales activity shall be immediately terminated and measures for correction shall be taken.

Article 32 Where the total face value of securities as issued to non-specified objects exceed RMB 50 million yuan, the said securities shall be underwritten by an underwriting syndicate. An underwriting syndicate shall be composed of a securities company acting as the principal underwriter and other participant underwriters.

Article 33 The term for sale by proxy or exclusive sale shall not exceed than 90 days at the most.

A securities company shall, within the term of sale by proxy or exclusive sale, guarantee the priority of the relevant subscribers in purchasing securities under sale by proxy or exclusive sale. A securities company shall not reserve in advance any securities under sale by proxy thereby or purchase in advance and sustain any securities under exclusive sale thereby.

Article 34 Where any stock is issued at a premium, the issuing price thereof shall be determined through negotiation between the relevant issuer and the securities company that engages in the underwriting.

Article 35 As for a public offer of stocks through sale by proxy, when the term of sale by proxy expires and if the number of stocks fails to reach 70% of the planned number in the public offer, it shall be deemed as a failure. The relevant issuer shall refund the issuing price plus interests as calculated at the bank deposit rate for the contemporary period of time to the subscribers of stocks.

Article 36 In a public offer of stocks, when the term for sale by proxy or exclusive sale expires, the issuer shall report the information on stock issuance to the securities regulatory authority under the State Council for archival filing within the prescribed term.

Chapter III Trading of Securities

Section I General Provisions

Article 37 The securities as purchased and sold by any party who is involved in any securities trading shall be the securities that have been legally issued and delivered.

Any securities that have been illegally issued shall not be purchased or sold.

Article 38 Any stocks, corporate bonds or any other securities that have been legally issued, where there are any restrictive provisions of laws on the term of transfer thereof, shall not be purchased or sold within the restricted term.

Article 39 Any stocks, corporate bonds or any other securities that have been publicly issued according to law shall be listed in a stock exchange as legally established or in any other places for securities trading as approved by the State Council.

Article 40 The means of public and centralized trading or any other means as approval by the securities regulatory authority under the State Council shall be adopted for the listed trading of securities in stock exchanges.

Article 41 The securities as purchased or sold by the parties involved in securities trading may be in paper form or in any other form as approval by the securities regulatory authority under the State Council.

Article 42 The securities trading shall be carried out in the form of spot goods as well as any other form as prescribed by the State Council.

Article 43 The practitioners in stock exchanges, securities companies and securities registration and clearing institutions, the functionary of securities regulatory bodies, as well as any other personnel who have been prohibited by any law or administrative regulation from engaging in any stock trading shall not, within their tenures or the relevant statutory term, hold or purchase or sell any stock directly or in any assumed name or in the name of any other person, nor may they accept any stocks from any other person as a present.

Anyone, before becoming any person as prescribed in the preceding paragraph herein, shall transfer the stocks he has held according to law.

Article 44 The stock exchanges, securities companies, as well as securities registration and clearing institutions shall keep confidential the accounts as opened for their clients according to law.

Article 45 A securities trading service institution and the relevant personnel that produce such documents as auditing reports, asset appraisal reports or legal opinions for stock issuance shall not purchase or sell any of the aforesaid stocks within the underwriting term of stocks or within 6 months as of the expiration of the underwriting term of stocks.

Except for the provisions as prescribed in the preceding paragraph herein, a securities trading service institutions and the relevant personnel that produce such documents as auditing reports, asset appraisal reports or legal opinions for listed companies shall not purchase or sell any of the aforesaid stocks within the period from the day when he accepts the entrustment of the listed company to the day when the aforesaid documents are publicized.

Article 46 The fee charge for securities trading shall be reasonable. The charging items, rates and methods shall be publicized.

The charging items, rates, and administrative measures of securities trading shall be uniformly formulated by the relevant administrative department of the State Council.

Article 47 Where any director, supervisor and senior manager of a listed company or any shareholder who holds more than 5% of the shares of a listed company, sells the stocks of the company as held within 6 months after purchase, or purchases any stock as sold within 6 months thereafter, the proceeds as generated therefrom shall be incorporated into the profits of the relevant company. The board of directors of the company shall take back the proceeds. However, where a securities company holds more than 5% of the shares of a listed company, which are the residual stocks after sale by proxy as purchased thereby, the sale of the foregoing stocks shall not be limited by the term of 6 months.

Where the board of directors of a company fails to implement the provisions as prescribed in the preceding paragraph herein, the shareholders concerned have the right to require the board of directors to implement them within 30 days. Where the board of directors of a company fails to implement them within the aforesaid term, the shareholders shall have the right to directly file a lawsuit with the people's court in their own names for the interests of the company.

Where the board of directors of a company fails to implement the provisions as prescribed in paragraph 1 herein, the directors in charge shall bear several and joint liabilities according to law.

Section II Listing of Securities

Article 48 An application for the listing of any securities shall be filed with a stock exchange and shall be subject to the examination and approval of the stock exchange according to law, and a listing agreement shall be concluded by both parties.

Stock exchanges shall, according to the decision of the department as authorized by the State Council, arrange for the listing of government bonds.

Article 49 For an application for the listing of any stocks, convertible corporate bonds or any other securities, which are subject to recommendation as is prescribed by any law or administrative regulation, an institution with the qualification of recommendation shall be hired as the recommender.

The provisions of paragraphs 2 and 3 of Article 11 of the present Law shall apply to the recommender of stock listing.

Article 50 A joint stock limited company that applies for the listing of its stocks shall meet the following requirements:

(1) The stocks shall have been publicly issued upon the approval of the securities regulatory authority under the State Council;
(2) The total amount of capital stock of the company shall be no less than RMB 30 million yuan;
(3) The shares as publicly issued shall reach more than 25% of the total amount of corporate shares; where the total amount of capital stock of a company exceeds RMB 0.4 billion yuan, the shares as publicly issued shall be no less than 10% thereof; and
(4) The company shall not have any major irregularity over the latest three years and there is no false record in its financial statements.

A stock exchange may prescribe the requirements of listing that are more strict than those as prescribed in the preceding paragraph herein, which shall be reported to the securities regulatory authority under the State Council for approval.

Article 51 The state encourages the listing of corporate stocks that comply with the relevant industrial policies and meet the relevant requirements of listing.

Article 52 As to an application for the listing of stocks, the following documents shall be submitted to a stock exchange:

(1) The listing report;
(2) The resolution of the general assembly of shareholders regarding the application for the listing of stocks;
(3) The constitution of the company;
(4) The business license of the company;
(5) The financial statements of the company for the latest three years as audited by an accounting firm according to law;
(6) The legal opinions as well as the Recommendation Letter of Listing;
(7) The latest prospectus; and
(8) Any other document as prescribed by the listing rules of the stock exchange.

Article 53 Where an application for the listing of stocks have been approved by the stock exchange, the relevant company that has concluded a listing agreement thereon shall announce the relevant documents for stock listing within the prescribed period and shall make the said documents available for public reference in designated places.

Article 54 A company that has concluded a listing agreement shall not only announce the documents as prescribed in the preceding Article herein but also announce the following items:

(1) The date when the stocks have been approved to be listed in a stock exchange;
(2) The name list of the top 10 shareholders who hold the largest number of shares in the company as well as the amount of stocks they hold;
(3) The actual controller of the company; and
(4) The names of the directors, supervisors and senior managers of the company as well as the relevant information on the stocks and bonds of the company they hold.

Article 55 Where a listed company is under any of the following circumstances, the stock exchange shall decide to suspend the listing of its stocks:

(1) Where the total amount of capital stock or share distribution of the company changes and thus fails to meet the requirements for listing;
(2) Where the company fails to publicize its financial status according to the relevant provisions or has any false record in its financial statements, which may mislead the investors;
(3) Where the company has any major irregularity;
(4) Where the company has been operating at a loss for the latest 3 consecutive years; or
(5) Under any other circumstance as prescribed in the listing rules of the stock exchange.

Article 56 Where a listed company is under any of the following circumstances, the stock exchange shall decide to terminate the listing of its stocks:

(1) Where the total amount of capital stock or share distribution of the company changes and thus fails to meet the requirements of listing, and where the company fails again to meet the requirements of listing within the period as prescribed by the stock exchange;
(2) Where the company fails to publicize its financial status according to the relevant provisions or has any false record in its financial statements, and refuses to make any correction;
(3) Where the company has been operating at a loss for the latest 3 consecutive years and fails to gain profits in last year;
(4) Where the company is dissolved or is declared bankrupt; or
(5) Under any other circumstance as prescribed in the listing rules of the stock exchange.

Article 57 A company shall, when applying for the listing of corporate bonds, meet the following requirements:

(1) The term of corporate bonds shall be more than 1 year;
(2) The amount of corporate bonds to be actually issued shall be no less than RMB 50 million yuan; and

(3) The company shall meet the statutory requirements for the issuance of corporate bonds when applying for the listing of its bonds.

Article 58 A company shall, when applying for the listing of its corporate bonds, report the following documents to the stock exchange:

(1) The listing report;
(2) The resolution as adopted by the board of directors regarding the application for listing;
(3) The constitution of the company;
(4) The business license of the company;
(5) The measures for financing through the issuance of corporate bonds;
(6) The amount of corporate bonds to be actually issued; and
(7) Any other document as prescribed in the listing rules of the stock exchange.

As to an application for the listing of convertible corporate bonds, the Recommendation Letter of Listing as produced by the relevant recommender shall be submitted.

Article 59 Where an application for the listing of corporate bonds has been approved by the stock exchange, the company that has concluded a listing agreement thereon shall, within the prescribed period, announce its report on the listing of its corporate bonds as well as the relevant documents, and make its application documents available for public reference in designated places.

Article 60 After any corporate bonds are listed, where the relevant company is under any of the following circumstances, the stock exchange may decide to suspend the listing of its corporate bonds:

(1) Where the company has any major irregularity;
(2) Where the company has any major change and thus fails to meet the requirements for the listing of corporate bonds;
(3) Where the funds as raised through the issuance of corporate bonds fail to be used according to the verified purposes of use;
(4) Where the company fails to perform its obligations according to the measures for financing through the issuance of corporate bonds; or
(5) Where the company has been operating at a loss for the latest 2 consecutive years.

Article 61 Where a company is under any of the circumstances as described in item (1) or (4) of the preceding Article and the consequences as incurred therefrom have been verified to be serious, or where a company is under any of the circumstances as described in item (2), (3), or (5) of the preceding Article and fails to eliminate the relevant consequences within a specified time limit, the stock exchange shall decide to terminate the listing of corporate bonds of the company.

Where a company is dissolved or declared bankrupt, the stock exchange shall terminate the listing of the corporate bonds thereof.

Article 62 Any company, which is dissatisfied with the decision of the stock exchange on disapproving, suspending or terminating its listing, may apply to the review organ as established by the stock exchange for review.

Section III On-going Disclosure of Information

Article 63 The information as disclosed by issuers and listed companies according to law shall be authentic, accurate and complete and shall not have any false record, misleading statement or major omission.

Article 64 For the stocks that have been publicly issued upon the verification of the securities regulatory authority under the State Council or for the corporate bonds that have been publicly issued upon the verification of the department as authorized by the State Council according to law, the prospectus or the measures for financing through the issuance of corporate bonds shall be announced. In an IPO of stocks or corporate bonds, the relevant financial statements shall be announced as well.

Article 65 A company whose shares or bonds have been listed for trading shall, within two months as of the end of the first half of each accounting year, submit to the securities regulatory authority under the State Council and the stock exchange a midterm report indicating the following contents and make a public announcement for it:

(1) The financial statements and business situation of the company;
(2) The major litigation the company is involved in;
(3) The particulars of any change concerning the shares or corporate bonds thereof it has already issued;
(4) The important matters as submitted to the general assembly of shareholders for deliberation; and
(5) Any other matter as prescribed by the securities regulatory authority under the State Council.

Article 66 A listed company whose shares or bonds have been listed for trading shall, within four months as of the end of each accounting year, submit to the securities regulatory authority under the State Council and the stock exchange an annual report indicating the following contents, and make a public announcement for it:

(1) A brief account of the company's general situation;
(2) The financial statement and business situation of the company;
(3) A brief introduction to the directors, supervisors, and senior managers of the company well as the information regarding their shareholdings;
(4) The information on the shares and corporate bonds it has already issued, including a name list of the top 10 shareholders who hold the largest number of shares in the company as well as the amount of shares each of them holds; and
(5) The actual controller of the company; and
(6) Any other matter as prescribed by the securities regulatory authority under the State Council.

Article 67 In the case of a major event that may considerably affect the trading price of a listed company's shares and that is not yet known to the investors, the listed company shall immediately submit a temporary report regarding the said major event to the securities regulatory authority under the State Council and the stock exchange, and make an announcement to the general public as well, in which the cause, present situation, and possible legal consequence of the event shall be indicated:

The term "major event" as mentioned in the preceding paragraph herein refers to any of the following circumstances:

(1) A major change in the business guidelines or business scope of the company;
(2) A decision of the company on any major investment or major asset purchase;
(3) An important contract as concluded by the company, which may have an important effect on the assets, liabilities, rights, interests or business achievements of the company;
(4) The incurrence of any major debt in the company or default on any major debt that is due;

(5) The incurrence of any major deficit or a major loss in the company;
(6) A major change in the external conditions for the business operation of the company;
(7) A change concerning directors, no less than one-third of supervisors or managers of the company;
(8) A considerable change in the holdings of shareholders or actual controllers each of whom holds or controls no less than 5% of the company's shares;
(9) A decision of the company on capital decrease, merger, division, dissolution, or application for bankruptcy;
(10) Any major litigation in which the company is involved, or where the resolution of the general assembly of shareholders or the board of directors have been cancelled or announced invalid;
(11) Where the company is involved in any crime, which has been filed as a case as well as investigated into by the judicial organ or where any director, supervisor or senior manager of the company is subject to compulsory measures as rendered by the judicial organ; or
(12) Any other matter as prescribed by the securities regulatory authority under the State Council.

Article 68 The directors and senior managers of a listed company shall produce written opinions to confirm the periodic reports of the company.

The board of supervisors of a listed company shall carry out an examination on the periodic report of its company as formulated by the board of directors and produce the relevant examination opinions in written form.

The directors, supervisors and senior managers of a listed company shall guarantee the authenticity, accuracy and integrity of the information as disclosed by the listed company.

Article 69 Where any of the prospectus, measures for financing through the issuance of corporate bonds, financial statements, listing reports, annual reports, midterm reports, temporary reports or any disclosed information that has been announced by an issuer or listed company has any false record, misleading statement or major omission, and thus incurs losses to investors in the process of securities trading, the issuer or the listed company shall bear the liabilities of compensation. Any director, supervisor, senior manager or any other person of the issuer or the listed company as held to be directly responsible shall take several and joint liabilities of compensation, unless he is able to prove that he has no fault therein. Where any shareholder or actual controller of an issuer or a listed company has any fault, he or it shall bear several and joint liabilities of compensation together with the relevant issuer or listed company.

Article 70 The information which must be disclosed as prescribed by law shall be publicized through the media as designated by the securities regulatory authority under the State Council and shall, at the same time, be made available for public reference at the company's domicile and the stock exchange.

Article 71 The securities regulatory authority under the State Council shall carry out supervision over the annual reports, midterm reports, temporary reports of listed companies as well as their announcements, over the distribution or rationing of new shares of such listed companies, and over the controlling shareholders and information disclosure obligors of the listed companies.

The securities regulatory body, stock exchange, recommender or securities company involved in underwriting as well as the relevant personnel thereof shall not, before an announcement is made by the company according to the provisions of the relevant laws and administrative regulations, divulge any content concerned before making the announcement.

Article 72 Where a stock exchange decides to suspend or terminate the listing of any securities, it shall announce the decision in a timely manner and report it to the securities regulatory authority under the State Council for archival filing.

Section IV Prohibited Trading Acts

Article 73 Any insider who has access to any insider information of securities trading or who has unlawfully obtained any insider information is prohibited from taking advantage of the insider information he holds to engage in any securities trading.

Article 74 The insiders who have access to insider information of securities trading include:

(1) Directors, supervisors, and senior managers of an issuer;
(2) Shareholders who hold more than 5% of the shares of a company as well as the directors, supervisors, and senior managers thereof, or the actual controller of a company as well as the directors, supervisors, and senior managers thereof;

(3) The holding company of an issuer as well as the directors, supervisors, and senior managers thereof;
(4) The personnel who may take advantage of their posts in their company to obtain any insider information of the company concerning the issuance and trading of its securities;
(5) The functionaries of the securities regulatory body, and other personnel who administer the issuance and trading of securities pursuant to their statutory functions and duties;
(6) The relevant personnel of the recommendation institutions, securities companies engaging in underwriting, stock exchanges, securities registration and clearing institutions, and securities trading service organizations; and
(7) Any other person as prescribed by the securities regulatory authority under the State Council.

Article 75 The term "insider information" refers to the information that concerns the business or finance of a company or may have a major effect on the market price of the securities thereof and that hasn't been publicized in securities trading.

All of the following information falls into the scope of insider information:

(1) The major events as prescribed in paragraph 2 of Article 67 of the present Law;
(2) The plan of a company concerning any distribution of dividends or increase of capital;
(3) Any major change in the company's equity structure;
(4) Any major change in the guaranty of the company's debt;
(5) Where the mortgaged, sold or discarded value of any major asset as involved in the business operation of the company exceeds 30% of the said asset at a single time;
(6) Where any act as conducted by any director, supervisor or senior manager of the company may be rendered to be responsible for any major damage and compensation;
(7) The relevant plan of a listed company regarding acquisition; and
(8) Any other important information that has been recognized by the securities regulatory authority under the State Council as having a marked effect on the trading prices of securities.

Article 76 Any insider who has access to insider information or has unlawfully obtained any insider information on securities trading may not purchase or sell the securities of the relevant company, or divulge such information, or advise any other person to purchase or sell such securities.

Where there is any other provision of the present Law on governing the purchase of shares of a listed company by a natural person, legal person or any other organization who individually holds or holds with any other person no less than 5% of the company's shares by means of an agreement or any other arrangement, such provision shall prevail.

Where any insider trading incurs any loss to investors, the actor shall make compensations according to law.

Article 77 Anyone is prohibited from manipulating the securities market by any of the following means:

(1) Whether anyone, independently or in collusion with others, manipulates the trading price of securities or trading quantity of securities by centralizing their advantages in funds, their shareholding advantages or taking their information advantage to trade jointly or continuously;
(2) Where anyone collaborates with any other person to trade securities pursuant to the time, price and method as agreed upon in advance, thereby affecting the price or quantity of the securities traded;
(3) Where anyone trades securities between the accounts under his own control, thereby affecting the price or quantity of the securities traded; or
(4) Where anyone manipulates the securities market by any other means.

Where anyone incurs any loss to investors by manipulating the securities market, the actor shall be subject to the liabilities of compensation according to law.

Article 78 It is prohibited for state functionaries, practitioners of the news media as well as other relevant personnel concerned to disturb the securities market by fabricating or disseminating any false information.

It is prohibited for stock exchanges, securities companies, securities registration and clearing institutions, securities trading service institutions and the practitioners thereof, as well as the securities industry associations, the securities regulatory bodies and their functionaries to make any false statement or give any misleading information in the activities of securities trading.

The securities market information as disseminated by any media shall be authentic and objective. Any dissemination of misleading information is prohibited.

Article 79 It is prohibited for a securities company as well as the practitioners thereof to commit any of the following fraudulent acts in the process of securities trading, which may injure the interests of their clients:

(1) Violating the entrustment of its client by purchasing or selling any securities on its behalf;
(2) Failing to provide any client with written confirmation of any transaction within the prescribed period of time;
(3) Misappropriating the securities as entrusted by any client for purchase or sale, or misappropriating the funds in any client's account;
(4) Unlawfully purchasing or selling securities for its client without authorization, or unlawfully purchasing or selling any securities in the name of any client;
(5) Inveigling any client into making any unnecessary purchase or sale of securities in order to obtain commissions;
(6) Making use of mass media or by any other means to provide or disseminate any false or misleading information to investors; or
(7) Having any other act that goes against the true intention as expressed by a client and damages the interests thereof.

Where anyone practices any trickery and thus incurs any loss to the relevant clients, the actor shall make compensations according to law.

Article 80 It's prohibited for any legal person to unlawfully make use of any other person's account to undertake any securities trading. It's prohibited for any legal person to lend its own or any other person's securities account.

Article 81 The channel for capital to enter into the stock market shall be broadened according to law. It's prohibited for any unqualified capital to go into the stock market.

Article 82 It's prohibited for any person to misappropriate any public fund to trade securities.

Article 83 The state-owned enterprises and state-controlled enterprises that engage in any trading of listed stocks shall observe the relevant provisions of the state.

Article 84 When stock exchanges, securities companies, securities registration and clearing institutions, securities trading service organizations as well as their functionaries discover any prohibited activities in securities trading, they shall report such activities to the securities regulation body in a timely manner.

Chapter IV Acquisition of Listed Companies

Article 85 An investor may purchase a listed company by means of tender offer or agreement as well as by any other legal means.

Article 86 When an investor, through securities trading at a stock exchange, comes to hold individually or with any other person 5% of the shares as issued by a listed company by means of agreement or any other arrangement, the investor shall, within three days as of the date when such shareholding becomes a fact, submit a written report to the securities regulatory authority under the State Council and the stock exchange, notify the relevant listed company and announce the fact to the general public. Within the aforesaid prescribed period, the investor may not purchase or sell any more shares of the listed company.

Once an investor holds individually or with any other person 5% of the shares as issued by a listed company by means of agreement or any other arrangement, he shall, pursuant to the provisions of the preceding paragraph herein, make a report and announcement for each 5% increase or decrease in the proportion of the issued shares of the said company he holds through securities trading at the stock exchange. Within the reporting period as well as two days after the relevant the report and announcement are made, the investor may not purchase or sell any more shares of the listed company.

Article 87 The written report and announcement as made according to the provisions of the preceding article shall include the following contents:

(1) The name and domicile of the shareholder;
(2) The description and amount of the shares as held; and
(3) The date on which the shareholding or any increase or decrease in the shareholding reaches the statutory percentage.

Article 88 Where an investor holds individually or with any other person 30% of the stocks as issued by a listed company by means of agreement or any other arrangement through securities trading at the stock exchange and continues the purchase, he shall issue a tender offer to all the shareholders of the said listed company to purchase all of or part of the shares of the listed company.

It shall be stipulated in a tender offer as issued to a listed company that, where the amount of shares the shareholders of the target company promise to sell exceeds the scheduled amount of stocks for purchase, the purchaser shall carry out the acquisition in proportion.

Article 89 Before any tender offer is issued pursuant to the provisions in the preceding article, the relevant purchaser shall issue an announcement a report on the acquisition of a listed company, which shall indicate the following items:

(1) The name and domicile of the purchaser;
(2) The decision of the purchaser on acquisition;
(3) The name of the target listed company;
(4) The purpose of acquisition;
(5) The detailed description of the shares to be purchased and the amount of shares scheduled to be purchased in schedule;
(6) The term and price of the acquisition;
(7) The amount and warranty of the funds as required by the acquisition; and
(8) The proportion of the amount of shares of the target company as held by the purchaser in the total amount of shares issued by the target company, when the report on the acquisition of the listed company is reported.

Article 90 The term for acquisition as stipulated in a tender offer shall be no less than 30 days but no more than 60 days.

Article 91 Within the term for acceptance as prescribed in the tender offer, no purchaser may revoke its tender offer. Where a purchaser needs to modify its tender offer, it must issue an announcement in a timely manner, stating the specific modification.

Article 92 All the terms and conditions of acquisition in a tender offer shall apply to all the shareholders of the target company.

Article 93 In the case of an acquisition by tender offer, a purchaser shall not, within the term for acquisition, sell any share of the target company, nor shall it buy any share of the target company by any other means that hasn't been stipulated bin its tender offer or that go beyond the terms and conditions as stipulated in its tender offer.

Article 94 In the case of an agreement-based acquisition, a purchaser may carry out share transfer with the shareholders of the target company by means of agreement according to the provisions of the relevant laws and administrative regulations.

In the case of an acquisition of a listed company by agreement, a purchaser shall, within three days after the acquisition agreement is reached, submit a written report on the acquisition agreement to the securities regulatory authority under the State Council and the stock exchange, and shall announce it to the general public.

No acquisition agreement may be performed before the relevant announcement is made.

Article 95 In the case of an agreement-based acquisition, both parties to the agreement may temporarily entrust a securities registration and clearing institution to keep the stocks as transferred and deposit the relevant funds in a designated bank.

Article 96 In the case of an agreement-based acquisition, where a purchaser has purchased, held individually or with any other person 30% of the shares as issued by a listed company through agreement or any other arrangement and if the acquisition continues, the purchaser shall issue an offer to all of the shareholders of the target listed company for purchasing all of or part of the company's shares, unless it is exempted from making a tender offer by the securities regulatory authority under the State Council.

A purchaser that purchases the shares of a listed company by means of tender offer according to the provisions of the preceding paragraph herein shall observe the provisions of Articles 89 through 93 of the present Law.

Article 97 Upon the expiration of a term for acquisition, where the share distribution of an target company fails to meet the requirements of listing, the listing of stocks of the said listed company shall be terminated by the stock exchange according to law. The shareholders that still hold the shares of the target company have the right to sell their shares in light of the equal terms as stipulated in the relevant tender offer, and the purchaser shall make the purchase.

When an acquisition is concluded, if a target company fails to meet the requirements for remaining a joint stock limited company any more, its form of enterprise shall be altered according to law.

Article 98 In the acquisition of a listed company, the stocks of the target company held by a purchaser shall not be transferred within 12 months after the acquisition is concluded.

Article 99 When an acquisition is concluded, if the purchaser merges with the target company by dissolving the target company, the original shares of the dissolved company shall be exchanged by the purchaser according to law.

Article 100 Where an acquisition is concluded, a purchaser shall, within 15 days, report the acquisition to the securities regulatory authority under the State Council and the stock exchange, and shall make an announcement for it.

Article 101 The purchase of the shares of a listed company as held by an organization that has been authorized by the state for investment shall be subject to the approval of the relevant administrative departments according to the provisions of the State Council.

The securities regulatory authority under the State Council shall formulate specific measures for the acquisition of listed companies according to the principles of the present Law.

Chapter V Stock Exchanges

Article 102 The term "stock exchange" refers to a legal person that provides the relevant place and facilities for concentrated securities trading, organizes and supervises the securities trading and applies a self-regulated administration.

The establishment and dissolution of a stock exchange shall be subject to the decision of the State Council.

Article 103 A constitution shall be formulated for the establishment of a stock exchange.

The formulation and revision of the constitution of a stock exchange shall be subject to the approval of the securities regulatory authority under the State Council.

Article 104 The words "stock exchange" shall be indicated in the name of a stock exchange. No other entity or individual may use the words "stock exchange" or its like in its or his name.

Article 105 The income at the discretion of a stock exchange which is generated from various commissions shall first be used to guarantee the normal operation of the place and facilities of the stock exchange as well as the gradual improvement thereof.

The gains as accumulated by a stock exchange that adopts a membership system shall belong to its members. The rights and interests of the stock exchange shall be jointly shared by its members. No accumulated gains of a stock exchange may be distributed to any member within its existence.

Article 106 A stock exchange shall have a council.

Article 107 A stock exchange shall have a general manager, who shall be subject to the appointment and dismissal of the securities regulatory authority under the State Council.

Article 108 Anyone, who is under the circumstance as prescribed in Article 146 of the Corporation Law of the People's Republic of China or any of the following circumstances, shall not assume the post of person-in-charge of a stock exchange:

(1) Where the person-in-charge of a stock exchange or securities registration and clearing institution or any director, supervisor or senior manager of a securities company who has been removed from his post for his irregularity or disciplinary breach and 5 years have not elapsed as of the day when he was removed from his post; or
(2) Where a professional of a law firm, accounting firm, or investment consulting organization, financial advising organization, credit rating institution, asset appraisal institution or asset verification institution who has been disqualified for his irregularity or disciplinary breach and 5 years have not elapsed as of the day when he was removed from his post.

Article 109 A practitioner of a stock exchange, securities registration and clearing institution, securities trading service organization or securities company or any functionary of the state organ, who has been dismissed for his irregularity or disciplinary breach, shall not be employed as a practitioner of any stock exchange.

Article 110 Anyone who enters into a stock exchange to engage in the centralized trading of securities must be a member of the stock exchange.

Article 111 An investor shall conclude an entrustment agreement with a securities company on securities trading, open a securities trading account in a securities company and entrust the securities company, in written form, by telephone or any other means, to purchase or sell securities on its behalf.

Article 112 A securities company shall, based on the entrustment of its investors, declare for securities dealings and engage in the centralized trading at a stock exchange according to the rules of securities trading and shall, on the basis of trading results, bear the relevant liabilities of settlement and delivery. A securities registration and clearing institution shall, on the basis of trading results and according to the rules of settlement and delivery, conduct settlement and delivery of securities and capital with the relevant securities company, and handle the formalities of transfer registration of securities for the clients of the relevant securities company.

Article 113 A stock exchange shall guarantee a fair centralized trading, announce up-to-the-minute quotations of securities trading, formulate the quotation tables of the securities market on the basis of trading days, and make announcements for it.

Without permission of the stock exchange, no entity or individual may announce any up-to-the-minute quotations of securities trading.

Article 114 Where any normal trading of securities is disturbed by an emergency, a stock exchange may take the measures of a technical suspension of trading. In the case of an emergency of force majeure or for the purpose of preserving the normal order of securities trading, a stock exchange may decide a temporary speed bump.

Where a stock exchange adopts the measure of technical suspension of trading or decides on a temporary speed bump, it shall report it to the securities regulatory authority under the State Council in a timely manner.

Article 115 A stock exchange shall exercise a real-time monitoring of securities trading and shall, according to the requirements of the securities regulatory authority under the State Council, report any abnormal trading thereto.

A stock exchange shall carry out supervision over the information as disclosed by the listed companies or the relevant obligor of information disclosure, supervise and urge them to disclose information in a timely and accurate manner according to law.

A stock exchange may, when it so requires, restrict the trading through a securities account where there is any major abnormal trading and shall report it to the securities regulatory authority under the State Council for archival filing.

Article 116 A stock exchange shall withdraw a certain proportion of funds from the transaction fees, membership fees and seat fees it has charged to establish a risk fund. The risk fund shall be subject to the administration of the council of the stock exchange.

The specific withdrawal proportion and use of the risk fund shall be provided for by the securities regulatory authority under the State Council in collaboration with the fiscal department of the State Council.

Article 117 A stock exchange shall deposit its risk fund into a special account of its opening bank and shall not unlawfully use it.

Article 118 A stock exchange shall, pursuant to the laws and administrative regulations on securities, formulate rules on listing, trading and membership administration as well as any other relevant rules, and shall report them to the securities regulatory authority under the State Council for approval.

Article 119 Where any person-in-charge and any other practitioner of a stock exchange has any interest relationship or any of his relatives has any interest relationship with the performance of his duties relating to securities trading, he shall withdraw.

Article 120 Any trading result of a transaction, which has been conducted in accordance with the trading rules as formulated according to law, shall not be altered. A trader who has conducted any rule-breaking trading shall not be exempted from civil liabilities. The proceeds as generated from the rule-breaking trading shall be dealt with pursuant to the relevant regulations.

Article 121 Where any staff member of a stock exchange who engages in securities trading violates any trading rule of the stock exchange, the stock exchange shall impose upon him a disciplinary sanction. Under any serious circumstances, the qualification thereof shall be revoked and the violator shall be prohibited from entering into the stock exchange to engage in any securities trading.

Chapter VI Securities Companies

Article 122 The establishment of a securities company shall be subject to the examination and approval of the securities regulatory authority under the State Council. No entity or individual may engage in any securities operations without the approval of the securities regulatory authority under the State Council.

Article 123 The term "securities company" as mentioned in the present Law refers to a limited- liability company or joint stock limited company that is established and engages in the business operation of securities according to the Corporation Law of the People's Republic of China as well as the provisions of the present Law.

Article 124 The establishment of a securities company shall meet the following requirements:

(1) Having a corporation constitution that meets the relevant laws and administrative regulations;
(2) The major shareholders having the ability to make profits continuously, enjoying good credit standing, and having no irregular or rule-breaking record over the latest 3 years, and its net asset being no less than 0.2 billion yuan.
(3) Having a registered capital that meets the provisions of the present Law;
(4) The directors, supervisors and senior managers thereof having the qualification for assuming such posts and its practitioners having the qualification to engage in the securities business;
(5) Having a complete risk management system as well as an internal control system;
(6) Having a qualified business place and facilities for operations; and
(7) Meeting any other requirement as prescribed by laws and administrative regulations as well as the provisions of the securities regulatory authority under the State Council, which have been approved by the State Council.

Article 125 A securities company may undertake some or all of the following business operations upon the approval of the securities regulatory authority under the State Council:

(1) Securities brokerage;
(2) Securities Investment consultation;
(3) Financial advising relating to the activities of securities trading or securities investment;
(4) Underwriting and recommendation of securities;
(5) Self-operations of securities;
(6) Securities asset management; and
(7) Any other business operations concerning securities.

Article 126 A securities company shall indicate the words "limited-liability securities company" or "joint stock limited securities company" in its name.

Article 127 Where a securities company engages in the business operation as prescribed in item (1), (2) or (3) of Article 125 of the present Law, its registered capital shall be RMB 50 million yuan at the least. Where a securities company engages in any of the business operations as prescribed in item (4), (5), (6) or (7) therein, its bottom-line registered capital shall be RMB 100 million yuan; Where a securities company engages in two or more business operations as prescribed in item (4), (5), (6) or (7) therein, its bottom-line registered capital shall be 500 million yuan. The registered capital of a securities company shall be paid-in capital.

The securities regulatory authority under the State Council may, according to the principle of prudent supervision and in light of the risk rating of all business operations, adjust the requirement of minimum amount of registered capital, which shall be no less than the minimum amount as prescribed in the preceding paragraph herein.

Article 128 The securities regulatory authority under the State Council shall, within 6 months as of accepting an application for establishing a securities company, carry out an examination according to the statutory requirements and procedures and on the basis of the principle of prudent supervision, make a decision on approval or disapproval, and thereafter notify the relevant applicant. In the case of disapproval, an explanation shall be given.

Where an application for establishing a securities company has been approved, an applicant shall, within the prescribed period, apply for registration of establishment with the organ in charge of corporation registration and collect its business license therefrom.

A securities company shall, within 15 days as of collecting its business license, apply for a Securities Business Permit with the securities regulatory authority under the State Council. Without a Securities Business Permit, a securities company shall not engage in any business operation of securities.

Article 129 Where a securities company establishes, purchases or cancels a branch, alters its business scope, increases its registered capital and the equity structure is changed greatly, reduces its registered capital, alters its shareholders who hold more than 5% of its stock rights or the actual controller, alters any important article of its constitution, has any merger or spilt, suspends its business operations, goes through dissolution or bankruptcy procedures, the approval of the securities regulatory authority under the State Council shall be obtained.

Where a securities company establishes or purchases a securities operation institution abroad or purchases the shares of any securities operational institution abroad, it shall be subject to the approval of the securities regulatory authority under the State Council.

Article 130 The securities regulatory authority under the State Council shall formulate provisions on the risk control indicators of a securities company such as net capital, the ratio between net capital and liabilities, the ratio between net capital and net assets, the ratio between net capital and operational scale of self-operation, underwriting and asset management, the ratio between liabilities and net asset, as well as the ratio between current assets and current liabilities.

A securities company shall not provide any financing or guaranty for its shareholders or any related person thereof.

Article 131 The directors, supervisors and senior managers of a securities company shall be honest and upright, have good morals, be familiar with the laws and administrative regulations on securities, and have the ability of operation and management as required by the performance of their functions and duties, and shall have obtained the post-holding qualification as verified by the securities regulatory authority under the State Council before assuming their posts.

Anyone who is under any circumstance as prescribed in Article 146 of the Corporation Law of the People's Republic of China or is under any of the following circumstances shall not hold the post of director, supervisor or senior manager of a securities company:

(1) Where a person-in-charge of a stock exchange or securities registration and clearing institution or a director, supervisor or senior manager of a securities company has been removed from his post for his irregularity or disciplinary breach and 5 years have not elapsed as of the day when he is removed from his post; and
(2) Where a professional of a law firm, accounting firm or investment consulting organization, financial advising organization, credit rating institution, asset appraisal institution or asset verification institution has been disqualified for his irregularity or disciplinary breach and 5 years have not elapsed as of the day when he is removed from his post.

Article 132 A practitioner of a stock exchange, securities registration and clearing institution, securities trading service institution or securities company or any functionary of the state organ, who has been dismissed for his irregularity or disciplinary breach, shall not be employed as a practitioner of a stock exchange.

Article 133 A functionary of any state organ and any other personnel as prohibited by any law or administrative regulation from taking any part-time job in a company shall not take any job in a securities company on a part-time basis.

Article 134 The state shall establish a securities investor protection fund. The securities investor protection fund shall be composed of the capital paid by securities companies and any other capital lawfully raised. The specific measures for financing, administration and use of the foregoing fund shall be formulated by the State Council.

Article 135 A securities company shall withdraw a trading risk reserve from its annual after-tax profits to cover any possible loss from securities trading. The specific proportion for withdrawal shall be prescribed by the securities regulatory authority under the State Council.

Article 136 A securities company shall establish and improve an internal control system, adopt effective measures of separation so as to prevent any interest conflict between the company and its clients or between different clients thereof.

A securities company shall undertake its operations of securities brokerage, underwriting, self-operation and asset management in a separate manner and may not mix them up.

Article 137 A securities company shall undertake its self-operations in its own name and shall not do so in the name of any other person or in any individual's name.

A securities company shall undertake its self-operations by using its own capital and funds it has lawfully raised.

A securities company shall not lend its self-operation account to any other person.

Article 138 A securities company may enjoy its right of independent management according to law and its legal operations shall not be interfered.

Article 139 The trading settlement funds of the clients of a securities company shall be deposited in a commercial bank and be managed through the separate accounts as opened in the name of each client. The specific measures and implementation procedures shall be formulated by the State Council.

A securities company shall not incorporate any trading settlement funds or securities of its clients into its own assets. Any entity or individual is prohibited from misusing any trading settlement funds or securities of its/his clients in any form. Where a securities company goes through bankruptcy procedures or is under liquidation, the trading settlement funds or securities of its client shall not be defined as its insolvent assets or liquidation assets. Under any other circumstance as irrelevant to the liabilities of its clients or under any other circumstance as prescribed by law, the trading settlement funds or securities of its clients shall not be sealed-up, frozen, deducted or enforced compulsorily.

Article 140 Where a securities company engages in any brokerage business, it shall arrange for a uniformly formulated power of attorney of securities trading for the entrusting party. Where any other means of entrustment is adopted, the relevant entrustment records shall be made.

For an entrustment of securities trading as made by a client, disregard whether the trading is concluded or not, the entrustment records shall be kept in the relevant securities company within the prescribed period.

Article 141 Upon accepting an entrustment for securities trading, a securities company shall, on the basis of the description of the securities, trading volume, method of quoting, price band, etc. as indicated in the power of attorney, undertake securities trading as an agent according to the trading rules and make trading faithful records. After a transaction is concluded, a securities company shall, according to the relevant regulations, formulate a transaction report and deliver it to the relevant clients.

The statements in check sheet made for confirming trading acts against the results of securities trading shall be authentic. Such statements shall be subject to the examination of an examiner other than the relevant transaction handler himself, on a transaction-by-transaction basis, so as to guarantee the consistency between the balance of securities in book account and the securities as actually held.

Article 142 Where a securities company provides any service of securities financing through securities trading for its client, it shall meet the provisions of the State Council and shall be subject to the approval of the securities regulatory authority under the State Council.

Article 143 A securities company that engages in brokerage operations shall not decide any purchase or sale of securities, class selection of securities, trading volume or trading price on the basis of full entrustment of its client.

Article 144 A securities company shall not make any promise to its clients on the proceeds as generated from securities trading or on compensating the loss as incurred from securities trading by any means.

Article 145 A securities company and the practitioners thereof shall not privately accept any entrustment of its client for securities trading beyond its business place as established according to law.

Article 146 Where any practitioner of a securities company violates the trading rules by implementing the instructions of his securities company or taking advantage of his post in any securities trading, the relevant securities company shall bear all the liabilities as incurred therefrom.

Article 147 A securities company shall keep the materials of its clients regarding account opening, entrustment records, trading records and internal management as well as its business operations in a proper manner. No one may conceal, forge, alter or damage any of the aforesaid materials. The term for keeping the aforesaid materials shall be no less than 20 years.

Article 148 A securities company shall, according to the relevant provisions, report the information and materials regarding its operations and management such as its business operations and financial status to the securities regulatory authority under the State Council. The securities regulatory authority under the State Council is empowered to require the securities company as well as the shareholders and actual controllers thereof to provide the relevant information and materials within a prescribed period.

The information and materials as reported or provided by the securities company and the shareholders and actual controllers thereof to the securities regulatory authority under the State Council shall be authentic, accurate and complete.

Article 149 The securities regulatory authority under the State Council may, when believing it is necessary, entrust an accounting firm or an asset appraisal institution to carry out an auditing or appraisal on the financial status, internal control as well as asset value of any securities company. The specific measures thereof shall be formulated by the securities regulatory authority under the State Council in collaboration with the relevant administrative departments.

Article 150 Where the net capital or any other indicator of risk control of a securities company fails to satisfy the relevant provisions, the securities regulatory authority under the State Council shall order it to correct in a prescribed period. Where a securities company fails to correct within the prescribed period or any act thereof has injured the sound operation of the securities company or has damaged the legitimate rights and interests of its clients, the securities regulatory authority under the State Council may take the following measures in light of different circumstances:

(1) Restricting its business operations, ordering it to suspend some business operations and stopping the approval of any new operations thereof;
(2) Stopping the approval for establishing or taking over any business branch;
(3) Restricting its distribution of dividends, restricting the payment of remunerations to or provision of welfare for its directors, supervisors or senior managers;
(4) Restricting any transfer of property or the setting of any other right to its property;
(5) Ordering it to alter its directors, supervisors and senior managers or restricting the right thereof;
(6) Ordering the controlling shareholders to transfer their stock rights or restricting its shareholders from exercising the shareholders' rights; and
(7) Revoking the relevant business license.

A securities company shall, upon rectification, submit a report to the securities regulatory authority under the State Council. The securities regulatory authority under the State Council shall lift the relevant measures as prescribed in the preceding paragraph herein within 3 days as of concluding the relevant examination and acceptance of the securities company that has met the requirements of risk control indicators upon examination and acceptance.

Article 151 Where a shareholder of a securities company makes any fake capital contribution or spirits away registered capital, the securities regulatory authority under the State Council shall order him to correct within a prescribed period and may order him to transfer the stock rights of the securities company it holds.

Before a shareholder as prescribed in the preceding paragraph herein corrects his irregularity and transfers the stock right of the securities company it holds according to the relevant requirements, the securities regulatory authority under the State Council may restrict the shareholders' rights thereof.

Article 152 Where any director, supervisor or senior manager of a securities company fails to fulfill his fiduciary duties and thus incurs any major irregularity or rule-breaking act or major risk to his securities company, the securities regulatory authority under the State Council may revoke the post-holding qualification thereof and order his company to remove him from his post and replace him with a new one.

Article 153 Where any illegal operation of a securities company or any major risk thereof seriously disturbs the order of the securities market or injures the interests of the relevant investors, the securities regulatory authority under the State Council may take such supervisory measures as suspending its business for rectification, designating any other institution for trusteeship, take-over or cancellation.

Article 154 During a period when a securities company is ordered to suspend its business for rectification, or is designated for trusteeship, or is being taken over or liquidated, or where any major risk occurs, the following measures may be adopted to the directors, supervisors, senior managers or any other person of the securities company as held to be directly responsible, upon the approval of the securities regulatory authority under the State Council:

(1) Notifying the exit administrative organ to prevent him from exiting the Chinese territory; and
(2) Requesting the judicial organ to prohibit him from moving, transferring his properties or disposing of his properties by any other means, or setting any other right to his properties.

Chapter VII Securities Registration and Clearing Institutions

Article 155 A securities registration and clearing institution is a non-profit legal person that provides centralized registration, custody and settlement services for securities trading.

The establishment of a securities registration and clearing institution shall be subject to the approval of the securities regulatory authority under the State Council.

Article 156 The establishment of a securities registration and clearing institution shall meet the following requirements:

(1) Its self-owned capital shall be no less than 0.2 billion yuan;
(2) It shall have a place and the facilities as required by the services of securities registration, custody and settlement;
(3) Its major managers and practitioners shall have the securities practice qualification; and
(4) It shall meet any other requirement as prescribed by the securities regulatory authority under the State Council.

The words "securities registration and clearing" shall be indicated in the name of a securities registration and clearing institution.

Article 157 A securities registration and clearing institution shall perform the following functions:

(1) The establishment of securities accounts and settlement accounts;
(2) The custody and transfer of securities;
(3) The registration of roster of securities holders;
(4) The settlement and delivery for listed securities trading of a stock exchange;
(5) The distribution of securities rights and interests on the basis of the entrustment of issuers;
(6) The handling of any inquiry relating to the aforesaid business operations; and
(7) Any other business operations as approved by the securities regulatory authority under the State Council.

Article 158 The way of nationally centralized and unified operations shall be adopted for the registration and settlement of securities.

The constitution and operational rules of a securities registration and clearing institution shall be formulated according to law and shall be subject to the approval of the securities regulatory authority under the State Council.

Article 159 The securities as held by the relevant holders shall all be put under the custody of a securities registration and clearing institution in a listed trading.

A securities registration and clearing institution shall not misappropriate any securities of its clients.

Article 160 A securities registration and clearing institution shall provide the roster of securities holders as well as the relevant materials to a securities issuer.

A securities registration and clearing institution shall, according to the result of securities registration and settlement, affirm the fact that a securities holder holds the relevant securities and provide the relevant registration materials to the securities holder.

A securities registration and clearing institution shall guarantee the authenticity, accuracy and integrity of the roster of securities holders as well as records of transfer registration, and shall not conceal, forge, alter or damage any of the aforesaid materials.

Article 161 A securities registration and clearing institution shall take the following measures to guarantee the sound operation of its business:

(1) Having the necessary service equipment and complete data protection measures;
(2) Having established complete management systems concerning operation, finance and security protection; and
(3) Having established a complete risk control system.

Article 162 A securities registration and clearing institution shall keep the original voucher of registration, custody and settlement as well as the relevant documents and materials in a proper manner. The term for keeping the aforesaid materials shall be no less than 20 years.

Article 163 A securities registration and clearing institution shall establish a clearing risk fund so as to pay in advance or make up any loss of the securities registration and clearing institution as incurred from default delivery, technical malfunction, operational fault or force majeure.

The securities clearing risk fund shall be withdrawn from the business incomes and proceeds of the securities registration and clearing institution and may be paid by clearing participants according to a specified percentage of securities trading volume.

The measures for raising and managing the securities clearing risk fund shall be formulated by the securities regulatory authority under the State Council in collaboration with the fiscal department of the State Council.

Article 164 The securities clearing risk fund shall be deposited into a special account of a designated bank and shall be subject to special management.

Where a securities registration and clearing institution makes any compensation by using the securities clearing risk fund, it may recourse the payment to the relevant person who is held responsible.

Article 165 An application for dissolving a securities registration and clearing institution shall be subject to the approval of the securities regulatory authority under the State Council.

Article 166 An investor who entrusts a securities company to undertake any securities trading shall apply for opening a securities account. A securities registration and clearing institution shall, according to the relevant provisions, open a securities account for the investor in his own name.

An investor who applies for opening an account shall hold the legitimate certificates certifying his identity of a Chinese citizen or its qualification of a Chinese legal person, unless it is otherwise provided for by the state.

Article 167 A securities registration and clearing institution shall, when providing netting service for a stock exchange, require the relevant clearing participant to deliver securities and funds in full amount and provide guaranty of delivery according to the principles of delivery versus payment (DVP).

Before a delivery is concluded, nobody may use the securities, funds or collaterals as involved in the delivery.

Where a clearing participant fails to perform the duty of delivery according to the schedule, a securities registration and clearing institution has the right to dispose of the properties as prescribed in the preceding paragraph herein according to the operational rules.

Article 168 The clearing funds and securities as collected by a securities registration and clearing institution according to the operational rules shall be deposited into a special account for settlement and delivery. The settlement and delivery that can only be applied to the securities trading as concluded according to the operational rules and shall not be enforced compulsorily.

Chapter VIII Securities Trading Service Institutions

Article 169 Where an investment consulting institution, financial advising institution, credit rating institution, asset appraisal institution, or accounting firm engages in any securities trading service, it shall be subject to the approval of the securities regulatory authority under the State Council and the relevant administrative departments.

The measures for the administration of examination and approval of the practice of securities trading services by the investment consulting institutions, financial advising institutions, credit rating institutions, asset appraisal institutions and accounting firms shall be formulated by the securities regulatory authority under the State Council and the relevant administrative departments.

Article 170 The staff of an investment consulting institution, financial advising institution or credit rating institution who engage in securities trading services shall have the special knowledge of securities as well as work experience in the securities business or securities trading services for more than 2 years. The standards for recognizing the securities practice qualification and the measures for administration thereof shall be formulated by the securities regulatory authority under the State Council.

Article 171 An investment consulting institution as well as its practitioners that engage in securities trading services shall not have any of the following acts:

(1) Engaging in any securities investment as an agent on behalf of its entrusting party;
(2) Concluding any agreement with any entrusting party on sharing the gains of securities investment or bearing the loss of securities investment;
(3) Purchasing or selling any stock of a listed company, for which the consulting institution provides services;
(4) Providing or disseminating any false or misleading information to investors through media or by any other means; or
(5) Having any other act as prohibited by any law or administrative regulation.

Any institution or person that has any of the acts as prescribed in the preceding paragraph herein and thus incurs any loss to investors shall bear the liabilities of compensation.

Article 172 An investment consulting institution or credit rating institution that engages in securities trading services shall charge commissions for the services it provides according to the rates of or measures for fee charging as formulated by the relevant administrative department of the State Council.

Article 173 Where a securities trading service institution formulates and issues any auditing report, asset appraisal report, financial advising report, credit rating report or legal opinions for the issuance, listing and trading of securities, it shall be assiduous and dutiful by carrying out examination and verification for the authenticity, accuracy and integrity of the contents of the documents applied as the base. In the case of any false record, misleading statement or major omission in the documents it has formulated or issued, which incurs any loss to any other person, the relevant securities trading service institution shall bear several and joint liabilities together with the relevant issuer and listed company, unless a securities trading service institution has the ability to prove its faultlessness.

Chapter IX Securities Industrial Associations

Article 174 A securities industrial association is a self-disciplinary organization for the securities industry and is a public organization with the status of a legal person.

A securities company shall join a securities industrial association.

The organ of power of a securities industrial association is the general assembly of its members.

Article 175 The constitution of a securities industrial association shall be formulated by the general assembly of its members and shall be reported to the securities regulatory authority under the State Council for archival filing.

Article 176 A securities industrial association shall perform the following functions and duties:

(1) Educating and organizing its members to observe the laws and administrative regulations on securities;
(2) Safeguarding the legitimate rights and interests of its members and reporting the suggestions and demands of its members to the securities regulatory body;
(3) Collecting and sorting out the securities information and providing services for its members;
(4) Formulating the rules that shall be observed by its members, organizing the vocational training for the practitioners of its member entities and carrying out vocational exchanges between its members;
(5) Holding mediation over any dispute regarding securities operation between its members or between its members and clients;
(6) Organizing its members to do research on the development, operation, etc. of the securities industry;

(7) Supervising and examining the acts of its members and, according to the relevant provisions, giving a disciplinary sanction to any member that violates any law or administrative regulation or the constitution of the association; and
(8) Performing any other functions and duties as stipulated by the constitution of the industrial association.

Article 177 A council shall be established within the securities industrial association. The members of the council shall be selected through election according to the provisions of the constitution.

Chapter X Securities Regulatory Bodies

Article 178 The securities regulatory authority under the State Council shall carry out supervision and administration of the securities market according to law so as to preserve the order of the securities market and guarantee the legitimate operations thereof.

Article 179 The securities regulatory authority under the State Council shall perform the following functions and duties regarding the supervision and administration of the securities market:

(1) Formulating the relevant rules and regulations on the supervision and administration of the securities market and exercising the power of examination or verification according to law;
(2) Carrying out the supervision and administration of the issuance, listing, trading, registration, custody and settlement of securities according to law;
(3) Carrying out supervision and administration of the securities activities of the securities issuers, listed companies, stock exchanges, securities companies, securities registration and clearing institutions, securities investment fund management companies and securities trading service institutions according to law;
(4) Formulating the standards for securities practice qualification and code of conduct and carrying out supervision and implementation according to law;
(5) Carrying out supervision and examination of information disclosure regarding the issuance, listing and trading of securities;
(6) Offering guidance for and carrying out supervision of the activities of the securities industrial associations according to law;

(7) Investigating into and punishing any violation of any law or administrative regulation on the supervision and administration of the securities market according to law; and
(8) Performing any other functions and duties as prescribed by any law or administrative regulation.

The securities regulatory authority under the State council may establish a cooperative mechanism of supervision and administration in collaboration with the securities regulatory bodies of other countries and regions and conducts trans-border supervision and administration.

Article 180 Where the securities regulatory authority under the State Council performs its duties and functions, it has the power to take the following measures:

(1) Carrying an on-the-spot examination to a securities issuer, listing company, securities company, securities investment fund management company, securities trading service company, stock exchange or securities registration and clearing institution;
(2) Making investigation and collecting evidence in a place where any suspected irregularity has happened;
(3) Consulting the parties concerned or any entity or individual relating to a case under investigation and requiring the relevant entity or person to give explanations on the matters relating to a case under investigation;
(4) Referring to and photocopying such materials as the registration of property right and the communication records relating to the case under investigation;
(5) Referring to and photocopying the securities trading records, transfer registration records, financial statements as well as any other relevant documents and materials of any entity or individual relating to a case under investigation; sealing up any document or material that may be transferred, concealed or damaged;
(6) Consulting the capital account, security account or bank account of any relevant party concerned in or any entity or individual relating to a case under investigation; in the case of any evidence certifying that any property as involved in a case, such as illegal proceeds or securities, has been or may be transferred or concealed; or where any important evidence has been or may be concealed, forged or

damaged, freezing or sealing up the foregoing properties or evidence upon the approval of the principal of the securities regulatory authority under the State Council;

(7) When investigating into any major securities irregularity such as manipulation of the securities market or insider trading, upon the approval of the principal of the securities regulatory authority under the State Council, restricting the securities trading of the parties concerned in a case under investigation, whereby the restriction term shall not exceed 15 trading days; under any complicated circumstance, the restriction term may be extended for another 15 trading day.

Article 181 Where the securities regulatory authority under the State Council performs its functions and duties of supervision or examination or investigation, there shall be no less than two people carrying out the supervision and examination, who shall show their legitimate certificates and the notice of supervision and examination as well as investigation. Where there are less than two people carrying out the supervision and examination or investigation or they fail to show their legitimate certificates and the notice of supervision and examination or investigation, the entity under examination and investigation has the right to refuse.

Article 182 The functionary of the securities regulatory authority under the State Council shall be duteous, impartial and clean, and handle matters according to law, and shall not take advantage of his post to seek any unjust interests or divulge any commercial secret of the relevant entity or individual it has access to in his performance of duty.

Article 183 Where the securities regulatory authority under the State Council performs its functions and duties according to law, the entity or individual under examination and investigation shall offer assistance, provide the relevant documents and materials in a faithful manner and shall not refuse any legitimate requirement, obstruct the performance of duties and functions or conceal any document or material concerned.

Article 184 The regulations, rules as well as the working system of supervision and administration as formulated by the securities regulatory authority under the State Council according to law shall be publicized to the general public.

The securities regulatory authority under the State Council shall, according to the results of investigation, decide the punishment on any securities irregularity, which shall be publicized to the general public.

Article 185 The securities regulatory authority under the State Council shall establish an information pooling mechanism for supervision and administration in collaboration with any other financial regulatory authority under the State Council.

Where the securities regulatory authority under the State Council performs its functions and duties of supervision and examination or investigation according to law, the relevant departments shall show cooperation.

Article 186 Where the securities regulatory authority under the State Council finds any securities irregularity as involved in a suspected crime when performing its functions and duties according to law, it shall transfer the case to the judicial organ for handling.

Article 187 The functionary of the securities regulatory authority under the State Council shall not hold any post in any organization under its supervision.

Chapter XI Legal Liabilities

Article 188 Where any company unlawfully makes any public issuance of securities or does so in any disguised form without the examination and approval of the statutory organ, it shall be ordered to cease the issuance, return the funds it has raised plus a deposit interest as calculated at the interest rate of the bank for the corresponding period of time and be imposed a fine of 1% up to 5% of the funds it has illegally raised. A company that has been established through any unlawful public issuance of securities or through any unlawful public issuance of securities in any disguised form shall be revoked by the organ or department that performs the functions and duties of supervision and administration in collaboration with the local people's government at or above the county level. The person-in-charge or any other person as held to be directly responsible shall be given a warning and be fined 30,000 yuan up to 300,000 yuan.

Article 189 Where an issuer fails to meet the requirements of issuance and cheats for the verification for issuance by any fraudulent means, if the relevant securities haven't been issued, it shall be fined 300,000 yuan up to 600,000 yuan; if the relevant securities have been issued, it shall be fined 1% up to 5% of the illegal proceeds it has unlawfully raised. The person-in-charge and any other person as held to be directly responsible shall be fined 30,000 yuan up to 300,000 yuan.

Any controlling shareholder or actual controller of an issuer that instigates any irregularity as prescribed in the preceding paragraph herein shall be subject to the punishments as prescribed in the preceding paragraph.

Article 190 Where a securities company underwrites or purchases or sells, as an agent, any securities which have been unlawfully issued in a public manner without examination and approval, it shall be ordered to stop its entrusted underwriting or purchase or sale. The illegal proceeds shall be confiscated and a fine of 1 up to 5 times its illegal proceeds shall be imposed. Where there is no illegal proceeds or its illegal proceeds is less than 300,000 yuan, a fine of 300,000 yuan up to 60,000 yuan shall be imposed. Where any loss has been incurred to any investor, the securities company shall bear several and joint liabilities of compensation together with the issuer. The person-in-charge and any other person as held to be directly responsible shall be given a warning and fined 30,000 yuan up to 300,000 yuan, and the post-holding qualification or securities practice qualification thereof shall be revoked.

Article 191 Where a securities company that engages in securities underwriting is under any of the following circumstances, it shall be ordered to correct and be given a warning. The illegal proceeds shall be confiscated and a fine of 30,000 yuan up to 600,000 yuan may be imposed concurrently. Under any serious circumstances, the relevant business license thereof shall be suspended or revoked. Where any loss has been incurred to any other securities underwriting institution or investor, it shall be subject to the liabilities of compensation according to law. The person-in-charge and any other person as held to be directly responsible shall be given a warning and may be concurrently fined 30,000 yuan up to 300,000 yuan. Under any serious circumstances, the post-holding qualification or securities practice qualification thereof shall be revoked:

(1) Conducting any advertising or any other publicity for recommendation, which is false or may mislead investors;
(2) Canvassing any underwriting business by any means of unjust competition; or
(3) Having any other irregularity in violation of the relevant provisions on securities underwriting.

Article 192 Where a recommender produces a recommendation letter with any false record, misleading statement or major omission, or fails to perform any other statutory functions and duties, it shall be ordered to correct and be given a warning. Its business income shall be confiscated and a fine of 1 up to 5 times its business income shall be imposed. Under any serious circumstances, the relevant business license shall be suspended or revoked. The person-in-charge and any other person as held to be directly responsible shall be given a warning and be fined 30,000 yuan up to 300,000 yuan. Under any serious circumstances, the post-holding qualification or securities practice qualification thereof shall be revoked.

Article 193 Where an issuer, a listed company or any other obligor of information disclosure fails to disclose information according to the relevant provisions or where there is any false record, misleading or major omission in the information it has disclosed, it shall be ordered to correct, given a warning and imposed a fine of 300,000 yuan up to 600,000 yuan. The person-in-charge and any other person as held to be directly responsible shall be given a warning and be imposed a fine of 30,000 yuan up to 300,000 yuan.

Where an issuer, a listed company or any other obligor of information disclosure fails to submit relevant reports or where there is any false record, misleading or major omission in any report it has submitted, it shall ordered to correct, given a warning and imposed a fine of 300,000 yuan up to 600,000 yuan. The person-in-charge and any other person-in-charge as held to be directly responsible shall be given a warning and be imposed a fine of 30,000 yuan up to 300,000 yuan.

The controlling shareholder or actual controller of any issuer, listed company or any other obligor of information disclosure instigates any irregularity as prescribed in the preceding 2 paragraphs herein shall be subject to the punishments as prescribed in the preceding 2 paragraphs.

Article 194 Where any issuer or listed company unlawfully alters the purpose of use of funds as raised through public issuance of securities, it shall be ordered to correct. The person-in-charge and any other person as held to be directly responsible shall be given a warning and be imposed a fine of 30,000 yuan up to 300,000 yuan.

The controlling shareholder or actual controller of any issuer or listed company who instigates any irregularity as prescribed in the preceding paragraph herein shall be given a warning and be imposed a fine of 300,000 yuan up to 600,000 yuan. The person-in-charge and any other person as held to be directly responsible shall be subject to the punishment according to the provisions of the preceding paragraph.

Article 195 Where any director, supervisor, or senior manager of a listed company or a shareholder who holds more than 5% of the shares of a listed company violates the provisions of Article 47 of the present Law by buying or purchasing any stock of the listed company, he shall be given a warning and be concurrently imposed a fine of 30,000 yuan up to 100,000 yuan.

Article 196 Any stock exchange as illegally established shall be banned by the people's government above the county level. Its illegal proceeds shall be confiscated and a fine of 1 up to 5 times its illegal proceeds shall be imposed. Where there is no illegal proceeds or the illegal proceeds is less than 100,000 yuan, a fine of 100,000 yuan up to 500,000 yuan shall be imposed, The person-in-charge and an other as held to be directly responsible shall be given a warning and be imposed a fine of 30,000 yuan up to 300,000 yuan.

Article 197 Any securities company that is unlawfully established or that unlawfully undertakes any securities operation without approval shall be banned by the securities regulatory body, the illegal proceeds shall be confiscated and a fine of 1 up to 5 times the illegal proceeds shall be imposed. Where there is no illegal proceeds or the illegal proceeds is less than 300,000 yuan, a fine of 300,000 yuan up to 600,000 yuan shall be imposed. The person-in-charge and any other person as held to be directly responsible shall be given a warning and be imposed a fine of 30,000 yuan up to 300,000 yuan.

Article 198 Where any personnel without a post-holding qualification or securities practice qualification is unlawfully employed as in violation of the provisions of the present Law, the securities regulatory body shall order it to correct, give it a warning and impose upon it a fine of 100,000 yuan up to 300,000 yuan. The person-in-charge and any other person as held to be directly responsible shall be given a warning and be imposed a fine of 30,000 yuan up to 100,000 yuan.

Article 199 Where any person who is prohibited by any law or administrative regulation from engaging in securities trading holds or purchases or sells any stock directly or in an assumed name or in the name of any other person, he shall be ordered to dispose of the stocks he unlawfully holds according to law. The illegal proceeds shall be confiscated and a fine of no more than the equivalent value of the stocks traded shall be imposed. In the case of any functionary of the state, an administrative sanction shall be given according to law.

Article 200 Where any practitioner of a stock exchange, securities company, securities registration and clearing institution or any functionary of any securities industrial association provides any false material or conceals, forges, alters or damages any trading record for the purpose of inducing investors to purchase or sell securities, the securities practice qualification thereof shall be revoked and a fine of 30,000 yuan up to 100,000 yuan shall be imposed. In the case of any functionary of the state, an administrative sanction shall be given according to law.

Article 201 Where a securities trading service institution and its staffs that produce any auditing report, asset appraisal report or legal opinions for the issuance of stocks violate the provisions of Article 45 of the present Law by purchasing or selling any stock, it shall be ordered to dispose of the stocks it or illegally holds according to law. The illegal proceeds shall be confiscated and a fine of no more than the equivalent value of the stocks traded shall be imposed.

Article 202 Where an insider who has access to insider information of securities trading or any person who has obtained any insider information purchases or sells the securities, divulges relevant information or advises any other person to purchase or sell securities before the information regarding the issuance or trading of securities or any other information that may have any big impact on the price of the securities is publicized, he shall be ordered to dispose of the securities he illegally holds according to law. The illegal proceeds shall be confiscated and a fine of 1 up to 5 times the illegal proceeds shall be imposed. Where there is no illegal proceeds or the illegal proceeds is less than 30,000 yuan, a fine of 30,000 yuan up to 600,000 yuan shall be imposed. Where an entity is involved in any insider trading, the person-in-charge and any other person as held to be directly responsible shall be given a warning and be imposed a fine of 30,000 yuan up to 300,000 yuan. Any functionary of the securities regulatory body that conducts any insider trading shall be given a heavier punishment.

Article 203 Where anyone violates the present Law by manipulating the securities market, he shall be ordered to dispose of the securities he illegally holds according to law. The illegal proceeds shall be confiscated and a fine of a fine of 1 up to 5 times the illegal proceeds shall be imposed. Where there is no illegal proceeds or the illegal proceeds is less than 30,000 yuan, a fine of 300,000 yuan up to 3,000,000 yuan shall be imposed. Where an entity manipulates the securities market, the person-in-charge and any other person as held to be directly responsible shall be given a warning and be imposed a fine of 100,000 yuan up to 600,000 yuan as well.

Article 204 Where anyone violates the relevant laws by purchasing or selling any securities during a period when the transfer of such securities is prohibited, he shall be ordered to correct, be given a warning and be imposed a fine of no more than the equivalent value of the securities as traded. The person-in-charge and any other person as held to be directly responsible shall be given a warning and be imposed a fine of 30,000 yuan up to 300,000 yuan.

Article 205 Where a securities company violates the present Law by providing any securities financing, the illegal proceeds shall be confiscated, the relevant business license shall be suspended or revoked, and a fine of no more than the equivalent value of the funds as raised through securities financing shall be imposed. The person-in-charge and any other person as held to be directly responsible shall be given a warning and be imposed a fine of 30,000 yuan up to 300,000 yuan, and the relevant post-holding qualification or securities practice qualification shall be revoked.

Article 206 Where anyone violates the provisions of paragraph 1 or 3 of Article 78 of the present Law by disturbing the securities market, the securities regulatory body shall order it to correct. The illegal proceeds shall be revoked and a fine of 1 up to 5 times of the illegal proceeds shall be imposed. Where there is no illegal proceeds or the illegal proceeds is less than 30,000 yuan, a fine of 30,000 yuan up to 200,000 yuan shall be imposed.

Article 207 Anyone who violates Paragraph 2 of Article 78 of the present Law by making false statements or providing misleading information in securities dealings shall be ordered to correct, and be fined 30,000 yuan up to 200,000 yuan. If the violator is a state functionary, he shall be given an administrative sanction, in addition.

Article 208 Where any legal person violates the present Law by opening any account in any other person's name or making use of any other person's account to purchase or sell any securities, it shall be ordered to correct and be imposed a fine of 1 up to 5 times the illegal proceeds. Where there is no illegal proceeds or the illegal proceeds is less than 30,000 yuan, a fine of 30,000 yuan up to 300,000 yuan shall be imposed. The person-in-charge and any other person as held to be directly responsible shall be given a warning and be imposed a fine of 30,000 yuan up to 100,000 yuan.

Where a securities company provides any securities trading account of its own or of any other person for any irregularity as prescribed in the preceding paragraph herein, he shall not only be subject to the punishments as prescribed in the preceding paragraph, the post-holding qualification or securities practice qualification of the person-in-charge or any other person as held to be directly responsible shall be revoked as well.

Article 209 Where a securities company violates the present Law by engaging in the self-operation of securities by assuming any other's name or any individual's name, it shall be ordered to correct. The illegal proceeds shall be confiscated and a fine of 1 up to 5 times the illegal proceeds shall be imposed. Where there is no illegal proceeds or the illegal proceeds is less than 30,000 yuan, a fine of 300,000 yuan up to 600,000 yuan shall be imposed. Under any serious circumstances, the business license of securities self-operation shall be suspended or revoked. The person-in-charge and any other person as held to be directly responsible shall be given a warning and be imposed a fine of 30,000 yuan up to 100,000 yuan, and the relevant post-holding qualification or securities practice qualification shall be revoked.

Article 210 Where a securities company purchases or sells any securities or carries out any trading in violation of the entrustment of its clients or handles any other non-trading matter in violation of the true intension as expressed by its clients, it shall be ordered to correct and be imposed a fine of 10,000 yuan up to 100,000 yuan. Where any loss has been incurred to its client, it shall be subject to the liabilities of compensation according to law.

Article 211 Where a securities company or securities registration and clearing institution misappropriates any fund or securities of its client, or unlawfully purchases or sells any securities for its client without any entrustment, it shall be ordered to correct. The illegal proceeds shall be confiscated and a fine of 1 up to 5 times the illegal proceeds shall be imposed. Where there is no illegal proceeds or the illegal proceeds is less than 100,000 yuan, a fine of 100,000 yuan up to 600,000 yuan shall be imposed. Under any serious circumstances, it shall be ordered to close or the relevant business license thereof shall be revoked. The person-in-charge and any other person as held to be directly responsible shall be given a warning and be imposed a fine of 30,000 yuan up to 300,000 yuan and the relevant post-holding qualification or securities practice qualification thereof shall be revoked.

Article 212 Where a securities company undertakes any brokerage business, accepts the full entrustment of any client to purchase or sell any securities or makes any promise on the proceeds as generated from securities trading or on the compensation of any loss as incurred from securities trading, it shall be ordered to correct. The illegal proceeds shall be confiscated and a fine of 50,000 yuan up to 200,000 yuan shall be imposed. The relevant business license may be suspended or revoked. The person-in-charge and any other person as held to be directly responsible shall be given a warning and be imposed a fine of 30,000 yuan up to 100,000 yuan. The relevant post-holding qualification or securities practice qualification thereof may be revoked.

Article 213 Where a purchaser fails to perform its obligations of announcing the acquisition of a listed company, issuing a tender offer. According to the present Law, it shall be ordered to correct, given a warning and be imposed a fine of 100,000 yuan up to 300,000 yuan. Before making any correction, for the stocks a purchaser holds individually or with any other person through an agreement or any other arrangement, the voting right thereof shall not be exercised. The person-in-charge and any other person as held to be directly responsible shall be given a warning and be imposed a fine of 30,000 yuan up to 300,000 yuan.

Article 214 Where a purchaser or the controlling shareholder of any purchaser takes advantage of the acquisition of any listed company to injure the legitimate rights and interests of the target company as well as the shareholders thereof, it shall be ordered to correct and be given a warning. Under any serious circumstances, a fine of 100,000 yuan up to 600,000 yuan shall be imposed. Where any loss is incurred to the target company or the shareholders thereof, it shall be subject to the liabilities of compensation according to law. The person-in-charge and any other person as held to be directly responsible shall be given a warning and be imposed a fine of 30,000 yuan up to 300,000 yuan.

Article 215 Where a securities company or any of its practitioners violates the present Law by privately accepting the entrustment of purchasing or selling securities from any client, it shall be ordered to correct and be given a warning. The illegal proceeds shall be confiscated and a fine of 1 up to 5 times the illegal proceeds shall be imposed. Where there is no illegal proceeds or the illegal proceeds is less than 100,000 yuan, a fine of 100,000 yuan up to 300,000 yuan shall be imposed.

Article 216 Where a securities company violates the relevant provisions by undertaking any trading of unlisted securities without approval, it shall be ordered to correct. The illegal proceeds shall be confiscated and a fine of 1 up to 5 times the illegal proceeds shall be imposed.

Article 217 Where a securities company fails to start its business operations 3 months after establishment without any justifiable reason, or suspends its business operations for a consecutive 3 months, the organ in charge of corporation registration shall revoke the business license of the company.

Article 218 Where any securities company violates the provisions of Article 129 of the present Law by unlawfully establishing, purchasing or revoking any branch, or unlawfully going through any merge, split-up, business suspension, dissolution or bankruptcy, or establishing, purchasing a securities operation institution abroad or purchasing the shares of any securities operation institution abroad, it shall be ordered to correct. The illegal proceeds shall be confiscated and a fine of 1 up to 5 times the illegal proceeds shall be imposed. Where there is no illegal proceeds or the illegal proceeds is less than 100,000 yuan, a fine of 100,000 yuan up to 600,000 yuan shall be imposed. The person-in-charge and any other person as held to be directly responsible shall be given a warning and be imposed a fine of 30,000 yuan up to 100,000 yuan.

Where any securities company violates the provisions of Article 129 of the present Law by altering any of the relevant items, it shall be ordered to correct and be imposed a fine of 100,000 yuan up to 300,000 yuan. The person-in-charge and any other person as held to be directly responsible shall be given a warning and imposed a fine of no more than 50,000 yuan.

Article 219 Where a securities company violates the present Law by engaging in any securities operation beyond its permitted business scope, it shall be ordered to correct. The illegal proceeds shall be confiscated and a fine of 1 up to 5 times the illegal proceeds shall be imposed. Where there is no illegal proceeds or the illegal proceeds is less than 300,000 yuan, a fine of 300,000 yuan up to 600,000 yuan shall be imposed. Under any serious circumstances, it shall be ordered to close down. The person-in-charge and any other person as held to be directly responsible shall be given a warning and be imposed a fine of 30,000 yuan up to 100,000 yuan, and the relevant post-holding qualification or securities practice qualification shall be revoked.

Article 220 Where a securities company fails to carry out its securities operation of brokerage, underwriting, self-operation or asset management in a separate manner according to law but mixes its own securities operation with other operations, it shall be ordered to correct. The illegal proceeds shall be confiscated and a fine of 300,000 yuan up to 600,000 yuan shall be imposed. Under any serious circumstances, the relevant business license shall be revoked. The person-in-charge and any other person as held to be directly responsible shall be given a warning and be imposed a fine of 30,000 yuan up to 100,000 yuan. Under any serious circumstances, the relevant post-holding qualification or securities practice qualification shall be revoked.

Article 221 Where a securities company submits any false document of certification or adopts any other fraudulent means to conceal any major fact so as to cheat for the securities business license or a securities company has any severe irregularity in the securities trading and thus, fails to meet the requirements of business operation any more, the securities regulatory body shall revoke its securities business license.

Article 222 Where a securities company or its shareholder or actual controller violates the relevant provisions by refusing to report or provide information or materials regarding its business and management to the securities regulatory body or in the case of any false record, misleading statement or major omission in the aforesaid information or materials as reported or submitted, it shall be ordered to correct, be given a warning and be fined 30,000 yuan up to 300,000 yuan. The relevant business license of the securities company may be suspended or revoked. The person-in-charge and any other person as held to be directly responsible shall be given a warning and be fined no more than 30,000 yuan, and the relevant post-holding qualification or securities practice qualification shall be revoked.

Where a securities company provides financing or guaranty for its shareholder or any person related to its shareholder, it shall be ordered to correct, be given a warning and be imposed a fine of 100,000 yuan up to 300,000. The person-in-charge and any other person as held to be directly responsible shall be imposed a fine of 30,000 yuan up to 100,000 yuan. Where a shareholder has any fault, the securities regulatory authority under the State Council may restrict his shareholders' right before he makes the correction according to the relevant requirements. Where anyone refuses to correct, he may be ordered to transfer the stock right of the securities company he holds.

Article 223 Where a securities trading service institution fails to fulfill its accountability in a diligent and dutiful manner so that any document it formulated or produced has any false record, misleading statement or major omission, it shall be ordered to correct. The proceeds as generated from its business shall be confiscated. Its securities business license shall be suspended or revoked. A fine of 1 up to 5 times its business income shall be imposed. The person-in-charge and any other person as held to be directly responsible shall be given a warning and be imposed a fine of 30,000 yuan up to 100,000 yuan, and the relevant post-holding qualification or securities practice qualification shall be revoked.

Article 224 Anyone that violates the present Law by issuing or underwriting any corporate bond shall be given a punishment by the department as authorized by the State Council according to the relevant provisions of the present Law.

Article 225 Where a listed company, securities company, stock exchange, securities registration and clearing institution, or securities trading service institution fails to keep the relevant documents and materials according to the relevant provisions, it shall be ordered to correct, be given a warning and be imposed a fine of 30,000 yuan up to 300,000 yuan. Where any relevant document or material is concealed, forged, altered or damaged, the violator shall be given a warning and be imposed a fine of 300,000 yuan up to 600,000 yuan.

Article 226 Where a securities registration and clearing institution is unlawfully established without approval of the State Council, it shall be cancelled by the securities regulatory body, its illegal proceeds shall be confiscated, and a fine of 1 up to 5 times of the illegal proceeds shall be imposed upon it.

Where an investment consulting institution, financial advising institution, credit rating institution, asset appraisal institution or accounting firm undertakes any securities trading service without the relevant approval, it shall be ordered to correct. The illegal proceeds shall be confiscated, and a fine of 1 up to 5 times of the illegal proceeds shall be imposed upon it.

Where a securities registration and clearing institution or a securities service trading institution violates the present Law or any operational rules it has formulated according to law, the securities regulatory body shall order it to correct, confiscate the illegal proceeds, and impose upon it a fine of 1 up to 5 times the illegal proceeds. Where there is no illegal proceeds or the illegal proceeds is less than 100,000 yuan, a fine of 100,000 yuan up to 300,000 yuan shall be imposed. Under any serious circumstances, it shall be ordered to close down or its securities business license shall be revoked.

Article 227 Where the securities regulatory authority under the State Council or the department as authorized by the State Council is under any of the following circumstances, the person-in-charge and any other person as held to be directly responsible shall be given an administrative sanction according to law:

(1) Verifying or approving an application for issuing securities or for establishing a securities company, which fails to comply with the present Law;
(2) Taking such measures as on-the-spot examination, investigation and evidence collection, consultation, freeze-up or seal-up as in violation of the provisions of Article 180 of the present Law;
(3) Giving any administrative sanction to the relevant institution or personnel as in violation of the relevant provisions; or
(4) Performing any other functions and duties in an unlawful manner.

Article 228 Where any functionary of the securities regulatory body or any member of the issuance examination committee fails to perform the duties and functions as prescribed in the present Law, abuses his power, neglects his duty, takes advantage of his post to seek any unjust interests or divulges any commercial secret of the relevant entity or individual as accessible in his performance, he shall be subject to legal liabilities.

Article 229 Where a stock exchange grants any approval to an application for securities listing that fails to meet the requirements as prescribed in the present Law, it shall be given a warning. Its business income shall be confiscated and a fine of 1 up to 5 times its business income shall be imposed. The person-in-charge and any other person as held to be directly responsible shall be imposed a fine of 30,000 yuan up to 300,000 yuan.

Article 230 Where anyone refuses or obstructs the securities regulatory body and its functionary in its or his performance of the functions and duties of supervision, examination and investigation by means of violence or threat, he shall be given an administrative sanction of public security according to law.

Article 231 Anyone who violates the present Law and constitutes a crime shall be subject to criminal liabilities according to law.

Article 232 Where anyone violates the present Law and shall be subject to civil liabilities of compensation and payment of fines and penalties, and if his properties are not sufficient to cover all the payment at the same time, he shall bear civil liabilities.

Article 233 Where anyone violates the relevant laws and administrative regulations or the relevant provisions of the securities regulatory authority under the State Council and is under any serious circumstances, the securities regulatory authority under the State Council may take measures to prohibit the relevant persons as held to be responsible from entering into the securities market.

The term "prohibition from entering into the securities market" as mentioned in the preceding paragraph refers to a system, whereby a person shall not undertake any securities practice or hold the post of director, supervisor or senior manager of a listed company within a prescribed term or for life.

Article 234 The fines as collected and the illegal proceeds as confiscated shall be all turned over into the State Treasury.

Article 235 Any party concerned that is dissatisfied with a decision of the securities regulatory body or a department as authorized by the State Council on punishment may apply for an administrative review or file a litigation with the people's court.

Chapter XII Supplementary Provisions

Article 236 The securities that have been approved for listed trading in a stock exchange according to the relevant administrative regulations before the present Law comes into force may continue to be traded according to law.

The securities operation institutions that have been approved for establishment according to the relevant administrative regulations and the provisions of the administrative department of finance of the State Council before the present Law comes into force but fails to completely comply with the provisions of the present Law shall meet the requirements as prescribed by the present Law within a prescribed term. The specific measures for implementation shall be separately prescribed by the State Council.

Article 237 An issuer that applies for verifying the public issuance of any stocks or corporate bonds shall pay the expenses for examination according to the relevant provisions.

Article 238 Where a domestic enterprise directly or indirectly goes abroad to issue any securities abroad or whose securities are listed abroad for trading, it shall be subject to the approval of the securities regulatory authority under the State Council according to the relevant provisions of the State Council.

Article 239 As to any subscription or trading of stocks of a domestic company in a foreign currency, the specific measures shall be separately formulated by the State Council.

Article 240 The present Measures shall come into force as of January 1, 2006.

Index

D. Yu, *Chinese Business Law*, The Palgrave Series on Chinese Law,
https://doi.org/10.1007/978-981-13-0902-1

H

I

J

L

M

The manufacturer's authorised representative in the EU is Springer Nature Customer Service Centre GmbH, Europaplatz 3, 69115 Heidelberg, Germany. If you have any concerns regarding our products, please contact ProductSafety@springernature.com

Printed and bound by CPI Group (UK) Ltd, Croydon, CR0 4YY
25/09/2026
02222902-0005